SfAA

Intellectual Property Rights for Indigenous Peoples,

• *A Sourcebook*

Tom Greaves
Editor

Society for Applied Anthropology
Oklahoma City, OK, USA
1994

The book is dedicated to the indigenous peoples
of the Western Hemisphere
who, for the first time in five centuries,
are winning.

Published by the Society for Applied Anthropology
P.O. Box 24083
Oklahoma City, OK 73124-0083 USA
1994

Intellectual Property Rights for Indigenous Peoples, A Sourcebook

Table of Contents

Table of Contents

Preface[1]

In today's world of high-speed communication, "intellectual property rights" (IPR) is at risk of becoming trendy and, thus, trivialized by its own importance. As with any other *cause célèbre* among op-ed intellectuals, corporate lawyers, and show-business personalities, intellectual property rights becomes a high profile item in the media (especially when politicians come on stage) which can bombard even the most sensitive citizen into inured disinterest.

The phrase "intellectual property rights" is much in the air these days. Hollywood writers and entertainers slug it out in court over "story ideas." Research-and-development scientists are lured from one company to another and the ownership of the knowledge in the researcher's head becomes a contested property. Software designers try to lay claim to their efforts but the "product" gets into the public domain on the "information highway" and old copyright laws for print media no longer seem adequate to protect the commercial interests of an electronic author. Interesting as these issues might be for the (sometimes) rich and famous, it is not on that bandwagon that this volume rides. Rather, as editor Tom Greaves and the very title of the work make clear, this collection aims to bring together ideas, examples, and experiences that might help tribal peoples and other "little societies" gain some benefit from their contributions to the commodities of the world economy, whether in pharmaceuticals or foodstuffs or traditional crafts or cool new sounds in popular music.

Industries, governments, and, increasingly, indigenous peoples themselves, country by country, seem to become ever more cognizant of the potential loss of control over not just the intellectual creations of gifted individuals but of possible forfeiture of the intellectual legacy of a whole people accumulated over time by countless, nameless ordinary people. Indigenous peoples' knowledge has been referred to as "the West's new 'frontier' in ... 'the last great resource rush' (Cultural Survival Quarterly, Summer 1991, p. 3). The comparison is apt.

The parallels between the dispossession of native peoples' land and dispossession of their intellectual products are riveting. Rapacious land-seekers and humanitarians alike have long struggled with trying to discover the appropriate legal fiction under which to alienate or secure the real estate of tribal peoples who operate under rules of land tenure utterly foreign if not incomprehensible to those who come from "state-level" societies. The alienation of incorporeal property of native peoples

[1] I thank Yolonda Youngs for the intellectual stimulation that her term paper provided me in the preparation of this preface.

is no less grievous. But, that which is taken seems so much more ephemeral than land ownership; no one is displaced, after all. Thus, native peoples and those who would work in their behalf are even more hard pressed than in the case of land to find a way to parcel out what massively more powerful societies may and may not take from them with impunity, at least without fear of recrimination from the "civilized nations of the world." If, however, western notions of land tenure were unworkable for a truly fair acquisition of native territories, western ideas of individual creativity imbedded in copyrights, patents, and trademarks seem even more problematic in any attempt to deflect expropriation of the artistic, medicinal, or botanical traditions of native peoples that have no individually identified creators or owners. Nonetheless, (to my never-ending amusement) western legal concepts can successfully sustain the convenient fiction that a group of people organized as a corporation is transformed into a single "person" before the eyes of the law. A curious idea, indeed.

Intellectual property rights for indigenous peoples is an issue about cultural differences of the most profound kind. In this sense, the question of who "owns" cultural knowledge penetrates to the very heart of human relations. Since its inception the Society for Applied Anthropology has been dedicated to the "scientific investigation of 'the principles controlling the relations of human beings to one another... and the wide application of these principles to practical problems'." In the area of intellectual property rights the Society stands steadfastly by this purpose. Historically the science of anthropology has been strongly tied to the fates of tribal peoples, and, certainly, applied anthropologists have a long-standing commitment to the protection of the rights of indigenous peoples. From the beginning, however, members of the Society have been equally attuned to what lessons might be learned from the study of little societies to help us better understand ourselves, that is, the large and powerful societies that produced anthropologists in the first place. Fittingly, then, editor Greaves' introduction draws attention to the fact that it is at the grass roots level that the most significant progress has been made in unraveling the knotty problems of intellectual property rights for indigenous peoples, rather than in the "big picture" of national and international efforts.

Grass roots does not mean quaint and simple. In this "post-modern" world the activities of indigenous peoples have a way of coming to center stage. For example, in January, 1994, the Principal Chief of the Cherokee Nation of Oklahoma, Wilma Mankiller, appeared in the Florida State University "Distinguished Lecture Series;" others in the series through the years have been such notables as Henry Kissinger, Carl Sagan, Alex Haley, and Richard Leakey. Chief Mankiller has become a media celebrity in her own rights (her distinctive surname, derived from the honorific title of an 18th century ancestor, hasn't hurt!). In an informal question-and-answer session with FSU faculty and staff someone asked Chief Mankiller how she felt about the commercialization of her tribe's name. In her response, Mankiller noted that previous attempts to curtail the use of their official name for products from jeeps to clothing were blunted by the legal opinion that the name "Cherokee" was in the "public domain." But, Mankiller continued hopefully, the tribe is considering revisiting the question of the commercial use of their name "as an issue in the area of intellectual property rights." IPR seems to crop up everywhere these days. In passing, I cannot resist expressing the thought that while in certain circles it might be chic nowadays to declaim against the "commodification" of native peoples, under the rubric of intellectual property rights, I would argue, indigenous peoples should retain the right to "market" themselves if they want to - no matter how crass it might seem to the upper middle-class liberal elite.

Intellectual property rights is, indeed, a complex issue. It challenges the creativity of us all, the "West" and "the Tribal World" alike. As current president of the Society for Applied Anthropology, I am much gratified that past-presidents Carole Hill and Tom Greaves had the foresight to bring the resources of the Society to bear on the global problem of intellectual property rights for indigenous peoples, an issue every bit as important as land rights for the cultural survival of the thousands of little societies which have been so much a part of the *raison d'être* of anthropology as a discipline and a profession.

On behalf of the Society of Applied Anthropology, I extend to the contributors to this sourcebook sincere appreciation for their pioneering efforts. To editor Tom Greaves, for the Society and for myself I express admiration, respect, and deep gratitude for his prodigious accomplishment in so quickly bringing this sourcebook together. I trust that in time this work by Greaves and his contributors will prove to be a milestone in the development of solutions to the profoundly human problems of protecting intellectual property rights for indigenous peoples.

J. Anthony Paredes, President
Society for Applied Anthropology
Tallahassee, Florida USA
January 31, 1994

Introduction

If there is one striking thing about intellectual property rights (IPR) for indigenous peoples[1] it is that the last three years have seen an astonishing burgeoning of interest in it, world wide. A glance at chapter footnotes and bibliographies in this volume and others reveals the enormous growth of publications, workshops, panels, papers, conferences and documents just since 1990. IPR for indigenous peoples has become a "hot button" issue.

Indigenous knowledge, historically scorned by the world of industrial societies, has now become intensely, commercially attractive. Indigenous societies find themselves poked, probed and examined as never before. The very cultural heritage that gives indigenous peoples their identity, now far more than in the past, is under real or potential assault from those who would gather it up, strip away its honored meanings, convert it to a product, and sell it. Each time that happens the heritage itself dies a little, and with it its people.

Indigenous communities, indigenous leaders, and advocates for indigenous rights have sought ways to gain some control in a rapidly worsening situation. At bottom, intellectual property rights consist of efforts to assert access to, and control over, cultural knowledge and to things produced through its application. The most urgent reason to establish that control is to preserve meaning and due honor for elements of cultural knowledge and to insure that these traditional universes, and their peoples, maintain their vitality. Subsidiary IPR goals are to manage the degree and process by which parts of that cultural knowledge are shared with outsiders and, in some instances, to be justly compensated for it.

IPR is a divided arena, with those who are seeking a usable and legal basis for indigenous IPR largely separate from those within indigenous groups who are seeking to protect their traditional knowledge. The former group include those who seeking ways to establish IPR through various national and international mechanisms, and laying strategies to bring that about.

---

[1] In the broader world of copyrights and patents, "intellectual property rights " (IPR) refers to the legal rights of ownership that individuals and corporations have over the products of individual creativity and inventiveness. In this book the meaning of IPR is different, in that it refers to the rights claimed by indigenous people over their traditional cultural knowledge. Thus, although in these chapters our more specialized use of IPR is frequently indicated by a qualifying phrase, elsewhere the use of an unqualified IPR or intellectual property rights is also intended in this more restricted sense.

Meanwhile, indigenous communities are experimenting with pragmatic ways to protect what is theirs. These ways can be *ad hoc*, may be vulnerable to later assaults, and show a wide range of approaches. Some communities seek control by imposing isolation and secrecy; others are working out avenues of partnership and linkage with the outside. Some are doing both.

IPR is divided in another way. There is a singular and sizable focus on IPR protections for biological products, which seems disproportionate to the range of cultural knowledge needing protection. The special salience of IPR attention to biological information partly reflects the large financial investments now being made by governments, the pharmaceutical, agricultural, and cosmetic industries in "biological prospecting." The emphasis on "biologicals" also reflects such factors as the parallel interest of the environmental movement in preserving biodiversity, the rather well developed specialty study of ethnobotany, the enormous size of the industries consuming novel biological materials (when they twitch others bounce), and the specialized structure of law that protects ownership rights to biological and biochemical materials.

From the view point of indigenous societies, however, the distribution of concern is *much* wider: protecting sacred lands, preserving spiritual wisdom and ceremonies, according respect to physical things and knowledge that should not be treated simply as grist for personal enrichment in the game of capitalism - these things make all the external interest in plants seem disproportionate. All who devote their energies to the campaigns for IPR need to remember that for indigenous peoples the scope of concern (and urgency) moves far beyond biological materials.

The Authors and Cases in this Volume

In bringing together the authors and chapters that compose the Sourcebook, I attempted to cast the net broadly. As will be said later, however, no network is all-inclusive and there are many who would have made important contributions who were either unable to accept a new writing obligation at this time, or were not contacted because of the deficiencies of my own network and knowledge, or whose work could not be accommodated within the length limitations of one Sourcebook.

In extending invitations to contribute, substantial efforts were made to seek authors among indigenous communities and their leaders. Some, directly or indirectly, agreed to contribute and I honor them and thank them for their generosity, time and effort. In other cases, indigenous leaders were clearly too pressed with the needs of community or organizational leadership to set aside the time required to produce a Sourcebook chapter. That's understandable. Today, indigenous societies and their leaders are in a frenetic race to defend what is still theirs, to address the urgent social and economic needs of their peoples, to join the rising voices of regional, national and international indigenous leadership, and to grasp political, economic and sovereignty possibilities that have recently developed in many countries.

The Design of the Sourcebook

A standard ordering of the book's selections would be to begin with the "big picture" - the international and national efforts to establish IPR-supportive institutions and structures - and then to move to the local level case material. This book consciously reverses that order. It is my conclusion that when one looks at what has been *achieved* in IPR, rather than at production of paper and talk, so far most of the truly important news is at the local level. IPR, in reality, is a grass roots process.

Meanwhile, the sizable efforts at the conceptual and international level are, clearly, making progress. If IPR is to be "entrenched" as our Canadian friends would say, both streams of effort will both need to contribute critical parts. It is clear, nonetheless, that the most fascinating, and under appreciated, IPR news is at the grass roots level. It is, I suggest, those local successes that will ultimately provide the additional energy necessary to break though intransigence at the national and international levels.

One of the purposes of the Sourcebook is to facilitate further explorations of IPR by interested parties. For that reason, a number of the Sourcebook's authors have provided chapter appendices of names and addresses of individuals, organizations, indigenous communities, and the publishers and distributors of key documents, so that readers can pursue the subject further. Also, ways to contact each contributing author are provided in the "About the Authors" section at the back of the Sourcebook. We hope the Sourcebook will be a passageway rather than a closed vault.

Goals for the Sourcebook.

The Society for Applied Anthropology has energetically fostered attention and dialog on indigenous peoples' IPR for the past four years, in symposia, workshops, a task force, and panels. At the same time, the Society's interest has been only one part of a much larger, now globally distributed stream of interest in the subject. A dysfunctional consequence of this rapidly expanding global interest is that communication and interaction on IPR now tends to be divided into discontinuous network clusters. Each cluster is doing important things, but word is slow to move beyond network edges. We intend the Sourcebook to help bridge network boundaries by broadening the shared stock of information, argumentation and experience.

Of special concern to the Society is that so much of the dialog and debate about IPR takes place largely out of earshot of its intended users, indigenous peoples. Comfortable conference rooms, auditoriums, and jargon-rich publications are distant from indigenous communities and most of their citizens. Ironically, as this volume will make clear, the most important advances in the use of IPR are occurring in just those local places. Consequently, we encouraged our authors to include real cases and specific experiences with IPR wherever they could. Further, the Society for Applied Anthropology is intentionally producing this volume at minimal cost, to give it the widest feasible availability to indigenous groups and leaders, and to indigenous advocacy organizations worldwide. It is the Society's hope that the Sourcebook, itself, can be a small instrument of change by making the discussions of IPR more inclusive and opening more cross-network channels of consultation.

The Sourcebook is not an attempt to "sell" IPR. Authors were encouraged not only to examine IPR's possibilities and successes, but also to expose IPR's failings, and the frustrations and blind alleys encountered in pursuing IPR. Naturally, the content, interpretations and views expressed in each chapter remain those of its author and do not reflect positions held by the Society for Applied Anthropology.

Whether IPR will be useful or not to indigenous societies, and what sorts of indigenous knowledge need protecting, are, indisputably, matters that each indigenous community will decide for itself. Hopefully the possibilities, hazards, successes, and failures depicted in this book, and the provision of contact addresses and written sources for follow up, will be useful as those decisions are made.

Acknowledgements

The leadership of the Society for Applied Anthropology, following traditions that resonate with the values of Margaret Mead, one of its early presidents, has been repeatedly attentive to the multiple vulnerabilities of indigenous peoples, and to the relentless destruction of their cultural knowledge and lifeways. Carole Hill, president of the Society from 1991 to 1993, was one of those who recognized at an early date the potential importance of IPR as a tactic and vehicle for strengthening the hand of indigenous peoples. Her steadfast attention to the Society's IPR efforts accounts substantially for this Sourcebook. The current president of the Society, Anthony Paredes, and the members of the SfAA Executive Committee, have nourished this priority and are directly responsible for the funding and publication of the Sourcebook. To each and all are due thanks for whatever value comes from this work.

As editor I owe heartfelt thanks to all of the Sourcebook's contributors, who accepted my compulsive editorial intrusiveness and tight deadlines to produce a finished manuscript ten months after receiving the Society's "green light." We all realized that IPR's astonishingly rapid evolution and the importance of conveying its nature to societies under siege precluded a less demanding pace of preparation. I also thank the many good-hearted people of Bucknell University for allowing me to devote much of a sabbatical semester to putting the Sourcebook together, covering many of its ancillary costs, and providing a supportive atmosphere for the project.

Most of all, I treasure the interest, help and love of my wife and life's colleague of 31 years, Margaret Harris Greaves, who gave up much quality time together -- not to mention long-postponed household projects -- in deference to the needs of getting the Sourcebook done.

Tom Greaves
Bucknell University
Lewisburg, PA., USA

Chapter
1

IPR, A Current Survey

Tom Greaves
Bucknell University

This chapter provides an introduction and overview to various questions that often arise when intellectual property rights are proposed as a means by which indigenous peoples can protect their cultural knowledge, control whether it may be used by outsiders, and, where possible, receive compensation for authorized use. - ed.

1

IPR, A Current Survey

Tom Greaves
Bucknell University

Introducing IPR

The scenario goes like this: Voracious Pharmaceuticals Inc.[1] is looking for a new, blockbuster drug. Hearing that tropical forests may have molecules with possibilities, the R&D director of Voracious sends a staff member to visit an Amazonian indigenous group for leads. The staffer befriends the local shaman who tells him of a plant that alleviates painful swelling of the joints. The staffer asks the shaman to show him the plant. The shaman obliges. The staffer collects samples, and takes them back to Voracious. The plant contains a heretofore unknown organic molecule that, ten years later, is approved as a new drug that earns Voracious tens of millions of dollars. Meanwhile the indigenous group has come under relentless pressure by local settlers. The only workable recourse is legal action but, unable to afford the costs of fighting the usurpation of their lands in court, the group is being dispersed and its culture extinguished. Although Voracious is making millions, the indigenous group whose knowledge contributed to this financial bonanza gets nothing.

This particular scenario so far has not happened, yet to different societies each of its components have occurred. Pharmaceutical companies are visiting tropical areas to engage in molecular prospecting.[2] Indigenous knowledge has led to the identification of commercially promising biological substances.[3] Indigenous societies are facing cultural extinction that could be avoided with leadership and cash. Can indigenous societies claim ownership of their cultural knowledge? Can they control whether it may be used by outsiders? Can they claim compensation for its permitted commercial use?

If plant extracts and potential pharmaceuticals were the only matters involved, the number of questions to ask would be manageably small. However, native knowledge with commercial possibilities is not limited to medicinals. Other commercially relevant indigenous

---

[1] An imaginary corporation.

[2] The scale of this activity is reflected, for instance, by Reid et al., 1993, and in Pollack 1992.

[3] See chapters by King and Laird

knowledge includes the location of local mineral and wild plant resources, domesticated plants with interesting genetic properties, musical instruments producing evocative sounds, new ingredients for cosmetics, new foods and spices, art designs and their potential use on all manner of salable products, mythic elements and stories, and sites for tour organizers. The list is enormous, and growing ever longer as entrepreneurs scour the world for remunerative opportunities. The great diversity of externally valuable indigenous knowledge infuses complexity in strategies to protect it.

Also at issue is the control of traditional ideas and knowledge that does not lead to a commercial product, but identifies places, customs and beliefs which, if publicly known, will destroy parts of a people's cultural identity. Sometimes it is knowledge entrusted only to properly prepared religious specialists. Disclosure to other, unqualified members destroys it. Sometimes it is knowledge shared among all of a society's members, but not with outsiders. Such knowledge charters a society's sense of self; to disclose it loosens the society's self-rationale. In a world of instantaneous global communication, with a planet-wide rate of information consumption now reaching gluttonous proportions, with isolation now disappearing for all indigenous societies, and with these societies subject to rapacious outside pressures, how to avoid the expropriation of cultural knowledge has become a problem with countless forms and urgencies.

Among those of us who seek equity for the world's indigenous peoples the thought arises, why couldn't indigenous peoples *own* their cultural knowledge, and then, if they allow it to be used elsewhere, secure a just share of the money it generates? At bottom, to seek intellectual property rights (IPR) for indigenous people is to seek a legally workable basis by which indigenous societies would *own* their cultural knowledge, *control* whether any of that knowledge may be used by outsiders, and for permitted uses, require acknowledgement as its source, and a *share* of any financial return that may come from its authorized commercial use.[4] Indigenous societies might well decide not to permit certain elements of their tradtional knowledge to be used by others, but for some the income generated from the allowed use of selected cultural information could strengthen their defense of their own cultural integrity.[5]

---

[4] In various instances in the American Southwest native groups have been more concerned that their contribution of, for example, cultigens be credited to them, rather than seeking financial return. Various traditional ethical systems resist financial transactions with nature's gifts. See, for example, Chapter 2 (Soleri, Cleveland et al.) for case material on this point.

[5] The 1990s are witnessing a dramatic increase in the number of indigenous societies who are waging aggressive campaigns against the predations of outsiders, and also in the frequency of success (see Greaves, 1992, 1993). The demand for cash to press these

The last three years have seen a truly astonishing rise in efforts to find ways of securing for indigenous societies mechanisms to control access to their cultural knowledge and to exact compensation for certain authorized uses by outsiders. How do we account for this sudden interest? The environmental movement is responsible for some of it. Thousands of environmentalist organizations on every continent seek to preserve natural settings and capabilities of the planet. It has finally dawned on some that calling for the protection of the life way of indigenous societies residing in those natural areas, and indigenous societies in general, adds greater strength to the demand that these natural areas be protected from development.[6] The international human rights movement has been a second factor focusing attention on indigenous IPR. The efforts of indigenous societies to preserve and continue their cultural heritages are, tragically, often linked to violence (as in the recent Yanomamo massacre)[7], destruction of the subsistence base, pollution of habitat, and other assaults. At bottom, one concludes, these predations comprise a gradualist form of ethnocide, mobilizing human rights organizations concerned with politically marginal peoples. IPR is a tool for reinforcing and defending cultural integrity against ethnocide. In part, too, IPR's strength derives from the emergence of indigenous-led advocacy groups in several countries with mature political skills and sufficient resources to insert the indigenous agenda into national political arenas. For these and other reasons, indigenous issues now have more salience generally, and IPR has benefited from that fact.

It is not enough, however, that indigenous IPR be an attractive, widely endorsed idea. IPR for indigenous cultural knowledge encounters a host of problems, both conceptually and practically.

Vehicles for IPR in Western Law and Practice

IPR entails looking for legal vehicles in Western law that could be used by indigenous societies and their advocates to establish their rights of cultural ownership. IPR is not for everyone. IPR is housed in *Western* law and in its system of courts, judges and lawyers. Advocacy of IPR assumes that indigenous societies or their advocates will use those Western institutions to secure and defend their rights. Many indigenous persons are uncomfortable with that. Why should an indigenous society, with its own concepts of property and civility, adopt

---

campaigns of cultural preservation is high. The channeling of casino-derived income from tribally controlled casinos in the United States into such campaigns reinforces this observation.

6 See the chapter by Kloppenberg and Gonzales for a detailed discussion of the advantages and cautions entailed in alliances with such non-governmental organizations. See also Kane, 1993, for a compelling account of an Ecuadorean case.

7 See, for example, Brooke 1993, A4.

the assumptions, rules and institutions of the dominant society in order to claim its rights? The pursuit of intellectual property rights forces indigenous people to play the dominant society's game. To date, many refuse.[8]

At the same time, indigenous societies are finding that each year they are less isolated and, in any case, that intrusions on their isolation are one-sided. Assaults on their land base, pollution of their habitat, decimation of their food supplies, the impacts of adjacent development projects, disease, the impoverishment of their children, the avaricious theft of their craft markets - these do not cease if one simply stops interacting. Today, an active offensive mounted on the turf of the outside world is central to survival. When indigenous societies seek intellectual property rights for their cultural knowledge it is an effort consistent with many the society is already making.

When legal mechanisms are sought for indigenous IPR, two central legal vehicles are most commonly mentioned: (1) the right to copyright or patent group ownership of cultural knowledge, and (2) the use of contracts granting access to specified elements of cultural knowledge or products under indigenous control. The next two paragraphs will briefly introduce these two general vehicles.

While we commonly think in terms of *copyrighting* indigenous knowledge, in Western law the ownership of intellectual property actually falls into four major legal types: copyrights, patents, trademarks, and trade secrets. The idea underlying each is that if a person originates ideas of value, that person should enjoy the benefits of ownership of those ideas, including the right to allow or deny others the use of them, and to share financially in profits stemming from their use in the marketplace.[9] Someone who steals those ideas (that is, uses them without consent and any required compensation) can be sued for damages and be required to stop using them. Copyrights, patents, trademarks and trade secrets are separate legal domains that together protect most of the sorts of intellectual property that people have heretofore sought to own and protect. Were these rights extended to indigenous cultural knowledge a

---

[8] Richard Deertrack, Taos Pueblo, eloquently descibed the feelings of those who hold this view point at the symposium, "Tropical Forest Medical Resources and the Conservation of Biodiversity", January 1992. At the same time, Western-style property guarantees are the top priority for most indigenous groups in seeking to establish a secure land base, however dissonant with traditional attitudes toward the landscape. The arena of Western institutions is played in when the stakes are high and there is no other choice.

[9] In the case of patents, copyrights and trademarks, this also entails placing the information in public circulation. For patents, others can then invent new, separately patentable things stimulated by the registered patent.

particular item might fall in any of these four domains, depending on its type. [10]

A contract is a simpler concept. If I have information you want, and if I can legally dispose of it, you can negotiate a contract with me that will specify what I will allow you to do with that information, for how long, and for what compensation. A contract can also be used to regulate what I will do for you, such as collect substances from my area to provide to you at a particular price. If you fail to follow the terms of the contract I can sue for damages in court. Using contracts to guarantee the terms for transfer of cultural knowledge requires, in many national settings, no new legal instruments. Not surprisingly, it is with contracts that most of the experimentation has thus far occurred.[11]

Each nation-state has its own structure of laws governing intellectual property. Although there is much similarity from country to country, there are also important differences. Consequently, IPR for indigenous societies will have to be secured separately in each country where indigenous peoples are found, and will have to fit within each country's existing system. Failing some international convention that induces signatory countries to uniformly redraw their IPR codes to accommodate the IPR protection for indigenous traditional knowledge, the indigenous leadership of each country will have to seek legal protections within the context of its host country's laws. It is hard to know whether this poses an obstacle or an advantage for indigenous societies seeking IPR. On the one hand, the struggle has to be waged numerous times; on the other, at least for certain countries waging a national-level campaign may be more promising than an international one. Either way, the struggles will be decidedly long term.

There is, in addition, an international dimension. Most countries are signatories to conventions and treaties which attempt to guard the ownership of intellectual property in one country against piracy in another.[12] For several years the United States has aggressively pressured other countries, especially in Asia, to adopt and enforce the western approach to intellectual property protections, thereby embedding further

---

[10] In industrialized countries such as the U.S. certain types of intellectual property have become so complex that elaborate bodies of specialized law have accumulated to protect ownership. Examples are pharmaceutical formulae, domesticated plant varieties, computer software, and the arts and crafts produced by native societies. These specialized legal domains can be relevant because some indigenous knowledge may fit within these specialized bodies of intellectual property law. See, for example, Chapter 12 by Stephenson.

[11] This is well illustrated by Chapter 6 (Cragg et al.) and Chapter 10 (Laird).

[12] Obvious examples are the 1888 Berne Convention for the Protection of Literary and Artistic Works (and its successors), the 1883 Paris Convention for the Protection of Industrial Property , the Universal Copyright Convention of 1955 and the Patent Cooperation Treaty of 1970.

the individualistic, capitalist principles on which it is based. The U.S. has also aggressively sought strengthening of IPR protections through the Uruguay Rounds of GATT.[13] Yet, as the chapters by Audrey Chapman (Ch. 14) and Darrell Posey (Ch. 15) make clear, there are some international avenues where IPR for indigenous culture might be pursued, although the obstacles are large. At the same time, Dean Suagee, in Chapter 13, makes clear that progress at the international level -particularly through the avenues open to the UN Working Group on Indigenous Populations - is essential if improvements at the national level are reasonably to be expected. But none of this is yet in place. For the present, no indigenous society, in the U.S. or any other country, is able to copyright its corpus of cultural knowledge. I want to turn now to some of the conceptual reasons why this is so.

Conceptual Issues of IPR

When lawyers first hear talk about according patent or copyright protection to indigenous culture, they roll their eyes. They see three immediate conceptual problems that make the whole plan seem ridiculous. The first problem is that copyrights and patents are for *new* knowledge, not for knowledge that already exists. If I write a new children's story I can copyright it, but I cannot copyright "Goldilocks and the Three Bears." That which is already in the public domain cannot be copyrighted. The second problem is that copyrights and patents are conferred on individuals (or corporations, legal entities acting as individuals). They give individuals ownership rights that are thereby *denied* to the other members of their society. Thus, copyrights and patents go to individuals, not to whole societies. The third problem is that copyrights and patents are supposed to confer temporary rights. Though the law allows for renewals, the fundamental principle is that author rights granted to the creator of intellectual property are for a finite number of years (currently the lifetime of the author plus 50 years). Thereafter, the rights of ownership lapse and the material goes into the public domain, owned by no one.[14]

None of these three problems is simply an arbitrary practice. Each of the three stems from a mainly Eighteenth Century European philosophy about social progress. In its barest form, the philosophy is this: A society thrives on progress. Creative people provide the innovations that generate progress. To foster creativity, creators must foresee the prospect of benefiting materially from their works. Within

---

[13] See Anon 1990:39.

[14] Trademarks and appellations of origin, however, may be maintained by the owner indefinitely. See Chapter 2 (Soleri, Cleveland et al.) for examples of experimentation in the American Southwest.

Eighteenth Century capitalism this meant (and still means) vesting creators with the rights of monopoly ownership in exchange for placing the information in the public domain. That monopoly remains in force for only a finite period of time, however, so as not to unduly impede further progress and price competition that comes when the innovation is available for all to use. Patents and copyrights, then, reward the innovator sufficiently to encourage creativity, but then lapse so that further development by others, and economic competitiveness, can supplant the temporary monopoly. This linkage between invention and social progress became a foundation of Euro-American social policy in the Eighteenth Century. The United States Constitution specifically provides for copyrights and patents in order "To promote the Progress of Science and useful Arts, by securing for limited Times to Authors and Inventors the exclusive Right to their respective Writings and Discoveries."[15]

Therefore, one can see that to propose allowing indigenous societies to patent and copyright their knowledge appears on its face to be nonsense. There is no identifiable inventor, all traditional culture is already in a public domain, and the monopoly benefits would, at best, be only for a finite number of years. The present purpose of patents and copyrights is to encourage change, not to maintain the traditional.

For those who are undaunted by lawyers, these objections merely define the problem. It indicates that what is needed is a *new legal instrument* - an instrument of the Twenty-first Century, that confers ownership and control of indigenous culture on those who practice it; an ownership and control that is society-wide rather than individual; that applies to what is already in the public domain; that, like ownership of property, confers an unending, monopoly ownership; and which is intended not to ensure progress, but to better enable indigenous societies to preserve and benefit from what is theirs.

The practical-minded among us recognize that establishing a new legal concept on a global basis is a goal that, at best, is decades away. Realistically it might never be achieved. A concept with fewer impediments is contracts. If an indigenous society were sufficiently aware, it could insist that before it shares any cultural knowledge with Voracious Pharmaceuticals' employee, that it must have a contract specifying what royalties it will receive in the advent of commercial success. Valid signatures by the two parties make it binding. Contracts can be applied to traditional knowledge, vested in a whole community, and can extend for as long as the contract specifies. Conceptually, then, a contract is a more ready-made instrument for control of an element of cultural knowledge than is a patent or copyright. As various chapters of this Sourcebook illustrate, many indigenous groups are already signato-

---

[15] Article 1, Chapter 8, Constitution of the United States of America.

ries to such contracts. As we will see later, however, contracts as guarantors of indigenous culture, too, have limitations.

In sum, those of us who pursue IPR generally think both concepts should be pursued and that, were both already at hand, that both would be useful. In this section I have limited myself to the conceptual issues. Many reading this will have already thought of many practical issues. Some will be addressed below, but it is prudent first to discuss what is evident thus far about the acceptability of IPR to indigenous groups.

The Acceptability of IPR to Indigenous Groups

The fact is that until now IPR as a concept and a goal has been almost entirely discussed among a few hundred non-indigenous people in industrial countries whose professional or personal concern has been with cultural preservation, with indigenous survival, with cultural rights, and with associated concerns in environmental conservancy, the preservation of biodiversity, human rights, molecular prospecting, and innovations in law. Regrettably, it cannot be said that there is either widespread awareness or support for IPR among indigenous societies, indigenous leaders, or indigenous advocacy groups. Indigenous leaders have been present at meetings on IPR held by the Rainforest Alliance, the Society for Applied Anthropology, the International Society for Ethnobiology, the National Science Foundation, and in other settings, but it remains true that IPR so far is neither a widely voiced objective of indigenous groups nor a rapidly spreading idea among indigenous societies. However, that may now be changing.[16]

At the same time, elements of IPR are emerging in indigenous settings in many places. The National Cancer Institute has implemented a model contract for use in molecular prospecting that accords future royalties to in-country institutions and, potentially, to indigenous societies assisting in the process (see chapter by Cragg et al.). Merck's widely publicized contract for molecular prospecting with Costa Rica's INBio institute is a parallel example from the corporate side.[17] The paper by Steven King of Shaman Pharmaceuticals illustrates the case of a company working directly with indigenous societies. Cultural Survival Inc. has already developed contracts with Amazonian societies

---

[16] Posey, however, argues that recent developments show that indigenous involvement in the search for IPR is rapidly taking hold. See his chapter (15) in this volume, and also Posey 1993 for further evidence on the point. See also Working Group on Indigenous Peoples, Report on Intellectual property rights for indigenous peoples, Year of Indigenous Peoples, United Nations, Geneva, 1993.

[17] The Merck-InBio agreement, however, involves no indigenous signatory or beneficiary. Prospecting in areas claimed by Costa Rica's indigenous groups is, for the present, avoided (Sittenfeld and Gamez 1993: 95-96).

for the supply of sustainable forest products, as has The Body Shop, a British, international cosmetics company committed to ecologically responsible products. For several years, now, the Native Americans of the Southwest have had exclusive ownership, guaranteed by federal laws, of tribal attributions, tribal trademarks, and similar designations for crafts in the Southwest. And finally, Canadian Inuit villages employ researchers under the stipulation that the villages retain authority over the information gathered, and own the copyrights to authorized publications containing their cultural information.[18]

The conclusion that may be drawn from this is that the pursuit of IPR should be continued. Without doubt, however, the involvement of indigenous people in the further development of this concept is urgent. This especially applies to multi-ethnic indigenous advocacy groups which have emerged in many countries of the hemisphere, including Brazil, Ecuador, Bolivia, Mexico, the United States and Canada. These groups have the legal expertise to orchestrate whatever effort may be launched for IPR and the opportunity to shape the agenda through grass roots input.[19]

Issues of IPR in Practice

Earlier I discussed conceptual problems that arise in applying copyright and patent concepts to indigenous cultural knowledge. In this final section I want to sketch some of the practical challenges that also arise.

The first problem is designating to whom IPR would apply. Presumably we would *not* want IPR to apply to traditional knowledge in industrial societies. Nobody should be able to copyright Goldilocks or patent a dinner fork. The goal is to accord IPR to *indigenous societies*, which means creating a special legal privilege, a category of people to whom it applies, and an apparatus for qualifying groups claiming inclusion. This would be messy, but not impossible.[20]

A more worrisome problem is to recognize that indigenous societies are not alone among peoples who perceive themselves under threat. The so-called "village peoples," the rural farmers inhabiting the rural areas of most Third World countries, are also demanding separate

---

[18] See, for example, Beilawski 1992.

[19] The draft Covenant on Intellectual and Cultural Property Rights currently circulating among indigenous and international organizations is a particularly good example of grassroots involvement. The Covenant is contained in Apendix 1 of Chapter 15 (Posey).

[20] For example, U.S. Native American societies are identified and accorded numerous rights unavailable to other citizens, such as a judicially affirmed hiring preference for positions in the Bureau of Indian Affairs, based on reasoning apart from affirmative action.

recognition and international status. They, too, are under assault, have cultural knowledge of potential or demonstrated economic value, and are seeking a voice apart from pronouncements madeby others in the national capital. Their role at the UNCED conference in Brazil of June, 1992, is just one indication of their rising ethnic self-consciousness. As we pursue IPR for indigenous peoples, we should anticipate a demand from organized villager groups for inclusion, and their demand has considerable persuasive force. Yet, widening IPR's special privilege to these groups may weaken the IPR prospects for indigenous societies, who include among their political assets the fact that they are usually seen by members of the dominant society as small, beleaguered, and for whom benefits can be accorded without significantly affecting the quality of life for members of the dominant society. When rural agricultural peoples are included, anxiety will rise that the dominant society's life way may be disrupted.

Returning to indigenous societies, it is worth mentioning that if IPR is in place, and royalty funds begin to accumulate, who gets the funds? A local "key informant"? A village chief? Indigenous village accounts? Multi-community ethnic groups? Regional indigenous advocacy organizations? The national treasury? McGowan and Udeinya's proposal for the sharing of proceeds in Nigeria explores some of the possibilities in Chapter 4, and another approach is illustrated in Moran's Chapter 7. In most writing dealing with IPR these potent practicalities are left unaddressed, as if these were practical matters best left to later. Not so. It would be helpful to have some workable models serving as points of reference as new cases of IPR are negotiated.[21]

Another issue is what to do when the same cultural knowledge is found among several distinct societies as is the case, for example, with knowledge of hallucinogens in the Amazon. Should IPR benefits flow only to the one that Voracious Pharmaceuticals happened to contact?

Then, too, all of the countries with significant indigenous societies have government mediator agencies to deal with them. In Brazil it's FUNAI, an agency with, to be overly generous, an exceedingly uneven record relative to the welfare of Brazil's indigenous groups. As authorized guardians of the welfare of indigenous peoples, these agencies will likely claim IPR funds. Other mediator agencies include the rapidly proliferating multi-tribal advocacy associations controlled by indigenous societies. Would IPR funds by-pass these intermediate organizations?[22]

---

[21] It should be noted, too, that in many - perhaps all - situations, the presense of such funds will itself produce internal change, such as centralization of power. For classic cases of this see Murphy and Steward 1956 and Fallers 1955.

[22] An interesting, relatively new player are the traditional healer associations. Now emerging in many countries, for commercial companies these urban-based associations are likely to be more attractive hosts for biochemical prospecting than visiting remote

Another question is, who monitors whether the terms of IPR contracts or copyrights are being fulfilled and royalties properly paid? And if piracy or fraud is discovered, who goes to court, who pays the lawyers, and who gets a fee for doing all this? Here I suspect that multi-tribal advocacy organizations have a logical role.

What is more important, however, is to agree that these issues are ones that indigenous people themselves will resolve. Non-indigenous advocates must respect the prerogative of indigenous peoples to supply their own answers to these questions. Meanwhile, the lack of easy answers should not restrain non-indigenous advocates from lending their help in securing IPR in those forms desired by indigenous communities, and on their terms.

Closing Thoughts

Another question, which is challenging existing intellectual property laws, is the rapidly developing technology for transforming any initial phenomenon into something else. Whether it's a new medicinal drug, or a novel sound from a musical instrument, increasingly it is the *idea*, not the phenomenon, that is of value. Chemists in the laboratory quickly seek out parallel compounds that do the same job more effectively, with fewer side effects, or for new applications the original substance couldn't address.[23] So, too, musical sounds need no longer rely on physical instruments, but on electronic synthesis. The group that sparks a surge of new innovation will face serious hurdles in claiming a share of the derivatives.[24] In my estimation, this is the most serious problem for IPR; knowledge that has been carefully guarded against change becomes profoundly weak in demonstrating consequential ancestry to the changes it stimulates.

Before closing, I want to offer one rather speculative thought that may be worth pursuing. Unlike the previous items in this section, this is not a problem but, rather, an effort to better delimit where IPR may best apply. In a conference two years ago sponsored by The Rainforest Alliance a man from an African society saw, for Africans,

---

villages. These associations are thus positioned to become key beneficiaries of pharmaceutical contracts even though the "ownership" of such cultural information is more broadly distributed. See McGowan and Udeinya (Chapter 4) for more on this point.

23 A clear example is the very rapidly developed laboratory synthesis of the anti-cancer drug, Taxol, previously available only from the Pacific Yew tree (cf. Culotta and Koshland 1993:1961).

24 A recent object lesson is the bitter, unsuccessful lawsuit by the computer maker, Apple, against the giant software manufacturer, Microsoft, over infringement on screen icons and other elements of software associated with Apple's products (see Wall Street Journal 1993).

little use for IPR.[25] In most African states, he argued, the larger tribal societies sees themselves as rightful elements of the nation's government. Owning their cultural knowledge is not the issue, owning a share of the central government is.

This may help us better understand where IPR is likely to be regarded most favorably, namely, where traditional societies understand themselves to be enclaves, however unwilling, within a dominant society, economy and legal system that is controlled by others. While this describes the structural position of most of the world's indigenous societies, it also happens to fits village-level communities on every continent where distinctive local knowledge of plants may be commercially interesting. The chapter by McGowan and Udeinya, gives a compelling example for Nigeria. On the other hand, IPR may be of particular utility to indigenous societies who, sovereignty claims notwithstanding, find themselves picked over by outsiders who invaded, subdued, and still control.

Despite this litany of issues, both conceptual and practical, IPR for indigenous peoples is a goal that is making progress. The progress is urgent because indigenous peoples remain under siege and badly in need of tools and income to protect themselves in a world where the last vestiges of protective isolation are evaporating like the morning mist.

Bibliography

Anon.
1990 Uruguay Round of GATT Provides New Forum for Debating Germplasm Ownership Issues. Diversity 6, 3-4: 39-40.

Bielawski, Ellen
1992 Indigenous Knowledge in Contemporary Inuit Culture. Presentation to the workshop, First Nations, A Current Event. Institute for the Humanities at Salado. Salado, Tx. October.

Brooke, James
1993 Gold Miners and Indians: Brazil's Frontier War. New York Times, September 7: A4.

Culotta, Elizabeth and Daniel E. Koshland, Jr.
1993 Molecule of the Year. Science 262 (24 December): 1960-61.

---

25 Symposium, "Tropical Forest Medical Resources and the Conservation of Biodiversity", New York: Rockefeller University, January 1992.

Fallers, Lloyd
1955 The Predicament of the Modern African Chief. American Anthropologist 57: 290-305.

Greaves, Tom
1992 The Indians are Winning. Paper presented to the annual meeting of the Society for Applied Anthropology, San Antonio, TX.

1993 Tribal Rights. Paper presented to the NSF/SfAA/AAAS workshop, Intellectual Property Rights and Indigenous Knowledge. Granlibakken, Lake Tahoe, CA. October.

Kane, Joe
1993 Letter from the Amazon: With Spears from All Sides. The New Yorker, October 17: 54-79.

Murphy, Robert F. and Julian H. Steward
1956 Tappers and Trappers: Parallel Process in Acculturation. Economic Development and Cultural Chantge 4: 335-355.

Pollack, Andrew
1992 Drug Industry Going Back to Nature. New York Times, March 5: D1,9.

Posey, Darrell A.
1993 International Agreements and Intellectual Property Right Protection for Indigenous Peoples. Paper presented to the NSF/SfAA/AAAS workshop, Intellectual Property Rights and Indigenous Knowledge. Granlibakken, Lake Tahoe, CA. October.

Rain Forest Alliance and New York Botanical Gardens
1992 Symposium: "Tropical Forest Medical Resources and the Conservation of Biodiversity" New York: Rockefeller University, January.

Reid, Walter V. et al.
1993 Biodiversity Prospecting: Using Genetic Resources for Sustainable Development. Washington, D.C.: World Resources Institute (and others).

Sittenfeld, Ana and Rodrigo Gamez
1993 Biodiversity Prospecting by INBio. In, Biodiversity Prospecting: Using Genetic Resources for Sustainable Development (Walter V. Reid et al., eds.) Washington, D.C.: World Resources Institute (and others). Pp. 69-97.

Wall Street Journal
1993 Apple's Claims Dismissed in Microsoft, H-P Case. June 2: B7.

Working Group on Indigenous Peoples
1993 Draft report, intellectual property rights for indigenous peoples. International Year of Indigenous Peoples. Geneva: United Nations.

Part One

IPR in Practice

Chapter
2

Gifts from the Creator: Intellectual Property Rights and Folk Crop Varieties

Daniela Soleri and David Cleveland,
with
Donald Eriacho, Fred Bowannie Jr., Andrew Laahty,
and Zuni Community Members

In this chapter the Zuni share their experience, range of views, and decisions affecting the use of their intellectual property by non-Zunis. Drawing on the expertise of the Center for People, Food and Environment and the Zuni Folk Varieties Project, the Zuni are raising the level of appreciation within the Zuni community for their traditional crop varieties. With this comes a heightened sense of concern for the disrespectful and commercial use of these resources. Through this process the Zuni are moving toward more effective control over who may use these varieties and for what purposes. Their situation also illustrates the added difficulty of imposing meaningful control when many varieties have already been acquired in commercial quantities by non-Zunis who have no legal obligation to observe Zuni wishes. The lessons are important.

Readers of this chapter will also find a clear analysis of the local complexities that impede Zuni use of federal laws to protect their cultural heritage, and an instructive example of the sort of questionnaire that can be effective for assessing and clarifying community attitudes toward the proper use of traditional cultural knowledge. - ed.

2

Gifts from the Creator: Intellectual Property Rights and Folk Crop Varieties

Daniela Soleri and David Cleveland, with Donald Eriacho, Fred Bowannie Jr., Andrew Laahty, and Zuni Community Members[1]

Introduction

Like many other indigenous farmers around the world, Zunis regard their folk crop varieties (also known as landraces or traditional varieties[2]) as sacred gifts from the Creator.[3] While the loss of folk varieties and their replacement through selection is part of the ongoing change of indigenous farming systems, there has been a dramatic decrease in folk varieties being grown by farmers (Cleveland et al. n.d.). Farmers' intellectual property rights to grow and to control their remaining folk variety seeds and food products is increasingly threatened by rapidly changing markets, laws, and biotechnologies largely controlled by industrial nations and corporations that also want to use folk varieties for their own purposes (Keystone 1991:4-6; Plucknett et al. 1987:3-4). intellectual property rights in folk varieties include rights to the information encoded in their DNA as a result of selection by farmers and their farming systems, as well as knowledge about production and use of folk varieties.

---

[1] The Zuni Folk Varieties Project is funded by grants from the C.S. Fund and the Jessie Smith Noyes Foundation, and is part of the Pueblo of Zuni Conservation Project. We thank the many farmers and others who shared their ideas with us, especially the Cultural Resources Advisory Team and Andrew Othole, their liaison, who worked with us to finalize the Team statements in response to the IPR survey; Jim Enote, Zuni Conservation Project Leader, for support and encouragement and his review of this chapter; Steve Smith and Hope Shand for comments on drafts of this chapter; and Hope Shand, Calvin Sperling and Darrell Posey for helping us to keep up with IPR issues.

[2] Folk varieties are the crop varieties of indigenous farmers, and were the *only* crop varieties until the advent of modern, formal plant breeding after 1900. They are genetically distinct local populations created through selection by the local environment and by farmers (Brown 1978:145; Harlan 1992:147-149).

[3] See Cushing (1979:361) for an outsider's account generally considered to be authentic: "As a mother of her own blood and being gives life to her offspring, so have these [corn maidens] given of their own flesh to you....ye shall treasure their gift...."

How do indigenous farmers' want to define intellectual property rights in their folk varieties, and how can they protect these rights in an age of gigantic multinational seed companies, genetic engineering in plant breeding, patents on plants and crop varieties, and a global marketplace hungry for exotic foods? These are the questions we begin to answer in this chapter, using Zuni as an example.

The Industrial World System and its Effect on Folk Varieties

In the industrial world the policy on intellectual property rights in crop genetic resources differs for folk varieties and modern varieties:

(1) free exchange of folk varieties with no recognition, control, or compensation to the farmer breeders who developed them, when outsiders collect their folk variety seeds, or when folk varieties or their genes are used to develop modern varieties,
(2) maximum legal protection and monetary compensation for individual scientists and corporations who manipulate folk varieties in their laboratories and experimental plots to create modern varieties.

For example, the current US guidelines for collecting folk varieties states only that collectors should "respect the local farmers" for their knowledge and encourage them to share it, with no mention of requesting permission to collect seed, or of any formal recognition or compensation (USDA 1992).

Two of the most important influences in promoting industrial world intellectual property rights policies in crops today are the legal provisions of the United States government and the Union *Internationale pour la Protection des Obtention Végétales* convention, created in 1961 by European nations and joined by the United States in 1980. What are generally referred to as plant breeders' rights are provided in the United States by the Plant Patent Act of 1930 for asexually reproduced crops for a period of 17 years, and the Plant Variety Protection Act of 1970 for seed and plants of sexually reproduced crops for a period of 18 years (Jondle 1989)[4].

In the United States utility patent protection (granted for 17 years) was extended in 1985 to plants, and is replacing PPA and PVPA protection for commercial purposes, since the utility patents offer the patent holder much greater control (Williams and Weber 1989; Williams 1991). Although there is confusion on the issue, the potential seems to exist that a slightly modified folk variety, or a trait from a folk variety,

---

[4] By 1988 over 6,500 plant patents and 2,133 plant variety protection certificates have been issued (Brown 1991:204-205).

could be patented. "The patenting of useful genes found in nature" could mean that Third World farmers would have to "pay royalties on biotechnology products which are based on their own knowledge and experience" (Shand 1991:137).

The Western industrial nations, the United States foremost among them, are exerting pressure on Third World countries, most of which do not recognize patents on living things, to accept industrial notions of intellectual property rights, and create and enforce national laws supporting them (Belcher and Hawtin 1991:14-15). This has been occurring in such international fora as the General Agreement on Tariffs and Trade (GATT), and the UN Conference on Environment and Development (Seedling 1992). The influential Consultative Group on International Agricultural Research (CGIAR) that spearheaded the "green revolution" and is dominated by industrial countries, holds a large proportion of all *ex situ* germplasm. It is looking for approval of a "trust" status of crop germplasm holdings, which may involve patenting (Seedling 1993a; Siebeck and Barton 1992). One CGIAR center, the International Rice Research Institute (IRRI) in the Philippines has stated that it will not seek any intellectual property rights on germplasm it holds in "trust," but leaves open the question of what happens when IRRI germplasm is used to develop new varieties (Seedling 1993b).

While no one knows how the expansion and extension of industrial nation concepts of intellectual property rights in plants could ultimately affect farmers and their folk varieties, it is likely that poor farmers will "be at a disadvantage without construction of proper safeguards" (Keystone 1991:12), and also "very likely that the profound and far-reaching questions raised by this issue will not even be evaluated before the decision is taken" (Belcher and Hawtin 1991:14). The United States has not even examined or resolved these issues as they relate to the indigenous Native American groups within its own borders. Desirable traits for commercial plant breeding and industrial agriculture continue to be borrowed in good faith from Native American folk varieties, but without apparent permission or compensation (e.g. Gulya 1992).

In addition to control over genetic information, the intellectual property rights of indigenous farmers in folk varieties are also being threatened by outsiders using folk variety names and foods without permission or compensation, or gaining legal control of names. This may restrict the marketing of seeds or food products by indigenous groups. In the US, for example, there is increasing consumer interest in Native American folk varieties and food products, and indigenous names are frequently used. One manufacturer of blue corn chips in the US states on the package that they are "dedicated to the Pueblo Indian tribes of the South West who *believed* this blue corn to be a sacred gift from the Kachinas, their gods" (emphasis added). There is no acknowledgment that any of these cultures and their beliefs are still in existence, for example that living Pueblo Indians continue to maintain blue corn folk varieties, much less any indication that they are in any way compensated. Legal control over indigenous names by outsiders, for example by trademarking, is also possible. For example, one company has trademarked the name "Hopi Blue," and uses it to market a blue popcorn purported to have been created by crossing "authentic" blue corn with white popcorn, stating that colored corn "was" grown by Hopis. There is no indication of compensation to the Hopi Native Americans who implicitly contributed the "authentic" blue parent in the cross, and who continue to produce their own blue corn folk varieties in large amounts (e.g. Soleri and Cleveland 1993).

Alternative Approaches to Intellectual Property and Folk Varieties

Many indigenous farmers disagree with the dominant industrial world viewpoint. One of the first questions a Hopi farmer in his 80s asked us suspiciously when we began talking with him about the Hopi bean folk varieties he was harvesting was "Are you going to take Hopi seeds away and make money with them?" (see Soleri and Cleveland 1993). The concern of indigenous farmers world-wide for safeguarding their intellectual property rights in crop genetic resources has increased as plant breeders' rights, patents, trademarks and other Western forms of intellectual property right threaten to alienate them from control of, and compensation for, these resources. While the industrial world is pressing for their version of intellectual property rights in crop genetic resources, indigenous farmers and their supporters see a need to safeguard the rights of farmers to (a) grow folk varieties and market folk variety seeds and food products, (b) be compensated when folk varieties, folk variety genes, folk variety food products and names are used or marketed by others, and (c) have a say in the manipulation and other uses of folk varieties by outsiders, which may violate the cultural and religious values with which folk varieties are often deeply imbued.

To those supporting farmers' intellectual property rights in their folk varieties, the effort and knowledge of indigenous farmers involved in creating and maintaining folk varieties implies the need for recognition on an equal footing with that of plant breeders and molecular biologists. They see the communal effort in developing folk varieties as an integrated part of making a living over generations to be as legitimate as the individual efforts of scientists in formal, segregated work settings in the laboratory or field plot. Thus, the effort to safeguard farmers' intellectual property rights in folk varieties is an attempt to reinterpret the dominant industrial system of intellectual property right using several different approaches.

The first approach is to protect the rights of farmer-breeders using industrial world intellectual property right concepts and methods such as contracts, trademarks, and patents. Plant breeders' rights or patents do not offer much promise for farm communities, in part because of the expense involved[5]. Another difficulty is that a large proportion of the genes in folk varieties of most crops probably already exists in *ex situ* collections or plant breeders' stock. An even greater complication is the likelihood that because of seed sharing between neighboring groups, there may be little or no genetic differences between folk varieties of some crops. Seeking protection of these varieties by applying the criteria of patents to them would be nearly impossible as it is doubtful that the historic and cultural complexities involved could be unraveled. Ultimately this could foster competition between communities in a region while the greater threat to control is external. There is a strong contrast between the approach to resource use of many indigenous groups and the emphasis on private ownership and commercialization of industrial societies. This has led a recent United Nations report on intellectual property and indigenous peoples to state that industrial world intellectual property right mechanisms are "inherently unsuitable" for indigenous peoples for philosophical reasons (Daes 1993, cited in Suagee, this volume). There is a difference, however, between the shorter-term, more expensive control primarily over specific genetic information offered by patents and plant breeders' rights, and the longer-term, less expensive, more general control offered by protocols, contracts and trademarks. Protocols, contracts, and trademarks could be used by indigenous communities to regulate the collection of folk variety seeds, and their subsequent use in ways much more amenable to indigenous cultures.

A second approach is to balance private plant breeders' rights with "farmers' rights" defined at a group level. Since 1987 the major international effort regarding intellectual property rights and folk varieties has been the promotion of "farmers' rights," which was endorsed in 1989 as part of the FAO Undertaking. This modified the original approach of the Undertaking, and was a concession to the predominance of private property in the world, making the Undertaking much more palatable to industrial countries. A fund has been established into which industrial countries and seed companies would contribute a fraction of a percent of the profit from sales of modern varieties, but few contributions have been made. The Keystone dialogue proposed that the money would be used at the national or regional level for "genetic

[5] Fees during the total 17 or 18 years of protection in 1989 for Plant Patent Act protection, a Plant Variety Protection Certificate, and a utility patent were US $405, $2,400 and $3,540 respectively (Knudson and Hansen 1991). This, however, may be a minor expense compared with the laboratory and legal work required before an application is filed.

conservation and utilization programs particularly, but not exclusively, in the Third World," but might also involve some sort of "technology transfer" to Third World countries (Keystone 1991:13, 25-33). This approach leaves out the local community, and ignores the widespread conflicts between local indigenous groups and nation states.

A third approach is the opposite of the first two in that it opposes control of crop genetic resources for profit, and aims to keep them freely available for everyone's use. Free access to all crop genetic resources was the original position of the 1983 FAO Undertaking on Plant Genetic Resources, which included not only folk varieties, but formal breeders' elite lines and finished varieties. This was vigorously opposed by Western industrial governments as directly opposed to notions of private property. Meanwhile, Seed Savers' Exchange of Iowa, USA, a grassroots network for heirloom seed conservancy, has systematically been publishing descriptions of their heirloom varieties (Whealy 1993). They believed, on the basis of information from the US Plant Variety Protection Office in Beltsville, Maryland, that published documentation should protect described varieties from subsequent plant breeders' rights protection. However, the strategy of publishing descriptions of folk varieties, which may serve to thwart plant breeders' rights protection, might possibly increase the chance of patenting folk varieties or their genes, if outsiders are alerted to desirable traits for the development of modern varieties.

A fourth approach is to protect folk varieties for indigenous peoples, but by very different means than those of industrial societies. This removes folk varieties from the same playing field as plant breeders' varieties, and attempts to force the world to recognize indigenous peoples' values as equal to those of the dominant society. One way is by defining protection of natural, cultural and intellectual property as part of the overall protection of indigenous peoples' human rights. For example, a recent United Nations report states that the most effective way for indigenous peoples to protect their intellectual property is to assert collective ownership of their land base (Daes 1993, cited in Suagee, this volume). This is also the approach of the report of the First International Conference on Indigenous Cultural and Intellectual Property Rights, which states that indigenous peoples are capable of managing their own traditional knowledge, but are willing to share with the rest of the world on condition that their rights to define and control their knowledge are internationally recognized and protected (Mataatua Declaration 1993). In regard to traditional plants and genetic resources, the Mataatua Declaration states that indigenous peoples must be in control of any commercialization or experiments.

More specifically, it has been suggested that folk varieties be treated as the cultural heritage of local communities under international law. For example it has been proposed (Shand 1991) that folk varieties could be protected under the *Model Law* of the United Nations World

Intellectual Property Organization (UNESCO/WIPO 1982), which recognizes the legal rights of communities to intellectual property in the form of folklore. For this reason some advocate referring to indigenous crop varieties as "folk varieties" rather than landraces or traditional varieties (Keystone 1990:26; Fowler and Mooney 1990:xvi). In 1989 UNESCO adopted a recommendation that the *Model Law* become a legally binding international convention, but it has not yet gone into effect.

Zuni Farming and Folk Varieties

Zuni folk varieties include varieties of ancient Native American crops like corn, beans, and squash. In recent generations, as Zuni farming declined, and as remaining Zuni farmers and gardeners planted more commercial varieties bought from mail order suppliers, stores, and nurseries, Zuni folk varieties began to disappear. Although new folk varieties and modern varieties are useful, existing folk varieties continue to play an important role in sustainable Zuni agriculture (Cleveland et al., n.d.; Soleri and Cleveland 1993). They are adapted to the climate and soils of Zuni, and can therefore usually produce good crops without chemical fertilizers or pesticides, and require a minimal amount of water. They are also important in making traditional Zuni foods, and in Zuni religious ceremonies.

Zunis are now revitalizing their agriculture and folk varieties are seen to be an essential ingredient for cultural and agroecological reasons. Zunis have previously been very successful in establishing rights to cultural property in case of *Ayayuda,* the twin war gods represented in wooden statues. However, no precedent in the US legal system has been established by Zuni in intangible, i.e. intellectual, property. It has not been well established in Zuni law either, according to the major study of Zuni law by outsiders (Smith and Roberts 1954). While that study did not deal with intellectual property rights, it pointed out that

> there is much evidence that in the ceremonial or religious realm a very clearly formulated notion of property in intangibles obtains. This is exemplified by the 'ownership' possessed by an individual or group in certain esoteric ritual procedures, songs or dances; or by a curer in certain methods of healing (65).

Seeds of Zuni folk varieties have been given in good faith to many outsiders, but Zunis presently have not established their rights in their folk varieties to compensation and control. Consequently, use of Zuni folk varieties by outsiders may violate these rights and be against Zuni wishes. Zuni seeds, Zuni foods, and even the name Zuni itself are used by people other than the Zuni. Many people in the Zuni community are familiar with this problem in the case of so-called "Zuni" jewelry being produced elsewhere and sold as a Zuni product. Zuni craftspeople neither make the pieces nor receive any benefits from such sales. What do the Zuni people think about this in the case of agricultural products? Should Zuni seeds, foods and the Zuni name be shared with all people? What if those people want to make money from them? Should those profits be shared with the Zuni people? These are some of the questions addressed in the intellectual property rights component of the Zuni Folk Varieties Project.

The Zuni Folk Varieties Project

The overall purpose of the Zuni Folk Varieties Project is to safeguard Zuni folk varieties for the revitalization of Zuni farming.[6] Though the project is not yet complete, we want to share some preliminary results regarding intellectual property rights in order to encourage interaction with other indigenous communities. The Project works with the Zuni community to achieve four goals. The first three concern supporting the role of folk varieties in sustainable agriculture at Zuni: improving the understanding of the role of folk varieties through documentation and education, including curriculum development with the Zuni schools; increasing the availability of folk variety seeds through encouraging a seed exchange network, and also through maintaining the Zuni Community Seedbank and searching for seeds of Zuni crops no longer available at Zuni[7]; and increasing the planting and diversity of folk varieties by working with the Zuni Sustainable Agriculture Project and exploring commercial opportunities if approved by the community.

The fourth goal is complementary to the first three: ensuring control by Zunis of their folk varieties by formulating policy options to establish intellectual property rights based on our documentation and the community's wishes. The Folk Varieties Project is breaking new ground as we work with members of the Zuni community, the Zuni Community Seedbank Board of Directors, the Zuni Cultural Resource Advisory Team, the Zuni Irrigation Association, the Tribal government, and legal consultants, to formulate new policies for protecting Zuni folk varieties.

---

6 The Folk Varieties Project builds in part on the Zuni Traditional Crops Project carried out by Carol Brandt of the Zuni Archeology Program, with the help of Jerome Zunie, in 1991 (Brandt 1992). That project asked 50 Zuni farmers about seed of Zuni folk varieties they were still growing, and accepted donations of seed to begin a seedbank. It also increased interest in a community seedbank, and raised questions about the future of Zuni folk varieties and how to safeguard them.

7 We have recently made a request to the US Department of Agriculture's National Genetic Resources Program to do a search for Zuni folk varieties that may have been removed from Zuni in the past and are presently being stored elsewhere, for example in the National Seed Storage Lab in Fort Collins, Colorado. They have already located seeds of several varieties (Sperling 1993), but none that is not currently grown at Zuni.

Policy options will cover 1) the collection of seeds at Zuni by outsiders, 2) the distribution of seed from the Zuni seedbank, 3) the use of Zuni folk variety seeds already removed from Zuni, and any that may be taken in the future, in regard to genetic manipulation, patenting, or commercial sales, and 4) the use of Zuni folk variety names, and other Zuni cultural symbols, in connection with the marketing of Zuni seeds or food products. We will also work with the Farmer Community Seedbank Board to help them prepare to take over control of the Community Seedbank by the end of the project.

We will discuss these options at open community meetings and in Project educational materials, and provide input to Tribal Council decision making on Zuni policy.

Zuni Attitudes Toward Intellectual Property Right and Folk Varieties

In addition to informal discussions with Zuni community members, questions about intellectual property rights in Zuni folk varieties are also included in four formal surveys. We present preliminary results from two of these below.

(1) The Peach Orchard Survey

We are interviewing Zuni families that have rights to land in peach orchards. These orchards became a major food sources for Zuni after the introduction of peaches, but are now mostly dead. We are responding to the great interest in the community to reestablish these orchards using Zuni peach varieties. Donald Eriacho is in charge of the interviewing, and so far we have completed 29 interviews. Two of the questions on the survey ask about the value of Zuni peach folk varieties and control over them.

The first question asks "Is it important to make sure that old Zuni peach varieties are not lost? Why?" Out of 25 answers, 24 were "yes," and 1 "don't know." Of the 17 who explained their answer, 10 said only that it was important to save Zuni peaches "for our children," 3 said Zuni peaches are part of Zuni culture, and the other four mentioned that Zuni peaches are more nutritious, easier to slice and dry than modern varieties, will help their children to make money, and are easier to care for now with modern technology.

The second question is "Should non-Zunis be given seeds of Zuni Peaches? Why?" Out of 24 answers, 17 said "no," 5 said "yes," and 1 said "don't know." Of the 19 who explained their answer, 9 said simply that Zuni peaches were only for Zunis, 4 added that outsiders would sell Zuni peaches for money or that Zuni peaches should not be commercialized. Other explanations of "no" answers included that the seeds were from the ancestors and that Zunis have given away too much already. One person qualified their "no" answer by stating that maybe it would be all right to give Zuni peaches to outsiders later if more information on how they would be used became available. Three people explained their "yes" answers by saying that Zunis could help outsiders out, that an arrangement could be worked out, and only if Zunis can control the peach seeds. In discussions during several of the interviews the image of Zuni farmers removing the pits before handing over the peaches to outsiders made us all laugh, but highlighted the practical problems of controlling seeds when selling or giving away fresh peaches, or dried chilies, corn or beans.

(2) The Intellectual Property Rights Scenario Survey

One of the main ways in which the Zuni Folk Varieties Project is documenting Zuni opinions about issues involving intellectual property rights is by asking people's opinions about four fictitious scenarios. Each scenario is followed by four responses by fictitious farmers, and we ask interviewees to choose the best response and comment on it, or give their own response if different.

We used this type of tool because intellectual property rights is an obscure and confusing term that is unfamiliar to many people both in and outside the Zuni community, although most are aware of the basic principle of intellectual property rights. These scenarios represent ways in which Zuni intellectual property rights in their folk varieties may be threatened, and they assist Zuni people in considering these specific issues and responding to them.

So far we have done the first survey with members of the Zuni Tribal Council, the Zuni Cultural Resources Advisory Team, and the Zuni Irrigation Association. We tell them that individual responses are confidential, but that the Folk Varieties Project will report the answers in the Project Newsletter (*Zuni Farming*) and other publications such as this, and on a community radio broadcast. A summary of the responses will also be included in the Folk Varieties Project final report that will be used to help the community and Tribal Council in discussing policy options.

While the scenarios, reproduced below, are fictitious, all of them describe things that have already happened or could easily happen at Zuni, and some have already happened in other Native American communities. For each scenario we ask: "Which farmer do you think had the best response?, "Why?, and "Is there another response not described above that you think is better? If so, what is it?"

> 1. Bill Barker is a seed collector with Kaleidoscope Seeds in California, a company that specializes in selling "old-time" seed varieties. His company is looking for new corn varieties to sell to their customers. Bill visits Zuni in October to collect seeds of

traditional blue and white corn. He drives around the fields and stops to talk with farmers while they are harvesting corn.

The first farmer, *Ted*, sells Bill five pounds of shelled Zuni white corn and five pounds of shelled Zuni blue corn that Kaleidoscope Seeds will plant on their California farm to get enough seed to sell. They will not need to return to Zuni for more seed.

The second farmer, *Elma*, sells Bill one fifty pound bag of shelled Zuni white corn and one fifty pound bag of shelled Zuni blue corn that Kaleidoscope Seeds will package into five ounce packets to sell directly to its customers. Elma also made Bill sign an agreement that any Zuni blue or white corn seed that Kaleidoscope sells will be purchased from Elma, not increased by Kaleidoscope on its California farm.

The third farmer, *Will*, refuses to give or sell any Zuni corn seeds to Bill, saying they are the gift of the Creator and should not be taken away from Zuni.

The fourth farmer, *Evan*, takes Bill to the Tribal Council, and together they agree on a contract between the Zuni Tribe and Kaleidoscope Seeds that guarantees that any Zuni corn seeds sold by Kaleidoscope will be purchased directly from Tribal members and none of these seeds will be increased by the company.

2. Ed Jones, a scientist with Better Seeds International, a large seed company, visits Zuni in October to collect seeds of traditional blue and white corn. His company is looking for corn varieties that are resistant to drought, so that they can use them in breeding programs to develop commercial corn varieties that Better Seeds would then sell. Ed drives around the fields and stops to talk with farmers while they are harvesting corn.

The first farmer, *Dan*, gives Ed Jones seed only after he makes Ed sign a contract stating that if Better Seeds International ever makes any money from the seeds he has given, that they will pay Dan a fair share.

The second farmer, *Ethel* sells him 10 ears of white and 10 ears of blue for a total of $20.

The third farmer, *Mary*, takes Ed to the Tribal Council, and together they agree on a contract between the Zuni Tribe and Better Seeds International that pays the individual farmer for the seeds, and gives the Tribe a share of any profits made by the Company based on use of the Zuni seeds.

The fourth farmer, *Jerry*, refuses to give Ed Jones any seed, saying that they are a gift of the Creator, and should not be given to non-Zunis.

3. Four Zuni farmers have been enlarging the area they plant to Zuni blue corn over the last several years. They now have more than enough to satisfy the needs of their families and extended families.

The first farmer, *Grace*, says that she would rather earn a little extra money by farming than washing dishes at the Pizza Shop every Friday, and she thinks they should sell blue corn in the village, but only to other Zuni people.

The second farmer, *Alfred*, agrees with Grace but says that there are a lot of outsiders and tourists who would be willing to pay for traditional Zuni blue corn, and that they should market it to these people also.

The third farmer, *Winston*, thinks they should stop expanding their blue corn production, since they have enough to meet family and extended family needs, and it's not right to sell traditional Zuni crops.

The fourth farmer, *April*, agrees with Alfred about marketing to both Zunis and non-Zunis except she thinks that only ground cornmeal should be sold to non-Zunis so that no traditional Zuni corn seed would be sold.

4. A group of four farmers has started a farmers' market at Zuni specializing in traditional Zuni crops like blue and white corn, chilies, string beans and squash. They have been very successful, selling to both Zuni and non-Zuni customers and some of them are selling some of these products off the reservation. A group of Anglo farmers in a nearby town has noticed the success of the Zunis, and they have begun growing Zuni crops and have started packaging blue corn meal and selling it as "Zuni Blue Corn Meal."

The first Zuni farmer, *Carol*, thought that their group should apply for a trademark on the name "Zuni" for use with farm produce. Then they would be the only one that could legally use the name.

The second Zuni farmer, *Bernice*, said that they should just ignore the Anglo farmers, and continue what they are doing.

The third Zuni farmer, *Victor*, agreed with Carol, but thought that they should work with the Tribe to get a trademark for use by any Tribal member.

The fourth Zuni farmer, *Neil,* said that they should tell the Anglo farmers to stop growing Zuni crops and selling them with the Zuni name, but if that didn't have an effect it wasn't worth doing anything else.

Among the three groups interviewed it was not uncommon to find an ideal position that Zuni folk varieties are only for Zuni people and should not be given, sold to, or used by outsiders. However, many people, including those who hold this position, believe that it is either too late or unrealistic to enforce this ideal, and that therefore Zuni folk varieties could be given or sold to or used by outsiders, within limits. We summarize the Tribal Council and Nutria Irrigation Unit responses in Table 1, and then present the comments of the Advisory Team. When discussing the first question many respondents in both groups pointed out the Zuni belief that "the crops grown are the gift or blessing of the Creator", and that "things should be kept in the Zuni tradition" (Will's response). Even so, the majority of people in each group selected the response (Evan) of a group contract through the Tribal Council or "some other body".

Table 1

Responses to the Intellectual Property Right Survey

Question	*Nutria Irrigation Unit Member*		*Zuni Tribal Council Members*	
#1	3rd farmer (Will)	= 6	3rd farmer (Will)	= 2
	4th farmer (Evan)	= 8	4th farmer (Evan)	= 3
#2	1st farmer (Dan)	= 3	1st farmer (Dan)	= 1
	3rd farmer (Mary)	= 2	3rd farmer (Mary)	= 3
	4th farmer (Jerry)	= 6	4th farmer (Jerry)	= 1
#3	2nd farmer (Alfred)	= 1.5*	2nd farmer (Alfred)	= 3
	3rd farmer (Winston)	= 2	4th farmer (April)	= 2
	4th farmer (April)	= 7.5*		
#4	1st farmer (Carol)	= 4	3rd farmer (Victor)	= 5
	3rd farmer (Victor)	= 4		
	4th farmer (Neil)	= 3		

* respondent gave two answers to this question, each one recorded as 0.5 votes.

Also in the second question many Nutria Irrigation Unit members supported the view of Jerry, as one wrote "our seeds are our children, I do not believe in selling any seeds to Zunis or non-Zunis". But respondents from both groups also selected answers that represented contracts between individual farmers and the company (Dan), and contracts between the Tribe and the company (Mary). Distinctions between these two approaches may not have always been clear. In addition, Tribal Council members in particular were concerned that the Council be involved in the approach and yet demonstrate that they recognize individual farmers' efforts. "The contract should be between the individual and the company but the Tribal Council should help write the contract. ..It might not be fair for just one person to hold the contract. There should be a one time payment to the individual and then long-term profits coming to the Tribe."

For the third question the idea of marketing Zuni corn while still controlling its fate by selling only corn meal to outsiders (April) was favored by many Nutria Irrigation Unit and some Tribal Council members. On the other hand, respondents from both groups also selected the approach of selling to outsiders without any special provisions for control (Alfred). A councilperson pointed out that "Not many young people would respond the way April did, but older men who are active in Zuni religion would recognize the difference between April and Alfred's responses." Another one said " Selling food to outsiders is different (than selling seeds); this is OK."

The distribution of answers to the fourth question may reflect a lack of clarity in the survey that made it difficult to see the difference between the first (Carol) and third (Victor) farmers' approaches: acquiring a trademark for a group of farmers vs. acquiring it for use by all tribal members. Others in this group selected a less formal and less powerful approach (Neil).

The Zuni Cultural Resources Advisory Team formulated the following response in a series of discussions on the survey with the Zuni Folk Varieties Program. The Advisory Team is a group of seven male Zuni religious leaders, recognized by the Zuni community. The Team, through the Cultural Preservation Officer who is their liaison, is active in developing recommendations for the care of Zuni resources in ways consistent with and supportive of Zuni cultural beliefs.

The Advisory Team felt it was important to make it clear that theirs is not a policy-making role, but rather to develop recommendations as a group that reflect Zuni cultural values concerning the resources being discussed. They feel that developing policy concerning these issues should be the responsibility of another community-based entity such as the Zuni Community Seedbank Board of Directors.

On the broad topic of rights to Zuni traditional crop seeds and the Zuni name for agricultural products the Advisory Team believes that:

> Zuni seeds should not be sold or given to outsiders for profit, resale, breeding, or trade marking because of their significance to the Zuni people. This statement applies to all long-time food crop varieties of the Zuni people including corn, beans, squash, melons, gourds, chilies, and peaches.

They stated that these seeds should not be used as a commodity for profit, and pointed out an event in Zuni oral narrative and history where their corn disappeared, and this was followed by a warning that the next time the Zuni people would not have a second chance. In addition, the Team added that once you let something as important as these seeds go you don't know how they will be used, because once they are out of your control, there are no guarantees.

It is important to point out that the Advisory Team made it clear that while their statement reflects an ideal that they believe in, it will not always reflect the changing world that the Zuni people live in and what is actually occurring in the Zuni community. Therefore when answering the following questions they always emphasized the above position and then discussed ideas that they felt best supported this position, but also responded in a realistic way to each of these scenarios, reflecting actual choices people must make.

Survey question #1. Advisory Team members indicated that in this situation there should be an agreement, but they felt that such an agreement should be between the company and a community-based entity whose work focuses on this topic, such as the Zuni Community Seedbank and its Board of Directors.

The Advisory Team realizes that sales of Zuni crops probably has and will occur, and they see their role as providing recommendations to the Zuni Community Seedbank Board of Directors. The Zuni Community Seedbank Board of Directors would have the responsibility of mediating the impact of these sales through policies to demand protection and compensation for the Zuni people. The Advisory Team feels it is extremely important that the Zuni Community Seedbank Board of Directors understand issues of cultural appropriateness concerning the use of these crops, and that the Zuni Community Seedbank maintain community support.

Survey question #2. This question was about the use of Zuni folk varieties as raw material for breeding new varieties, instead of using them directly as was the case in question #1. The Advisory Team does not support the idea or practice of "crossbreeding", that is mixing two varieties to make a new variety. They feel that this is inappropriate for Zuni farming and would result in a loss of the distinct varieties that are important to the Zuni people. They stated that they know the special qualities of Zuni corn are desirable, but this kind of crossing is only done for making money, and the Zuni people never get any of that money.

The Advisory Team believes there should be recognition and compensation not only for breeding using Zuni crop varieties that is occurring now and in the future, but also for what has already happened in the past. They feel that this is a policy question that the Team would be willing to make recommendations on, but that is the responsibility of the Zuni Community Seedbank Board of Directors.

Survey question #3. The Advisory Team pointed out that there is a need within the Zuni community for increased quantities of traditional Zuni farm products such as blue corn. How to make them more available and whether or not they should be available to outsiders were considered policy issues that should be addressed by an entity such as the Zuni Community Seedbank and its Board of Directors.

If sales were considered as one way of increasing the availability of these products, Team members felt it was important to know if farmers would be selling their corn and other goods themselves, that is directly to customers vs. to a retailer. If the farmers are not selling directly then it would be very easy for them to lose control of how their corn or other farm products would be sold or used.

The Advisory Team felt that making a decision about the availability of Zuni seeds and farm products to outsiders is difficult because different outsiders have very different histories and intentions. For example, the Team pointed out that there is a long history of sharing these goods with the other Pueblos, especially the Hopi. On the other hand, there are many examples of Anglos who have used Native American seeds, foods, or tribal names for their own profit. Perhaps this means that the policy would need to depend on who the outsiders are, how they intend to use the farm products, and if they actually use them in the way that they claim.

One suggestion that the Advisory Team had was that the Zuni Community Seedbank could act as a marketing board for Zuni farm products both within and outside the community. The Zuni Community Seedbank could purchase surplus corn or other Zuni farm products from farmers for a fair price, the corn could then be resold in the community with a minimal price increase. The Zuni Community Seedbank would not do this for profit but as a community service. The Advisory Team stated that they would be willing to provide recommendations to the Zuni Community Seedbank Board of Directors concerning these policies. By doing this, and actively seeking community input, the policies could best reflect Zuni concerns and interest.

The Advisory Team believed that such an arrangement could offer the following advantages: community members would have a source for Zuni farm products that they know are Zuni and of good quality, farmers would know they have a way to market their surpluses, and both those buying from and selling to the Zuni Community Seedbank would have the assurance that these transactions would be done in a way that was supportive of Zuni cultural and religious values. Options could be considered such as selling whole seed only within the community and fresh produce such as sweet corn or processed foods such as cornmeal or parched corn to non-Zunis to insure that no viable seed would be sold to them.

Survey question #4. This question focused the discussion on the issue of trademarking. The Advisory Team favors protection of the Zuni name for use by tribal members only. Protecting cultural resources such as Zuni crops, foods and the Zuni name for use by tribal members was seen by the Team as a sovereignty issue that should be addressed. They felt that how this protection was achieved is a policy issue and the responsibility of an entity directly concerned with the topic such as the Zuni Community Seedbank Board of Directors.

Conclusion

Complex and heated debates have enveloped questions of natural resources, such as rights to certain quantities and quality of water and air, that we all thought of as freely available to all. The same is happening with folk varieties.

Developing policy options for dealing with intellectual property rights in folk varieties is a very complicated task. Zuni farmers, like most farmers, have traditionally shared seeds freely with each other and with their neighbors. The increasing private control and manipulation of seeds by companies for profit has changed this situation and many indigenous peoples like the Zuni are becoming reluctant to share their folk varieties freely. Lack of formal policies concerning these issues does *not* mean that these communities are unaware or unconcerned about them. Indigenous groups must learn more about the issues and their options, so that they can at least decide whether they want to do anything or not. Otherwise, those with the most influence in the government, the courts, and the market place will dominate the scene for their own interests.

An important part of the Zuni Folk Varieties Project is exploring alternatives that can protect the rights of indigenous communities and their farmers in their folk varieties. None of the four alternative approaches that we outlined above is an easy and satisfactory strategy. A common basic approach by indigenous communities globally seems to be emerging and is a necessary foundation to assuring recognition of basic human rights within which folk varieties can be protected. Many groups, including the Zuni, are in fact taking greater control over the use of their culture and creating new precedents. Each community, however, will probably develop its own specific strategies, some of which may be brand new. This will depend to some extent on the power relationships within the community, and between community and outside groups.

During the rest of the Zuni Folk Varieties Project we will continue to work with the Tribal Council, Cultural Resources Advisory Team, and other community members to develop agreement on how Zunis wish to protect their intellectual property rights in their folk varieties. We will consult with lawyers and other outside experts on specific ways in which Zuni can get this protection. For example, protocols (rules) for outsiders collecting Zuni seeds, contracts with outsiders using Zuni seeds, and trademarking of the use of the Zuni name in selling Zuni seeds, produce and food products. This work will be continued by the Zuni Community Seedbank Board and the Zuni Sustainable Agricultural Project with the goal of establishing Zuni Tribal policy to protect Zuni folk varieties.

Bibliography

Belcher, Brian and Geoffrey Hawtin

1991 A Patent on Life: Ownership of Plant and Animal Research. Ottawa, Ontario, Canada: International Development Research Center.

Brandt, Carol

1992 Sustaining Traditional Crops of the Zuni Pueblo Indians of West-Central New Mexico: A Harvest for the Local and Global Agricultural Community. Ethnobiological Technical Series. Number 92-8. Zuni, New Mexico: Zuni Archeology Program.

Brown, A.H.D.

1978 Isozymes, Plant Population Genetic Structure and Genetic Conservation. Theoretical and Applied Genetics 52:145-157.

Brown, Bart, ed.

1991 Biotechnology in a Global Economy. Washington, D.C.: US GPO for the Office of Technology Assessment, US Congress.

Cleveland, David A., Daniela Soleri, and Steven E. Smith

n.d. Safeguarding Folk Crop Varieties for Sustainable Agriculture. ms.

Cushing, Frank H.

1979 Selected Writings of Frank Hamilton Cushing. Jesse Green, ed. Lincoln, Nebraska: University of Nebraska Press.

Daes, Erica-Irene (Special Rapporteur)

1993 Study on the Protection of the Cultural and Intellectual Property Rights of Indigenous Peoples. E/CN.4/Sub. 2/1993/28. Sub-Commission on Prevention of Discrimination and Protection of Minorities, Commission on Human Rights, United Nations Economic and Social Council.

Fowler, Cary, and Pat Mooney.

1990 Shattering: Food, Politics and the Loss of Genetic Diversity. Tucson, AZ: University of Arizona Press.

Gulya, T.J.

1992 Native American Variety May Provide Sunflower Crop with Crucial Resistance. Diversity 8,4: 29-30.

Harlan, Jack R.
1992 Crops and Man. 2nd ed. Madison, Wisconsin: American Society of Agronomy, Crop Science Society of America.

Jondle, Robert J.
1989 Overview and Status of Plant Proprietary Rights. In, Intellectual Property Rights Associated with Plants. ASA Special Publication No. 52. Madison, WI: CSA, ASA, SSSA. Pp. 5-15.

Keystone Center, The
1990 Final Consensus Report of the Keystone International Dialogue Series on Plant Genetic Resources. Madras Plenary Session. Washington, D.C.: GRCS, Inc.

1991 Final Consensus Report: Global Initiative for the Security and Sustainable Use of Plant Genetic Resources. Oslo Plenary Session. Washington, D.C.: GRCS, Inc.

Knudson, Mary and LeRoy Hansen
1991 Intellectual Property Rights and the Private Seed Industry. Agricultural Economic Report Number 654. Washington, DC: Economic Research Service, US Department of Agriculture.

Mataatua Declaration
1993 The Mataatua Declaration on Intellectual and Cultural Property Rights of Indigenous Peoples. First International Conference on the Cultural and Intellectual Property Rights of Indigenous Peoples, 12-18 June, 1993, Whakatane, Aotearoa. Draft ms.

Plucknett, Donald L., Nigel J.H. Smith, J.T. Williams, and N. Murthi Anishetty
1987 Gene Banks and the World's Food. Princeton, NJ: Princeton University Press.

Seedling
1992 Biodiversity at Rio: Conservation or Access? Seedling 9,2&3: 2-5.

1993a IARC Genebanks under Auspices of FAO. Seedling 10,2: 6-9.

1993b IRRI Adopts Intellectual Property Right Policy. Seedling 10,2: 10.

Shand, Hope
1991 There is a Conflict between Intellectual Property Rights and the Rights of Farmers in Developing Countries. Journal of Agricultural and Environmental Ethics 4,2: 131-142.

Siebeck, Wolfgang, and John H. Barton
1992 The Implications of Applying the Legal Concept of Trust to Germplasm Collections at CGIAR Research Centers. Diversity 8,3: 29-35.

Smith, Watson, and John M. Roberts
1954 Zuni Law: A Field of Values. Papers of the Peabody Museum of American Archaeology and Ethnology, Harvard University, No. 1. Cambridge, Massachusetts: Peabody Museum, Harvard University.

Soleri, Daniela and David A. Cleveland
1993 Hopi Crop Diversity and Change. Journal of Ethnobiology 13,2 [In press]

Sperling, Calvin (Plant Exploration Officer, National Germplasm Resources Laboratory, US Department of Agriculture)
1993 Personal communication.

UNESCO/WIPO
1982 WIPO Model Provisions for National Laws on the Protection of Expressions of Folklore Against Illicit Exploitation and other Prejudicial Actions. Geneva: WIPO.

USDA (United States Department of Agriculture)
1992 Guidelines for Plant Exploration Proposals - 1993. Beltsville, Maryland: Plant Exploration Office, USDA/ARS.

Whealy, Kent (Director, Seed Savers Exchange, Decorah, Iowa, USA)
1993 Personal communication.

Williams, J.T.
1991 Plant Genetic Resources: Some New Directions. Advances in Agronomy 45:61-91.

Williams, Sidney B., Jr. and Kenneth A. Weber
1989 Intellectual Property Protection in Plants. In Intellectual Property Rights Associated With Plants. ASA Special Publication No. 52. Pp. 91-107. Madison, Wisconsin: CSA, ASA, SSSA.

Chapter
3

Tribal Sovereignty and the Control of Knowledge

Sandra Lee Pinel
Urban and Regional Planner, Santa Fe, NM, USA

Michael J. Evans
University of Arizona
Bureau of Applied Research in Anthropology

The struggle to gain control of indigenous intellectual property is especially difficult where the potential for commercial gain by non-Indians runs high. The Pueblos and their neighbors from the American Southwest are a particularly instructive case. Pinel and Evans describe three areas where Pueblo groups have sought to prevent the use of their sacred symbols by outsiders in mundane and disrespectful settings, and the difficulties that those efforts have encountered. Exasperation is strongly felt over the intractable nature of Western principles of law and rules supporting concepts of public domain and the rights of an entrepreneur. Increasingly many have concluded that their best strategies are to enter the market place on their own terms, and to avoid telling any outsider anything. - ed.

3 Tribal Sovereignty and the Control of Knowledge

Sandra Lee Pinel
Urban and Regional Planner, Santa Fe, NM

Michael J. Evans
University of Arizona Bureau of Applied Research in Anthropology

Introduction

Most of the discussion of intellectual property rights has centered on plants and the indigenous knowledge of their useful properties. However, in American Indian populations, intellectual property rights are being defined in a much broader sense. While plants and knowledge of their uses are considered important, other aspects of culture, particularly those that center around religious and spiritual knowledge, are also considered intellectual property worth of special protection. The reason for this expansion of the concept of intellectual property rights is pragmatic -- cultural knowledge acquired from American Indian populations is often used by outsiders in activities considered inappropriate or exploitative by the group that originated the information. We here examine three examples from the Southwest: the marketing of native seed and blue corn products, efforts to protect the authenticity of Native American arts and crafts, and efforts to protect the petroglyphs located west of Albuquerque, New Mexico. The three illustrate the broad challenge entailed in protecting and controlling the use of native cultural knowledge. The efforts of Native American tribes and Pueblos to use the principles of sovereignty to assert their own values and control access to, and the use of, native cultural knowledge point to the need to broaden and revise the meaning of intellectual property rights. One can also see more clearly the roles anthropologists and other non-Indian professionals should take to assist in the protection of native cultural knowledge.

Sovereignty and Cultural Property

In the United States, American Indian tribes have a degree of sovereignty that other groups around the world often do not have. Tribal sovereignty in the United States is based not on absolute and indivisible power, but on divided and respectable power. Wilkinson defines tribal sovereignty as:

> [presupposing] a culturally distinct people within defined territorial limits, it connotes legal competence rather than absolute power. It is used in the narrow sense of the power of a people to make governmental arrangements to protect and limit personal liberty by social control (Wilkinson 1987:54-55).

Since 1978, the U.S. Supreme Court has made it clear that "tribal powers trace to inherent sovereignty, not grants from the United States," since powers of self government preceded colonization. (Wilkinson 1987:61-62). However, federal law can limit the exercise of those rights and can overlay or compete with other rights protected by the U.S. Constitution.

One way that American Indian tribal governments exercise sovereignty is by passing laws and ordinances that govern conduct within their land and communities. Tribal governments also have the sovereign power to set limits on ethnographic, archaeological, and other types of research that entails asking tribal members to divulge knowledge.

In addition to the power to govern activities on-reservation, recent laws, such as the Native American Graves Protection and Repatriation Act (NAGPRA) and the American Indian Religious Freedom Act (AIRFA), specify situations in which agencies must consult with tribal governments before taking actions concerning cultural materials or resources located off-reservation. Although there is little legal protection of non-material Native American knowledge once that knowledge is shared beyond the context of the community, Native American tribes are using the principle of tribal sovereignty to define and control the use of culturally based knowledge to exercise their intellectual property rights.

The legal recognition of tribal sovereignty is in essence the recognition of communal or group rights. In the Pueblo Indian context and with many other tribes, activities that fit within a realm of important traditional or religious knowledge are regulated by the elders or other groups with responsibility for such knowledge. The transmission of such information is full of rules of process and responsibilities of use. There are various levels of knowledge and strict procedures for passing this knowledge on to other Indian people. History has demonstrated to the Pueblo people that once photos, designs, stories, or ceremonies are public, a Pueblo Indian tribe cannot stop their use for individual gain. The inherent difficulty is that the tribal members must keep secret the same information that must be shared in the process of trying to protect sacred sites and religious objects threatened by external change. The various federal laws require some element of disclosure, thereby exposing the information to inappropriate commercial users, and consequently destroying the very same sacred qualities that give the site or object its meaning in the first place.

The following examples will illustrate that protection of intellectual property in the Indian tribal context requires that we first honor tribal definitions of cultural property. While there may presently be little formal legal recognition of group intellectual property, anthropologists, entrepreneurs and others using this knowledge can conduct themselves in such a way that the future opportunities for the group to protect its rights remains, rather than be destroyed by unauthorized sharing of the intellectual property.

Blue Corn and Native Seeds

The Pueblos and many other groups in the Southwest have farmed for thousands of years and have developed drought resistant and unique seed varieties. One of these crops is blue corn.[1]

Since 1984, blue corn has become the basis of numerous expensive gourmet and health food products due to its nutritional value and unusual appearance. Although the seed stock is continued primarily by the Hopi, Zuni, and the Rio Grande Pueblos, the seed is open pollinated. Therefore, once a commercial farmer obtains the seed, that farmer can continue to produce seed and new crops without buying additional seed from those who developed the variety over generations. Most blue corn is grown on small plots for subsistence use, not for commercial sale. Production has decreased as tribal members substitute wage employment for a subsistence life style. However, there are several efforts to revive interest in the cultivation of blue corn by developing markets and income opportunities, and also to preserve and attribute sources of seed stocks.

Native Seeds/SEARCH, a non-profit seed conservation group located in Tucson, Arizona, buys seeds from individual Indian people and then contracts reproduction to provide a larger supply for sale. The catalog includes varieties of corn, beans, and squash that were collected from elders and others who had saved seed stock. Such seeds are also marketed internationally as suitable for arid areas. Although there is some reciprocity, such as providing seeds for free from their catalog to Indian people and helping tribes set up their own seed banks, there is as yet no mechanism to protect the long term rights of the farmers and Pueblos as the market for these varieties grows. Buyers can freely develop commercial production with the seeds. The inherent risks of publicly selling traditional seed are evident in the efforts of the Pueblos to develop their own market for blue corn products.

---

[1] The value of blue corn to the Pueblos is not only for food, but also for ceremonial activities and prayers, and for special dishes such as piki bread served at these times. The number of individuals growing blue corn has decreased with the increased dependence on urban employment that takes members away from the community during the day. In the Southwest there are several efforts to revive interest in the cultivation of blue corn and provide income to the Pueblo farmers who have continued these varieties.

Five Sandoval Indian Pueblos, Inc. (FSIP), a consortium of five Rio Grande Pueblos located north of Albuquerque, New Mexico, began an agricultural project in 1984 to encourage cultivation through cooperative marketing assistance to individual Pueblo families. The State Department of Agriculture helped secure a contract with a new company in Santa Fe that was selling mail order gift packages of native foods. The packaged southwest image meant a price two thirds higher than what was then charged for blue corn meal by New Mexico grocers. The company promised to buy the crop when the harvest was pooled and ready for delivery, but then later abandoned the agreement because the owner was able to obtain a similar grain, hybridized blue and white corn, at half the wholesale price of New Mexico blue corn. Native, open pollinated blue corn cannot be harvested by machine and is therefore more costly to produce. Hybridized blue and white corn is grown commercially in large quantities in Texas and Colorado. Processors routinely buy the hybridized corn and then label it as blue corn.

As a solution, FSIP established a dryer and mill to produce and directly market value added products such as roasted blue corn meal. At about this time the health food industry discovered blue corn. Blue corn cereal, pancake mix, and other products labeled as "Hopi Blue" or "Indian" lined the shelves but the actual origins of the corn ingredients were not identified. Given the difficulty of patenting an open pollinated seed, the Pueblo growers tried distinctive trade marking and labeling. Thus, Santa Ana Pueblo labels its corn "Tamaya Blue;" "Navajo Blue" is grown on the Navajo reservation. However, these labels do not bring a price any higher than that charged for products originating with hybridized corn because consumers do not understand the difference between blue corn and hybridized corn. In this case, value added products added no value for Pueblo farmers who maintained the seed stock and who cultivate, harvest and process using costly, labor intensive methods.

Native Seeds/SEARCH pays a higher $3.00 a pound for seed stock, but once the seeds are purchased they are in the public realm. Therefore, that $3.00 a pound will not be paid again by a buyer. In contrast, the Pueblo of Zuni has its own folk varieties project to preserve and classify native seeds. The Pueblo is developing tribal policies to exercise control over the distribution of seed varieties. (See Chapter 1 for further discussion of this point. - ed.)

Blue corn is only one of many native crops in the world that cannot be patented (Axt, Corn, Lee, and Ackerman 1993). Therefore, the approach is now through the use of trademarks and direct marketing of value added items. However, even these approaches have been usurped by enterprises that do not have formal business agreements with those from whom they obtained the seeds or product ideas. Tribal enterprises must become strong enough to compete for niches in the specialty crops market.

Indian Arts and Crafts

In the case of Indian arts and crafts, trademarks are being tried to ensure that Indian artists and craftsmen receive full value for their work. Labeling laws are used in New Mexico to protect the market value. The sale of arts and crafts provides one of the few opportunities for the Pueblo people to both be in business and participate in a traditional cycle of activities within the community. In New Mexico, Indian arts and crafts are an $800 million annual industry. The annual weekend Santa Fe Indian Market alone contributes $125 million to the local economy. The protection of the market from those who would imitate Indian art and crafts is critical for both Indian people and the state economy.

In 1988, the New Mexico State Commission on Indian Affairs sponsored hearings to evaluate the effectiveness of the 1978 New Mexico Indian Arts and Crafts Protection Law before proposing amendments. Traditional drum makers from Cochiti, among others, testified at hearings on the amendments. Cochiti and Taos make almost all the Pueblo drums and their quality is well known. A Cochiti drum maker described how someone with Cochiti blood but without an Indian name (thereby being not fully accepted into the Cochiti Pueblo community) was using a chain saw to hollow out aspen for drums, instead of the slow drying and carving process, and was selling them as Cochiti Drums. "Someone is coming in and taking our heritage which our forefathers have left to us. We survived by making drums," the drum maker testified.

Cultural heritage was being misrepresented in two ways. First, a person was identifying himself as Cochiti even though he was not tied to the cultural life of the community. Second, he was using techniques that result in a poor quality, thus confusing customers as to how a real Cochiti drum should be made.

The production methods and styles of designs on pottery, silver, and other arts and crafts are traceable to specific Pueblos and families. Zuni craftsmen, for example, recognize that certain designs belong to certain families and no one other than that family can use them. This is, in effect, an intra-group "cultural copyright" recognized by the members, but having no force in external U.S. law.

The efforts of Pueblo people and others to bring their definitions of "Indian" and "art" into state law is illustrative. While New Mexico law cannot deal with these intra-group rights, it does aim to stop non-Indians and mass producers from undercutting genuine Indian artists and craftsmen in the market. The law makes it the duty of anyone who is showing or selling Indian arts and crafts to inquire into the origin of objects to determine a) if the maker was an Indian as defined by tribal enrollment or certificate of Indian blood, b) if the object is hand made or machine made, and c) if materials are authentic (naturalness) or semi-processed. If the item can meet this test, then it can be labeled as an authentic, Indian, hand made piece. However, a label is not required so long as there is no misrepresentation. The law allows artists, consumers, and the Attorney General to pursue violations.

Although the final act was supported by a coalition of Indian artists, wholesalers, and retailers, there was a three year battle over the definitions of "Indian" and "authentic" before its passage. Cases such as the Cochiti Drum where the craft had a direct tie to a tribal tradition were clear and fit within the legislative language. However, Indian artists were not enrolled in a federally recognized tribe objected to the idea that tribal governments had the right by law to certify their work's authenticity. Also, Indian artists who had moved on to contemporary materials and forms objected to their work being simply labeled "Indian," because the artist was Indian, rather than as "fine art" which was their preferred designation. If the purpose is to protect art forms that had their origin in a culture, then these artists felt that the law should be limited to protecting traditional styles, workmanship and materials. The attempt to bring tribally defined rights into a law impacting individuals creates some problems.

Enforcement of such laws immediately raises the questions of to what extent a piece is a product of cultural knowledge and its sale can therefore be controlled by the tribes known for such items, and to what extent art is an individual creation. Does the label "Indian made" point to an Indian as an individual or to group identity? Are distinct tribal traditions cultural attributes that need special protection, or can they be used by any Indian person in a generic identification of "Indian culture?" Navajos, for example, are now selling "Navajo Storytellers" at a lesser price than what is charged for Pueblo Storytellers.[2] To protect "cultural copyrights" the Pueblos and other tribes may need to pursue their own trademarks of designs or symbols within their own laws because a state cannot distinguish between different cultural traditions within the generic
label of "Indian". However, without state law, most of the market would not be affected.

Petroglyphs

Preventing the misuse of symbols is also a major concern in the case of the Petroglyph National Monument. More than 17,000

[2] The Pueblo Storyteller, as an artistic expression of a Puebloan cultural concept, was first introduced by Helen Cordero at Cochiti Pueblo. In its most common form, a Storyteller is a piece of pottery made in the shape of a woman, with a number of smaller figures of children on her lap. Variations are possible, all based on the theme of a story being passed on to a new generation. "Navajo Storytellers" are the same basic figure, but the maker of the piece is Navajo, not Pueblo. There is no cultural connection between the Puebloan cultural concept represented by the Storyteller and Navajo culture.

petroglyphs found on volcanic escarpments west of Albuquerque, New Mexico, are now within the newly established Petroglyph National Monument where they will be protected by the National Park Service (NPS) and interpreted to the public.

The statute establishing the monument required that in the development of a management plan the NPS consult with the Rio Grande Pueblos whose ancestors are thought to have created most of the images. NPS and the State of New Mexico contracted for an ethnographic assessment to identify cultural resources within the new monument's boundaries needing protection and to identify how American Indian and Hispanic groups wanted to be included in a long-term consultation process with the NPS for the development of the monument.

Petroglyph images are the latest southwest design trend. Jewelry, dinnerware, postcards, business promotional literature, and tee shirts all show actual symbols copied from petroglyphs found in the Southwest, many of them in New Mexico. One artist was quoted in an Albuquerque newspaper as saying that everything he makes with petroglyph designs sells and that he has changed his entire line to reflect this new opportunity (Sanchez 1993).

This type of business behavior was considered exploitative by the Pueblo people who participated in the ethnographic assessment. They did not want such behavior encouraged by the NPS through the sale of such items in the future monument gift shop. Those individuals obtaining a profit from the use of such symbols, however, maintain that symbols within the monument are now part of the public domain and not the property of contemporary peoples living in the area.[3]

The Pueblo position is that many petroglyphs are sacred symbols. Although made long ago, the symbols have contemporary associations with stories and ceremonies and have current religious meaning. The Pueblo people want these symbols accorded the deference and respect accorded to other religions' sacred symbols. These symbols are connected to specific religious ceremonies still practiced and they remain part of the pool of individual and collective Puebloan cultural knowledge (Evans, Stoffle, and Pinel 1992).

An aspect of knowledge, in this case, is knowing the appropriate context for placing and using the petroglyph images. Although sale of such images for individual profit is considered highly inappropriate by the Pueblos, there is little they can do to collectively "own" such

[3] One of the more vexing problems is that non-Indian people are copyrighting the images along with their own interpretations of the symbols. Examples include cards with photos and stories that were copyrighted by an individual who had done ethnographic research and published on the petroglyphs.

symbols. One store in downtown Santa Fe sold a plate of dinner ware for $28. The same plate with the symbols formed into the sides of the plate sold for $100. The commercial use of these symbols added to the reticence of Pueblo people to share information on the petroglyphs with the researchers even though that information was necessary to recommend restricting non-Indian access to sacred sites protected under AIRFA (American Indian Religious Freedom Act).

Even if it was possible to protect a monetary share of this activity for the Pueblo tribes, this would not protect rights to cultural knowledge. That protection would have to include the right to prevent inappropriate use of the symbols in the wider society. During the ethnographic assessment, Pueblo people did not want to share information with the NPS interpretative ranger or with us as researchers because they could not be assured that the information or the items will be used only in the appropriate context of respect.

Group Rights Vs Individual Rights

The U.S. recognition of tribal sovereignty is an implicit recognition that the group's rights supersede the individual's rights. In the cases presented, items and ideas spring from a well of cultural knowledge and experience and from individual creativity. A conflict arises when one tries to assert group rights off-reservation or when a third-party researcher, artist, or business person enters the picture. The artists and researcher perceive their work as individual creations, as intellectual property, although the sources of original data may have been tribal. When tribal governments attempt to control the scope and process of social research, social scientists often claim that their academic freedom and the right to pursue the truth take precedence over sovereignty, not recognizing that such a "right" is culturally biased (Axt, Corn, Lee, and Ackerman 1993:32, Klesert and Powell 1993:350, Meighan 1986:9-12).

Intellectual property represents a complex bundle of rights that will take significant time to sort out. In the interim, the future opportunity for Indian people to retain and benefit from their knowledge is being eroded by the open market system that recognizes individual and corporate rights over property, but does not recognize group rights over cultural property (Byrne 1993). Mechanisms are needed to assure group rights off reservation where much of the knowledge is now dispersed. Researchers who insist that the right to research supersedes the right of the tribe to control the distribution of group knowledge can damage the chances for a tribe to protect its intellectual property.

Intellectual Property

The cases illustrate a broad concept of intellectual property -- one that encompasses other than western cultural concepts. Symbols, ideas, and cultural uses and interpretations are all part of intellectual property from a cultural resource standpoint. American Indians are searching for ways to have their own emphasis on group ownership, and uses in appropriate context, recognized in efforts to protect their cultural resources. This was quite evident in the Pueblo peoples' insistence that protection of the petroglyphs was not just a matter of protecting images and sites, but of protecting the entire area connecting them to shrines, spirit trails, the volcanoes nearby and the mountain ranges (Evans, Stoffle, and Pinel 1992). When the Pueblo concepts of group property meet the world of individual rights to possess and sell knowledge and information, there is a conflict that has no easy answer. These differing concepts of property and of collective rights present an inherent difficulty in defining intellectual property rights for indigenous knowledge (Axt, Corn, Lee, and Ackerman 1993)

Tribal Approaches to Controlling Cultural Knowledge

Given these limitations, tribal governments are taking a number of steps to protect the right to control the use of cultural information by building on their own sovereign right to define how they will interact with the larger society, by educating society, and by creating their own enterprises and ordinances.

In the blue corn case, Santa Ana Pueblo took over the processing operation and developed some new ways to control marketing. It developed a direct business relationship with The Body Shop, a company based in England and known for natural cosmetics made with plants, clay and other substances purchased from indigenous peoples throughout the world. The Body Shop buys blue corn meal for a new line of soap and purchased a new grinder for the Pueblo. The Body Shop committed itself to help Santa Ana Pueblo develop its own enterprise, something that may have a more direct benefit than trying to legally protect an interest in hybridized corn varieties.

In the case of Indian arts and crafts the tribes both participated in revising a state law to recognize their right to define who is Indian and what is genuine. In order to exert more control over the benefits of the market, the eight Northern Indian Pueblos consortium now holds a show each year featuring the work of 800 artists and sets the criteria for authentic entries. Some of the Pueblo tribes are looking into the possibility of protecting their unique designs through trademarks. State law is being supplemented with direct tribal enterprises and ordinances.

The petroglyph case is difficult in that the petroglyphs have been defined as being in the public domain and under the control of the NPS. The Pueblos have taken the position that the symbols cannot be discussed out of the context of their total environment and creation and have largely refused to divulge meanings and interpretations to outsiders, including the National Park Service, until mechanisms to protect sacred and religious information are in place. From the Pueblo viewpoint, the NPS would be protecting their cultural property rights if it embraced and communicated the broader relationship the Pueblos have to the area rather than demanding specific interpretations of symbols.

Some of the Pueblos and other tribes are defining how information will be shared before it becomes part of the public domain. These efforts have implications for how anthropologists, scientists, journalists and others do research. For example, during Christmas, 1991, a television film crew had permission from the Pueblo of Jemez to film a religious event for a public interest story. Each year a family sponsors the Christ Child in the home and the community participates in processions and other ceremonial activities. A tribal member then invited a second crew without authorization from the tribal government. Upon learning of the second film crew, Pueblo officials sent it away and then passed a resolution forbidding their own members or others to invite journalists and researchers into the Pueblo without formal permission from the tribal council. The resolution restricts the rights of tribal members as individuals and asserts tribal or group rights over the sharing of cultural information. Outsiders who do not abide by the resolution are asked to leave and the tribal members who invited them are called before the tribal council.

Native American tribes have participated in defining how cultural information will be presented by the Smithsonian Institution in the new Museum of the American Indian. In a southwestern consultation session tribal leaders and cultural resource staff expressed their historic concern with the practice of museums, but went on to redefine the purpose of the museum as one of communicating the Native American world views by creating the proper spaces and experiences in which to context objects. The Smithsonian is also planning to give access to tribes to feed and care for religious objects archived in Washington and to use the new museum as a vehicle for strengthening their own cultural protection and education efforts. This is illustrative of a potential partnership between researchers and native peoples that can strengthen efforts to protect cultural resources, including intellectual property.

What Can Social Scientists or Other Professionals Do To Support This Process?

The most important step a researcher or other professional can take to advance intellectual and cultural property rights in the United States is to respect and work within tribal sovereignty. Before engaging in any type of work with tribal members or within the land area controlled by a tribal government, one asks permission from authorized tribal government representatives. By following this practice, the cultural group can feel confident it has some control over its cultural knowledge. Once information is out, as the Pueblos would say, there is no control, hence the extreme reluctance and often outright refusal of Pueblo people to divulge any kind of information to anyone. It is to the advantage of both the outside professional and to the cultural group if the reports of information are limited to that which the group feels is appropriate for a given situation. In this way, uncontrolled broadcasting of information that can be used by others for private gain is limited and the people whose knowledge is being documented retain the maximum leverage to benefit from its future uses.

Within Pueblo societies, there are ethical obligations of reciprocity and responsibility when one receives cultural knowledge. By clearly understanding that information is valued and used differently in the tribal, academic, and business world, professionals can responsibly inform the indigenous communities of those values so that a fair system of reciprocal exchange can be negotiated.

Conclusions

Rather than providing legal models for patents, copyrights, or trademarks, the examples discussed in this paper illustrate the more fundamental rights of indigenous peoples to define the appropriate use of their cultural knowledge and to participate in decisions as to its dissemination. Translation of indigenous concepts of "ownership" into national and international law will require a sustained effort. Unless there is legal recognition of group or tribal rights, there is no foundation for the control of the subsequent use of cultural knowledge in the production and marketing of products. The cultural systems for transferring and continuing knowledge of crops, art forms, songs, dances, and other innovations have been primarily oral and reciprocal. Written documentation is needed to build recognition of indigenous knowledge.

Although some 14 laws were passed in United States during the 1980's to strengthen corporate rights to patents, copyrights, and trademarks, these laws have not been applied to tribal governments as "corporations". However, Native American tribal governments are using their sovereign status to define how cultural knowledge should be used or marketed. Within the context of tribal sovereignty, there are many potential partnerships between tribal governments and researchers that could position indigenous people to better define and protect their own cultural resources for the benefit of future generations.

Bibliography

Axt, Josephine R., M. Lynne Corn, Margaret Lee and David M. Ackerman

1993 Biotechnology, Indigenous Peoples, and Intellectual Property Rights: Congressional Research Service Report for Congress. Washington, D.C.: U.S. Government Printing Office.

Byrne, Christopher S.

1993 *Chilkat Indian Tribe v. Johnson* and NAGPRA: Have We Finally Recognized Communal Property Rights in Cultural Objects? Journal of Environmental Law and Litigation 8: 109-131.

Evans, Michael J., Richard W. Stoffle, and Sandra Lee Pinel

1992 Petroglyph National Monument Rapid Ethnographic Assessment Project. Report submitted to New Mexico State Historic Preservation Office, September 30, 1992. Tucson, AZ: Bureau of Applied Research in Anthropology, University of Arizona.

Klesert, Anthony L. and Shirley Powell

1993 A Perspective on Ethics and the Reburial Controversy. American Antiquity 58,2: 348-354.

Meighan, C. W.

1986 Archaeology and Anthropological Ethics. Calabasas, CA: Wormwood Press.

Sanchez, Isabel

1993 "A Fork in the Road," Albuquerque Journal, April 4, 1993, p. A1, A12.

Wilkinson, Charles

1987 American Indians, Time, and the Law: Native Societies in a Modern Constitutional Democracy. New Haven: Yale University Press.

Sources Of Additional Information

Blue Corn and Native Seeds:

Santa Ana Pueblo Agricultural Project
Attn: Gerry Kinsman
Star Route
Bernalillo, NM 87004
(505) 867-3301

Native Seeds/SEARCH
2509 N. Campbell Ave. # 325
Tucson, AZ 85719
(602) 327-9123

Arts and Crafts law

New Mexico Office of the Attorney General
Attn: Roberta Jo
Bataan Memorial Building
Santa Fe, NM 87503
(505) 827-6000

New Mexico Office of Indian Affairs
La Villa Rivera Building
Santa Fe, NM 87501
(505) 827-6440

Petroglyphs

National Park Service
Southwest Regional Office
Office of American Indian Programs
1220 St. Francis Drive
P.O. Box 728
Santa Fe, NM 87501-0728

Chapter
4

Collecting Traditional Medicines In Nigeria: A Proposal For IPR Compensation

Janet McGowan
Cultural Survival Inc.
and
Iroka Udeinya
Howard University

It is easier to talk about the equity and compensation principles that should be in an IPR compensation contract than to draft an actual contract. It is also easy to overlook the reality that conditions for drafting a contract may preclude some, or even any, real consultation between the parties before a grant proposal must be written, illogical as that seems. This chapter by McGowan and Udeinya describes a contract developed under such conditions. While the unique aspects of any actual project insure that every IPR contract will be different from the rest, readers should find an interesting inventory of the ideas within this proposed contract. The specifics of the step-by-step incremental compensation, the participation of both village-level and regional organizations, the fee percentages assigned, and the trust disbursement mechanism are among many interesting features of this proposal. - ed.

4

Collecting Traditional Medicines In Nigeria: A Proposal For IPR Compensation

Janet McGowan
Cultural Survival Inc.
and
Iroka Udeinya
Howard University

In 1992, three U.S. agencies announced a novel program to collect and experiment on plants and the traditional medicines used throughout the world. Seeking cures for AIDS, cancer, heart disease and mental illness, the National Cancer Institute, National Science Foundation and Agency for International Development invited individuals and groups to apply to the International Cooperative Biodiversity Groups (ICBG) Program. The ICBG program is unusual in its focus on traditional medicines and plants as a source for cures - but also in that each ICBG team had to link and promote drug development with the "interdependent issues" of biodiversity conservation, sustainable economic development, and the protection of the intellectual property of indigenous peoples. These are four issues not commonly addressed in the same sentence, much less a government program, and each team applying to the ICBG program had to advance all four goals.

The purpose of this paper is to present the parts of our team's proposal to collect traditional medicinal plants in rural southeast Nigeria which dealt with the difficult issue of compensating local people for the use of their traditional knowledge of these plants. Although our team was not picked to be an ICBG team, hopefully this proposal and our thinking as we wrote it will help others as they deal with the practical problems of compensating people for traditional knowledge. These issues are complex and difficult, we think, to work out in a practical way, particularly when many different communities and people share knowledge.[1] Ultimately we decided on a three-part arrangement: one, the team would make sure specific money benefits went to the local communities at each stage of its research; two, representatives from these communities would decide how

1 The team members were: Dr. Iroka Udeinya of Howard University, Dr. Nina Etkin of University of Hawaii, Professor Paul Obiekwe Okonokwo of University of Nigeria and Dr. Martha Knight, President of Peptide Technologies. Attorney Janet McGowan was a consultant to the team.

this money would be spent; and three, a legal trust would be created to make sure the representatives' decisions were actually implemented.

The focus of the ICBG program on traditional medicines and the medicinal properties of plants reflects a greater interest in plant medicines by researchers around the world. The media is filled with stories on the importance of tribal or native knowledge and the potential pharmacopeia in the world's rainforests.[2] Drug companies are spending more on their research of plants, microbes, bacteria and fungi in the hopes of finding new medicines. Government and university researchers are doing the same.

While many have a positive view of this renewed interest in nature and traditional knowledge, many tribal and indigenous peoples are noticeably less enthused. The resources of indigenous peoples have long been a target of state governments and commercial enterprises. Gold, timber, crops, land, oil, minerals, water, fisheries and art have all been sought or taken from native peoples. Now indigenous knowledge - of complex healing systems combining plant medicines, local ecology and spiritual care - is yet another resource being taken and used by others. For many indigenous peoples, it looks like more of the same. Many indigenous peoples and healers refuse to share their cultural knowledge with outsiders, viewing this use of their cultural knowledge as yet another resource appropriation without permission, payment, recognition or proper respect.

It was with this understanding and within this context, we tried to address the indigenous intellectual property issues raised by collecting traditional medicinal plants. Our team wanted to make sure that the local tribal communities we worked with were informed participants in our project, and that they received compensation for the information and plants they shared with us. Fair compensation to these communities was a key goal of our proposed team. If the ICBG teams were paid for their research, it was only fair that the local communities also be paid. Although the chance was remote, if our team's research led to the discovery and creation of a commercial drug, the team could license its work to a drug company and earn large royalties on drug sales. Another important goal of our team was informed consent: we wanted the people we worked with to know the potential commercial value of their information, their right to control this knowledge, how this information would be used, and that access to drugs developed by our project could be restricted by patents.

With these admirable goals, we immediately ran into problems.

---

[2] E. Linden, "Lost Tribes, Lost Knowledge," Time, September 23, 1991, p. 46-56; C. Joyce, "Prospectors For Tropical Medicines," New Scientist, 19 October 1991, p. 36-40; J. Wallace, "Rainforest RX," Sierra, July/August 1991, p. 36-41; D. Lewis, "The Gene Hunters," Geographical Magazine, January 1991, p. 36-38.

Lack of Models of Fair Compensation and Exchange

First of all, we had no examples or models. Indigenous peoples rarely are full partners in the search for new drugs. Because it is easier, less confusing and familiar, drug companies and research institutions generally avoid working directly with indigenous peoples. Drug companies prefer instead to collect plant samples, medicines and information from established botanical gardens, university researchers inside developing countries or to simply buy samples from plant collectors in the field. Often information on traditional medicines and plants can be found in a library. Some healers work with ethnobotanists or anthropologists in a spirit of collaboration and do not want payment. Finally, even though enthnobotanists recognize the need to compensate traditional healers and their communities, few payments have been made.

While some botanical gardens have informal policies to share royalties with the organizations they are working with in developing countries, we knew of none which directly had compensated an indigenous group. Of the two deals we knew about, where a drug company and a researcher had agreements with indigenous groups, we had few details. The often-discussed Merck-INBio agreement does not address the use of plants or knowledge possessed by indigenous peoples in Costa Rica.

In the past, researchers have avoided paying indigenous communities, either directly or under contracts, for several reasons. Indigenous peoples often have special or unclear legal statuses under national laws, making contracts more complicated and difficult to create and enforce. Many people have raised questions about who would sign a contract or be paid if more than one person or group uses a medicine or plant. Also, some feel giving money to healers and communities is inappropriate or culturally destructive, and earmark funds for conservation projects or local non-profits organizations.

Who Is Paid For Shared Knowledge?

The second, more difficult problem we faced was that it simply was not clear who to compensate for plants and information. Obviously, we could not speak to and pay everyone in the project area. Even if only people who knew the medicinal plants were paid, the allocation task was still difficult. In southeast Nigeria, traditional medicine is practiced by both lay people and traditional healers. Many people know about healing plants, although one person in a family usually has greater healing knowledge and administers medicines. So, many local people in the project area either are practitioners or know medicinal plants and merit compensation.

Traditional healers are specialists or professionals who are consulted in more complex or unfamiliar cases. While traditional healers' associations exist in each Nigerian state, their members generally are from urban areas. Even though it would have been easier to negotiate arrangements with the traditional healers' associations, and the team planned to consult with them, the associations would not necessarily represent the people working with the team.

Other differences between the traditional healers and local people exist. The issue of intellectual property rights and proper compensation has been discussed more widely among traditional healers and at several conferences in Nigeria. In the past, the knowledge of healers has been used as the basis of patent applications by others. As a result, many traditional healers are more likely to keep information from researchers, or to require that they are directly paid or that contracts are signed, before they will share information. A Brazilian pharmacognosist, collecting in Nigeria this past year, encountered several different responses during two weeks of field collections. Some healers refused to share information, others insisted on contracts, some wanted up-front payments and still others shared freely. In contrast, the debate over proper payment for, and protection of, traditional knowledge certainly has not raged through rural communities in southeast Nigeria. Few people in small villages would be aware of these issues and rarely would see any problem in freely sharing their knowledge.

Adding to the confusion was the fact that the local people and traditional healers all work from a general body of knowledge. We thought it was unfair to pick one group over the other or to give benefits to individuals for collective or cultural knowledge. On the other hand, individuals do continue to experiment with new plants and medicines. This suggested to us that an individual, village or town which gave the team unique plant medicines should be compensated. But then again, without an extraordinarily detailed survey of healing plants and their uses the team would not always know when a plant or medicine was unique.

Adding to the difficulty in establishing a fair, consistent compensation scheme, was the fact that many tribal groups lived in the project area. This raised a whole host of issues about decision-making in these groups, their view of healing and how they viewed property, etc.

All these problems tied into a fourth, key problem--the fact that our proposed team controlled the money, who would get it and when. The teams applying to the ICBG program had to resolve all patent and other intellectual property issues at the time they applied, not while the project was being implemented. So, the team did not have the chance to discuss its work, and the compensation and intellectual property issues raised by it, with some of the people in the project area. This timing problem seemed almost fatal. Our team would make key decisions about the treatment of the rights of others, as much as they exist legally or ethically, on its own.[3]

The question of who should receive payment defied logical resolution. Whatever compensation scheme we developed, it seemed, inevitably, it would be unfair to a group or wrong in other important ways. Giving money to one group meant another group did not get money. Despite this, we put together a plan--with the hope it would improve on past and current collecting efforts. We also understood this plan might change as the project was implemented and we discussed these issues with the people with whom we worked.

How Much Compensation? Who Would Get It and How?

First, the team agreed to make a series of financial commitments. The team agreed that, at *each* stage, the communities with whom it worked would benefit. This philosophy of returning benefits at each stage was borrowed from Cultural Survival's marketing project. In practice, this meant that benefits would go to the communities when plants and medical information were collected, when more plant supplies were collected (if needed for further tests), if the team licensed or sold its research results or if a commercial drug was developed. Second, the team decided to talk with different groups, or local representatives, in these communities who would decide how to spend this money. Third and finally, the team decided to establish a trust to implement these decisions, and to sign contracts to bind the team to its commitments. In this way, the team agreed to give benefits at each stage of their research, local representatives would decide where benefits would go, and an impartial body, a legal trust, would execute both these decisions.

Up-Front In-Kind Payments and Future Sourcing of Plants

To implement its commitment of returning benefits to these communities at each project stage, the team agreed to the specific financial

---

[3] It is hard to establish intellectual property rights in a body of knowledge shared by many people. Trade secret protection can attach to any collection of information with commercial value, so the information known by a healer or group could be protected by U.S. law if proper steps were taken (see Gollin, 1993). Also, deep ethical issues are not always raised every time a person collects indigenous knowledge or a medicinal plant. Much information about these medicines and plants is public and was freely given, just as many researchers, scientists, academics, lay people and members of other cultural groups share their insights, knowledge and discoveries with each other.

arrangements. Five percent of project funds ($25,000) would be set aside for in-kind, up-front support to the villages and towns in which the team directly worked. This would mare sure each community received a concrete, immediate benefit from working with the team, since it was unlikely that a commercially valuable drug would result from the team's research. If a plant medicine were promising and more plants were needed, the team would buy all future plant supplies from the communities which originally gave the plant, creating another source of income for the communities.

If a commercial drug were discovered and developed, the team also would require the drug manufacturer to purchase future plant supplies from the project region, so long as consistent and sufficient plant supplies were provided. If a plant was endangered, or not enough were available, the team agreed to work with communities to solve these problems by farming the plant, changes in harvesting techniques, or by addressing any broader causes, such as deforestation, which caused the shortage.

Royalties and Profits

The team members also agreed to share, with the people in the project area, 25% of whatever royalties or profits they earned. Royalties could be earned in several ways. The size of the royalty would depend on what the team sold to a drug company and the success of the drug sales. If the team simply sold a dried plant sample to a drug company, it could expect to receive the standard royalty share of 1 to 2% of the sales of any commercial drug developed from this sample. If the team sold an extract from a plant, the expected royalty would be larger, potentially 3 to 5% of sales. If the team sold a chemical compound and the compound were promising, the team could get a greater royalty, ranging from 5 to 15%. The amount would depend on how much testing the team had done and what disease the drug was for - a cure for AIDS would be worth more than one for athlete's foot.

Of this 25% royalty share for local communities, half would go to the Local Government[4] area from which the plant was collected and half would go to the village or town where the plant was collected. This 50-50 split between the Local Governments and the villages was a compromise between two goals -- to reward individual, local innovation and collective, traditional knowledge -- and all the different suggestions about who to pay. We decided this after a long, circular debate over who should receive royalties--individuals, families, villages, Local Governments, the entire project area, local non-profits and so on. Unfortunately we made good, logical arguments in support of every position.

---

4 Local Governments are the equivalent of U.S. county governments.

The team also dedicated 5% of all commercial drug profits (if a drug were created) to projects in southeastern Nigeria which promoted rural health, traditional medicines, biodiversity conservation and sustainable economic development. This 5% requirement meant any drug company that sold the drug had to agree to turn over 5% of its profits to benefit the project area. This 5% requirement would be part of the licensing contract between the team and the drug company. The drug company also had to make the drug available, at cost, to all Nigerians afflicted with the disease helped by the drug. This guaranteed that all Nigerians benefitted from the biodiversity and community knowledge in their country.

How To Spend Royalties and Up-Front Payments

Who would decide about how the 5% up-front, in-kind payment and the potential 25% royalty share would be spent? We felt these important decisions should not be made by the team, but by the people we worked with in Nigeria. The initial, in-kind benefits for the villages and towns the team collected in was appropriately the decision of the elders and chiefs in these communities. Elders and chiefs also would decide where the half of the 25% of royalties would go. In each community it worked in, the team would discuss the project, funding, goal of drug discovery, the drug discovery process, the potential value of new drugs, the right to limit access created by patents, and other legal issues.

For the half royalty share that would go to the Local Government, the team decided to set up, in each local government, an advisory group consisting of a local government administrator, town chiefs and traditional healers. The team would discuss these same issues with each advisory group. The advisory groups each would decide how royalties would be spent in their area if a commercial drug was developed from their area. The team hoped that the advisory groups would, periodically, meet with each other and exchange ideas.

Contracts and Distribution of Proceeds

The decisions of the advisory groups and the villages' leaders would be incorporated into binding legal contracts. The contracts would be between the team members, the team and drug companies, and the team and each village or advisory group. To receive and distribute the royalties and the 5% of profits (again, if there were any), the team planned to set up a trust through Howard University in the United States. A United States trust was chosen because it was the safest and most stable way to guarantee that royalties would go where they were promised. We felt Nigerians would concur.

The scheme we created divided decisions and responsibilities into three parts. Generally, no one group controlled more than one aspect of the money. The team decided how much money went to the project area. Representatives from the region and the village elders and chiefs determined how this money would be spent. A trust would track royalty payments and profits, and make sure these decisions were implemented.

The team's work with the advisory groups, elders and chiefs was not intended to substitute for direct talks with local residents and healers. The team members planned to discuss their work, goals, funding, the effects of sharing information, etc. with them. No plants or information would be collected without consent. People would be told that publication of their information likely would jeopardize whatever intellectual property rights they may have in this knowledge, but did not prevent their own use of their medical knowledge. Obviously, individuals and villages could decide not to work with the team.

Other aspects of the project are worth mentioning because they address related issues of acknowledgement, respect, exchange and secrecy. The team agreed to acknowledge individuals and communities in all of its publications. Individuals or groups would be listed on the patent application for a drug compound (or a chemical derivative), if this was possible legally and the information they gave was proven by the team's research. The team would exchange information about medicinal uses of local plants by publishing a guide in local languages. The guide would list plant names, descriptions, medical conditions, and the physical preparations of the plant compounds. The guide would not reveal the process of healing used by different healers and practitioners since this often involved confidential information or spiritual practices. Because it is difficult to keep confidential, the team decided not to collect secret information from individuals and healers. The team would try to confirm appropriate dosages of plant medicines that healers and villagers could use and to spread this information.

Looking back at this proposal some months later, it seems to achieve the team's goal of bettering current collection practices. We were constrained by the fact that we planned to collect from many different villages and peoples, and the fact that our proposal was submitted before we discussed and debated these issues with the project communities. As a result, we could not get away from the fact that the team, and not the village elders, chiefs, healers and local representatives, determined the amount of royalties, up-front payments and the percentage of profits dedicated to the project region. But, we hoped that novel and fair solutions would result from open discussion among traditional healers, village elders, chiefs, government officials and local residents, enough time to discuss these complex issues fully, and a collective search for answers.

Bibliography

Belcher, B. & Hawtin, G.
1991 A Patent on Life: Ownership of Plant and Animal Research. International Development Research Centre.

Cultural Survival Quarterly
1991 The Politics of Ownership. Vol. 15, No. 3. Summer.

Cunningham, A.B.
1989 Indigenous plant use: balancing human needs and resources. Biotic Diversity in Southern Africa: concepts and conservation. London: Oxford University Press.

Elisabetsky, E.
1990 The Pharmacopeia From The Forest. Garden p. 4-6.

Frazer, L.
1992 The Treasure of Healing Knowledge. Student Lawyer. March: 38-44.

Gollin, Michael A.
1993 An Intellectual Property Rights Framework for Biodiversity Prospecting. Biodiversity Prospecting (Walter Reid et al.). Washington, D.C.: World Resources Institute and others. Pp. 159-197.

Joyce, C.
1991 Prospectors For Tropical Medicines. New Scientist. 19 October: 36-40.

Lewis, D.
1991 The Gene Hunters. Geographical Magazine. January, Pp. 36-38

Linden, E.
1991 Lost Tribes, Lost Knowledge. Time. September 23, 1991: 46-56.

Pickersgill, D.
1992 Indigenous Knowledge and Rainforest Medicinal Plants: Intellectual Property and Natural Resources. (unpublished paper).

Rural Advancement Foundation Int'l.
1990 Lifelore: Toward a Third World Trade Union for Biological Intellectual Property. July. Manitoba, Canada.

Reid, W. et al.
1993 Biodiversity Prospecting: Using Genetic Resources for Sustainable Development. WRI/IUCN/UNEP Global Biodiversity Strategy. Washington, D.C.: World Resources Institute (and others).

Wallace, J.
1991 Rainforest RX. Sierra. July/August. Pp. 36-41.

Chapter
5

Establishing Reciprocity: Biodiversity, Conservation and New Models for Cooperation Between Forest-Dwelling Peoples and the Pharmaceutical Industry

Steven R. King
Shaman Pharmaceuticals

Shaman Pharmaceuticals, Inc., has pioneered a pattern of corporate relationships directly with indigenous societies and organizations, and the commitment by contract to direct, staged compensation. The practical dilemmas of distributing IPR compensation are numerous, and Shaman's solutions are here described in detail. The Shaman approach involves up-front return and at each further stage of the product development process. The company has built into its practices its concern with overall biodiversity maintenance within the potential producing areas, a concern Shaman has found strongly held also by the indigenous communities with which it works. This chapter details a highly original, and widely applauded approach to collaboration which can be used in its present form, or adapted as circumstances require. Contracts along these lines could be insisted upon by other indigenous groups when they are approached for botanical prospecting, or adopted by other corporations as preferred practice. - ed.

5

Establishing Reciprocity: Biodiversity, Conservation and New Models for Cooperation Between Forest-Dwelling Peoples and the Pharmaceutical Industry

Steven R. King
Shaman Pharmaceuticals

Introduction

Shaman Pharmaceuticals develops new therapeutic agents by working with indigenous and forest-dwelling peoples of tropical forests and in the process, Shaman contributes to the conservation of biocultural diversity (King 1991, 1992a,b). The term, "forest-dwelling peoples" refers to local people such as the caboclos or mestizos who live along the Amazon river or who are of mixed ethnic descent but interdependent with the tropical forest environment. Shaman is committed to the compensation of intellectual property rights for the use of plant resources to the indigenous peoples and governments with whom we work. Increasingly native people, scientists and international policy advocates have discussed the rationale for providing reciprocal benefits to indigenous people for their role in developing new natural products (Boom 1990a,b; Cunningham 1991, 1993; Elisabetsky 1991; Moran 1992; Padoch and Boom 1991; Posey 1990). The question is no longer whether indigenous and forest-dwelling people should benefit from products developed based on their knowledge and forest management technology, but rather how to provide these benefits in the most fair and effective method. Shaman has responded to this question by stipulating that the contribution of all parties to the development of a therapeutic agent must be taken into account.

Indigenous and Laboratory Technology

The knowledge of indigenous and forest-dwelling peoples is a vital part of Shaman's process of drug discovery and development. The knowledge, skills and technological advances developed by our scientists and scientific advisors is also extremely important to the success of the process. This linkage of indigenous and western science requires reciprocity.

Shaman's Reciprocal Benefits

We have established a policy that provides benefits to local people, communities and the proper agencies in three ways, spanning the short-, medium- and long-term horizon. We feel that our method is one of the most appropriate and balanced solutions for providing reciprocal benefits to all the parties due acknowledgement for their contributions to new drug development. There are two case studies in this paper that describe how we provide first, short-term and second, medium-term benefits to local people, driven by the expressed needs of the people with whom we work.

The issue that has preoccupied the majority of participants and outside observers has been how and through what mechanism will resources be returned once a product reaches the market. Our approach involves three parts. First, we have committed the company to provide a portion of the profits of any and all products to all of the communities and countries in which we have worked. This spreads out the risk and assures a more rapid return of resources for all of our collaborators. This would include a portion of profits derived from a product that may enter the company via a separate route, including a product licensed from another company.

The second part of the solution is the mechanism. We created, at the formation of the company, a non-profit conservation organization, now called the Healing Forest Conservancy, to help determine, with an independent board of advisors, the appropriate distribution of these resources to the communities and government organizations. Representatives from the various countries will participate in this process of discussion and decision making. A database on countries and cultures with which Shaman has collaborated is one of the primary tracking tools managed by The Healing Forest Conservancy. The Executive Director of the Healing Forest Conservancy, Ms. Katy Moran, is currently supporting a number of projects through outside fund raising efforts to support the maintenance of biological and cultural diversity in tropical countries.

The third part of returning benefits involves the creation of new natural product supply industries in the countries in which we work. One specific example is described in Case II, an example of our helping to create a direct sustainable supply network for a specific natural product. We have established similar relationships with other forest-dwelling peoples in four countries in Latin America. Our approach has focused on local and indigenous peoples.

Government and Non-Governmental Analysis

In April and May of 1993, two detailed studies were released on the challenges facing all parties concerned with the ethics and prospects for international new product development in the post 1992 "Earth Summit" global community. One was published by the United Sates Congressional Research Service (CRS) and the other by the World Resources Institute (WRI) in Washington, D.C. (Axt et al. 1993; Reid et al. 1993). These two reports undertook an in-depth analysis of the issues surrounding intellectual property rights, indigenous knowledge, biotechnology and the conservation of global biodiversity. Both reports examine the role of industry, indigenous people, and methods for returning benefits to the countries that provided research material. Both of these reports offer similar conclusions. Contracts and agreements for the return of benefits should be provided to stimulate conservation and respect for biological and cultural diversity. The two reports praise respectively the Merck and Co. Inc. agreement with INBio, a Costa Rican biological research organization and the National Cancer Institute's program and "Letter of intent" which outlines guiding principles for the compensation of countries that have sourced material to the NCI program.

Our policies and activities were initiated in 1990, before the United Nations Earth Summit took place in Brazil in 1992. Our approach and philosophy predates the much publicized Merck and INBio agreement, which specifically excludes indigenous knowledge and indigenous participation. We have forcefully reminded our colleagues and observers about the value and importance of indigenous knowledge prior to the inclusion of the term "traditional knowledge" in the NCI program or letter of intent. We salute these other initiatives and encourage others to follow the pattern. We recommend that our approach be better integrated by these and other programs. We place a greater emphasis on the return of immediate and appropriate benefits to the local people and communities with which we work.

We believe that there is one other vital aspect which is not addressed adequately by the above mentioned studies. One of the most important pieces of information required to make decisions about returning benefits is the expressed needs and desires of local and native people throughout the world. Discussions with the leaders of indigenous and forest-dwelling people need to be conducted at the beginning of any programs aimed at developing new natural products for commercial markets. These discussions require time and need to focus on the problems, goals and aspirations of the members of the specific communities as part of ongoing dialogues with a wide diversity of people within and between local groups.

New Models for Reciprocity

Shaman Pharmaceuticals is working to establish a new set of reciprocal guidelines for the pharmaceutical industry and any other industry working directly with tropical forest peoples. In the pharmaceutical industry, there is a 5-10 year development period for any potential new product, but indigenous people typically have immediate - often urgent - needs to which Shaman responds. Consequently, Shaman advocates that reciprocal benefits not be limited to the commercialization of a specific product.

We have adopted a program of reciprocity that will return benefits from any product to all the groups and countries with whom we have worked in any given geographic region. For example, we have worked in more than 30 indigenous communities and countries in Latin America, Africa and Southeast Asia; all of these communities and countries will benefit when we bring our first and all subsequent products to the market. Shaman believes that this is a more appropriate method of distributing compensation than returning benefits to only one or two specific communities, indigenous groups, or countries. This view has also been expressed in the conclusions of the Congressional Research Service document mentioned above (CRS 1993).

The mechanism by which we will return those benefits is the non-profit conservation organization, The Healing Forest Conservancy. This organization will determine, with an independent multi-lateral advisory board and representative members from the regions that we have sourced the product, how and specifically which organization will receive those resources. According to CRS, this is a more appropriate method of reciprocity than arranging return benefits with one institution because traditional knowledge is shared and safeguarded by many individuals and organizations. Most importantly, this approach will provide for those benefits to go back to the people and places from whom that knowledge arose. When Shaman succeeds, all our collaborators will also succeed.

Shaman also believes strongly that because of the long development period for any pharmaceutical product it is important to return benefits immediately to any and all groups with which we work. It is very easy to do this if an organization simply asks the people that they work with what their immediate needs may be, and this should be done in advance of any given research project. To demonstrate this, two case examples follow that may be useful to other individuals and/or organizations collaborating with or initiating research and development relationships with indigenous and forest-dwelling peoples in the tropics. The first case describes a research and collecting expedition that was conducted in the past year. The second case describes a long-term supply arrangement that we are developing with a number of indigenous and forest-dwelling peoples at this time. We hope that these two cases provide a bases for subsequent relationships by other groups.

Case I: Immediate Reciprocity

In December, 1991 Shaman began discussions with one Quichua community in the Ecuadorian Amazon. We were planning an expedition to do primary research with this group and asked permission from the leaders of the village to come and work with these people. This is part of our standard procedure before any collaboration is initiated. As part of the process, we asked this group what specific and immediate reciprocal benefits we could provide as part of our research expedition. We also asked what specific ongoing reciprocity we could provide as part of this relationship.

This group told us they needed to expand the length of an airplane landing runway they use for emergency medical evacuations and infrequent air departures to the nearest town of Puyo, Ecuador. The runway was inadequate to safely fly out more than one person at a time. This meant that anyone who required emergency care in the regional medical facility would have to go alone, without a family chaperone during and after emergency medical attention. In April, 1992 we provided $1500 U.S. dollars to the community and, utilizing our resources and tools, organized a series of communal labor parties to expand their airstrip.

Our actual expedition reached the area in October, 1992. Upon our arrival the community thanked us for the airstrip support and asked for further projects. First, they requested one large cow to feed the entire community during our visit. This was done. They also requested quarterly or semi-annual visits of a culturally sensitive physician and dentist to provide health care over the next two years. We agreed to this and have supported the visit of health professionals to this village since our departure in 1992. We receive updates on the medical visits as part of our follow-up activity.

The community also had a young man who had been working with their shaman as an apprentice over the past several years. However, he periodically left the village to go to a nearby tea plantation to earn money to purchase goods required by his family. We agreed to provide a reasonable stipend for both the shaman and apprentice so that the apprentice's training could continue uninterrupted by his need to work elsewhere. This has continued since our departure and has provided a means by which this individual did not have to leave his family or his village to earn wages via outside labor.

The village also requested a number of over-the-counter medicines such as aspirin and other goods that could be used to treat minor ailments. We provided a modest supply of these materials, but had a discussion with the community about the value of their traditional medicine and showed them a book which listed their materia medica in Spanish and Quichua with specific information on the plants they used to treat the minor ailments with which they were concerned. Most of the people in the village were familiar with many of these plants and their use, but they were not familiar with this particular book, which could serve as a highly appropriate local health care manual. We agreed to acquire enough copies of this publication so that each family would have a personal copy to help treat the specific minor conditions that they had discussed with us.

At the end of our research we participated in a community meeting where the leaders discussed their goals and concerns about our research activities. The predominant concern of this community was access to periodic health care and access to emergency health care. They also expressed an interest in access to wage-earning opportunities to purchase goods that they required for day-to-day subsistence such as household wares, tools and clothing. During our research we employed roughly thirty individuals performing a variety of research and support activities. Several individuals had some previous training in botanical specimen preparation. We added further guidance and technical training to enhance their skills in plant collection and processing. This was viewed in a positive way, and we have subsequently employed one of these people to do more plant collections, processing and identification. We also agreed to provide follow-up information about the results of our research on the plants which we had collected with them. This information was provided in Spanish which is of use to the ongoing documentation of their culture's medicinal plant knowledge.

Our relationship to the community continues today. In-country collaborators monitor the commitments that we made for the short- and medium-term reciprocity to ensure continuance. The Ecuadorian Quichuas will also receive compensation when our first product is commercialized, and they will also be recipients of benefits from any other product that we develop in the future. We follow this process of discussing reciprocity with each of the communities in which we work. Benefits vary since each region, area, culture and situation is unique. Members of the communities determine priorities and reciprocal benefits that they most require. Since this process has proven successful, Shaman and the communities we work with advocate that this approach be taken by organizations working with forest-dwelling peoples and communities in the tropics.

Case II: Indigenous Supply Management Among the Aguaruna Huambisa Federation

This case describes our long-term activities to establish and maintain sustainable supply of our lead anti-viral products. These two products, Provir and Virend, are sourced from multiple countries in Latin America. This case describes the steps that we have taken over the past two-and-a-half years to work directly with forest-dwelling peoples who harvest and supply this product. We view one of the immediate and medium-term reciprocal benefits of developing natural products from the forest to be the establishment of long-term supply industries where the proceeds go directly to communities that are sourcing this material. In 1990 we began discussion with the members representing the Pan Amazonian Indigenous Peoples Federation (COICA) of Amazonian South America. This is a region from which a portion of our supply comes. We began discussions about our company's philosophy, commitments and goals to bring to market two specific products, Provir and Virend, derived from a well-known, widely abundant natural product from Latin America. These discussions initially entailed our mutual concern about long-term sustainability, conservation and the return of benefits to the peoples with whom we are working. Initial discussion involved negotiations over the details of price and mechanisms of supply, including the transport costs and the export of material.

We provided upon request, the airfare and transportation expenses for one member to return to his federation in the northern Peruvian Amazon to discuss with the leaders of the federation our proposal to source material directly from their communities. The indigenous leaders stated that if we were in a great hurry to establish this supply agreement we should move to another geographic region. They expressed to us their experience of international and national programs that work too quickly on settling agreements. They had told us that many of the programs sponsored by international development agencies were unsuccessful and had led to decreased environmental integrity with a negative impact on the indigenous federations. We agreed that in order for our proposal to suceed, a lengthy, time-consuming process of discussions that included many federation and community leaders would be required.

We received enthusiasm and interest to proceed from this federation of nearly 70,000 people. Discussions and negotiations continued at a pace that reflected the distances, time and concensual process that this federation deemed important to any successful agreements.

During this process initial research activities were conducted with their consent to ascertain the quantity and quality of the material that we were interested in sourcing. This involved forestry scientists traveling in and around the region to collect small samples of herbarium specimens and material to confirm the suitability of this region as an area of supply. One of the conditions that was set by this group was that the results of our research on the suitability of this material be returned to the group along with much detailed information about our program and the therapeutic activities of the plant with which we were working.

One of the frequently expressed desires and concerns of this group was that proper acknowledgment be given to the indigenous peoples as the source of knowledge about this plant. It was clearly expressed by all parties that this plant was by no means solely discovered by one group, but was very well known by literally dozens of forest-dwelling peoples throughout Peru and many other countries. It was continuously expressed by this group that they should be acknowledged and given credit by scientists, educators and the general public for the scientific discovery of this material in not only monetary terms but also in intellectual terms as well.

Discussions continued and a second visit was made during one of the annual meetings of this federation. This meeting was attended by roughly 138 delegates of communities in this region of northern Peru. A representative from Shaman Pharmaceuticals and a Peruvian citizen, attended that meeting to discuss with the entire federation our interests, plans and goals to proceed with an experimental purchase of a large quantity of material from this group. The goals were expressed to the federation and translated from Spanish to their local language and then discussed within their group.

The conclusion of the group was positive. They sent to Shaman Pharmaceuticals, Inc., a letter confirming their agreement to supply an initial experimental quantity of material with specific terms laid out regarding the responsibilities for purchase, transport, payment and other critical details. One of their major concerns was the actual logistics and cost breakdown of who would pay for the various aspects of the purchase and transport to a central city for ultimate export. Those specific terms were written down and agreed to with the assistance of legal counsel so that there would be no ambiguity about who would bear the cost of the various phases in addition to the actual purchase price. The purchase price agreed to was a premium price above any of the prices currently paid by existing independent commercial middlemen. That aspect was well received and was one of the negotiating points that were important to this particular group. We, in turn, required that the group guarantee the quality and integrity of the product that they were to supply in order for us to agree to the enhanced value paid for the material. The initial agreement that we made was documented by a letter from this federation and accompanied by signatures of 138 delegates of this federation.

The experimental purchase of a large quantity of material was carried out in a satisfactory matter as agreed by all parties concerned. The next major issue facing both Shaman Pharmaceuticals and this indigenous federation was the export of this material out of the country.

Sustainable Management Commitments

All the parties involved in this agreement agreed to the importance of the sustainability and long-term management of this and any other resource to be marketed. Part of the discussion has always involved the importance of managing this resource. Shaman Pharmaceuticals, Inc., in order to continue purchasing material from that region, has requested that the group initiate and conduct the proper reforestation and management activities reflecting the current state of knowledge about this species. The indigenous federation in return has requested from Shaman Pharmaceuticals any and all information regarding the management and technical data that could enhance their management activities. An exchange is strongly recommended by the International Union for the Conservation of Nature (IUCN). We have conducted to date more than a dozen studies on many aspects of the marketing, management and conservation of this natural forest species. We have provided to the PanAmazonian indigenous organization, COICA, the local Peruvian indigenous organization, AIDESEP, and the Peruvian Foundation for the Conservation of Nature (FPCN) a number of these studies are in Spanish so that they may utilize them as they progress with their management and reforestation programs. This is one of the obligations that we have undertaken with a number of countries and forest-dwelling peoples. We have extended and acknowledge our obligation to include returning this information to the regional conservation organizations as well as to government ministries involved with the control and management of agricultural and forest resources.

Expanding the Approach

We are pursuing similar experimental supply and purchase agreements with other groups in the Peruvian Amazon and the countries of Colombia, Mexico and Ecuador. These discussions have similar types of short- medium- and long-term commitments to bring value-added purchasing and the integration of the management and conservation of this particular species. This is a slow and time consuming process which in order to be successful must be carefully conducted by all parties involved. One of the benefits of the pharmaceutical industry's relatively long product development time is that these programs can be conducted in a rational and thoughtful process.

Discussions regarding management, supply agreements and long-term purchasing are continuing. In May, 1993, the president of Shaman Pharmaceuticals, Inc., Ms. Lisa Conte and this author, met directly with seven indigenous leaders of AIDESEP in Peru to discuss our company's long term goals, commitments and programs for the next several years. Since this process has so far proven fruitful for both Shaman and AIDESEP, we recommend it for collaboration between the management of pharmaceutical companies and the elected indigenous representatives or managers of tropical forest environments. During these discussions, several recurring themes were agreed upon. The indigenous leaders expressed their ongoing concern about the integrity of the environment and the conservation of their useful species. They also explicitly expressed a desire to prevent short-term gains and monetary benefits that compromised the long-term integrity of their traditional plant resources and acknowledgment of their intellectual property rights.

Scientific and Intellectual Acknowledgment

One of the other major points expressed to Shaman Pharmaceuticals officials at this meeting was the issue of intellectual property rights and scientific credit. We were told that one of the ongoing concerns of the indigenous community is not only the financial credit but also the scientific and intellectual credit for their scientific discoveries and achievements. It was pointed out to us that historically all the modern medicines that were based on plants used by indigenous people have come into the pharmacopoeia without proper acknowledgment and credit to the initial scientists and experimenters who discovered and developed them in-situ. They requested that we be certain that this aspect be accentuated in the process of bringing our product to the market. They said that as indigenous inhabitants of the tropical rain forest of South America they should be accorded proper intellectual credit for the discovery and use of these plant medicines. This would extend to education and information concerning the origin of the new therapeutic agents which would be included in historical, educational and promotional information about the new medicine. This proper acknowledgment can serve to help strengthen their cultural identity. They were quite adamant that this could no longer be omitted from any process that brings a new tropical forest species into the world of modern therapeutic drugs.

Conclusion

We have provided three specific ways to return reciprocal benefits to the peoples with which we have been collaborating in a number of regions in the tropics of Asia, Africa and in this case, Latin America. We hope that these three specific methods and two cases illustrate our overall philosophy and approach to the issues of reciprocity and intellectual property rights and that they will serve as useful templates for other individuals and organizations. We know that there is room to modify and improve some of our approaches, but we advocate a more direct participation with forest-dwelling peoples in all these processes. This would imply that the appropriate government organizations not be the only parties in these discussions. It is critical for forest-dwelling peoples to be equal participants in negotiations over appropriate reciprocal benefits involved in the development of pharmaceuticals or any natural product.

Bibliography

Axt, Josephine R., M.L. Corn, M.Lee, D.Ackerman

1993 Biotechnology, Indigenous Peoples and Intellectual Property Rights. Congressional Research Service, The Library of Congress.

Boom, B.M.

1990a Giving Native People a Share of the Profits. Garden 14,6: 28-31.

1990b Ethics in Ethnopharmacology. In, Ethnobiology: Implications and Applications. Proceedings of the First Congress of Ethnobiology, Vol. 2, Part F. (D. Posey et al., eds.). Belém, Pará: Museu Paraense Emilio Goeldi. Pp. 147-153.

Cunningham, A.B.

1991 Indigenous Knowledge and Biodiversity: Global Commons or Regional Heritage? Cultural Survival Quarterly, Summer: pp. 1-4.

1993 Ethics, Ethnobiological Research, and Biodiversity. WWF/ UNESCO/KEW "People and Plants" Initiative, Gland, Switzerland.

Elisabetsky, E.

1991 Folklore, Tradition or Knowhow? Cultural Survival Quarterly 15,3: 9-13.

King, Steven R.

1991 Source of Our Cures. Cultural Survival Quarterly. 15,3: 19-22.

1992a Pharmaceutical Discovery, Ethnobotany, Tropical Forests and Reciprocity: Integrating Indigenous Knowledge, Conservation and Sustainable Development. In, Sustainable Harvest and Marketing of Rainforest Products (Mark Plotkin and Lisa Familore, eds.). Washington, D.C.: Island Press. Pp. 231-239.

1992b Conservation and Tropical Medicinal Plant Research. HerbalGram #27. Austin, Texas.

Moran, Katy

1992 Ethnobiology and U.S. Policy. In, Sustainable Harvest and Marketing of Rainforest Products (Mark Plotkin and Lisa Familore, eds.). Washington, D.C.: Island Press.

Padoch, C. and Boom, B.

1991 Draft Code of Ethics: Society for Economic Botany. Unpublished Draft, Society of Economic Botany.

Posey, D.A.
1990 Intellectual Property Rights and Just Compensation for Indigenous Knowledge. Anthropology Today 6,4: 13-16.

Reid, Walter, S.A. Laird, C.A. Meyer, R. Gámez, A. Sitenfeld, D. Janzen, M. Gollin, C. Juma
1993 Biodiversity Prospecting: Using Genetic Resources for Sustainable Development. WRI/IUCN/UNEP Global Biodiversity Strategy. Washington, D.C.: World Resources Institute (and others).

Suggested Contacts

Congressional Research Service, ML-213, The Library of Congress, Washington D.C., 20540-7210 (202/707-5700)

World Resources Institute, 1709 New York Avenue, NW, Washington, D.C. 20006 (202/638-6300)

Chapter
6

Policies for International Collaboration and Compensation in Drug Discovery and Development at the United States National Cancer Institute: The NCI Letter of Collection

Gordon M. Cragg, Michael R. Boyd,
Michael R. Grever and Saul A. Schepartz

*Developmental Therapeutics Program,
Division of Cancer Treatment,
National Cancer Institute, Bethesda, Maryland*

Using the earth's plants for potential drugs to treat the maladies of our species is as familiar as quinine and centuries old. The more recent awareness that the number of plant species is rapidly shrinking, that biodiversity is imperiled, has brought with it the realization that the human species stands in danger of exterminating its own well being. Even though it is well known that the traditional medicine systems in countries such as China and India have played key roles in the primary health care of the peoples of those countries for centuries, it is only relatively recently that awareness has spread that other indigenous societies have knowledge of medicinal plants, what ailments they address, and, equally important, when the plants should be collected, prepared and applied. And even more recently, thought began to be given to what sort of rights source countries and indigenous peoples might have over this knowledge.

(continued)

NCI, a major player in worldwide plant screening for cancer and AIDS, has been a pioneer in recognizing that simply expropriating these plant substances and knowledge without recognizing the rights of the countries and peoples of origin must stop. The NCI Letter of Collection is a benchmark in the widening practice of establishing these rights. The authors of this chapter present the NCI Letter, indicating that it can be used not only between the NCI and national institutions in host countries, but also with indigenous societies. - ed.

6

Policies for International Collaboration and Compensation in Drug Discovery and Development at the United States National Cancer Institute, The NCI Letter of Collection

Gordon M. Cragg, Michael R. Boyd,
Michael R. Grever and Saul A. Schepartz
Developmental Therapeutics Program, Division of Cancer Treatment, National Cancer Institute, Bethesda, Maryland

Plants have a long history of use in the treatment of cancer, and the discovery of plant-derived anticancer drugs, such as vinblastine and vincristine from the Madagascar periwinkle (*Catharanthus roseus*), prompted the U.S. National Cancer Institute (NCI) to initiate a program for the systematic testing of plants for anticancer activity. Between 1960 and 1982 the United States Department of Agriculture (USDA) and the NCI collaborated in the collection and testing of approximately 35,000 plant samples collected mainly from temperate regions in some sixty countries.

In 1985 the NCI decided to focus its plant collection program in tropical and sub-tropical regions worldwide. In selecting these regions as the new focus for plant collections, the NCI recognized several important factors. Firstly, tropical forests contain well over 50% of the world's estimated 250,000 plant species, and only a very small fraction of these has been investigated as a source of potential new drugs; in particular, relatively few had been tested for their anticancer activity in the NCI program. The implementation in 1987 of a major new program within the NCI for the discovery and development of drugs for the treatment of acquired immunodeficiency syndrome (AIDS) provided further impetus and resources for this initiative. Secondly, the rapid destruction of tropical forests emphasized the importance of studying these valuable resources before they have been too severely depleted. Last, but not least, ethnobiologists and anthropologists have warned that the valuable indigenous knowledge associated with the use of many plants is disappearing with the emergence of a new generation of indigenous people which places less reliance on their longstanding traditional medicine systems. Recognition of these factors prompted the

NCI to formulate policies for collaboration with, and compensation of, countries and peoples which agreed to participate in the NCI collection program. These policies have formed the basis for agreements with organizations in seven countries, and are discussed later in this paper.

Historically, pharmaceutical companies and research organizations have shown little interest in investigating plants as sources of potential new drugs, and the NCI natural products drug discovery program has been the world leader in this area. While the NCI program continues to be the leader in this endeavor, attitudes are changing, and several large companies, such as Glaxo Chemicals, Merck Pharmaceuticals, Monsanto Company and Smith Kline Beecham are testing plants and other organisms for a range of biological activities. In most cases, collections for these companies are carried out by botanical institutions (e.g. Missouri Botanical Garden, New York Botanical Garden, the Royal Botanical Garden at Kew) or intermediary organizations such as the National Biodiversity Institute (INBio) in Costa Rica. Generally these companies recognize the rights of source country organizations and peoples, and agreements for compensation have been finalized, either directly or through the intermediary organizations. The small company, Shaman Pharmaceuticals, Inc., bases its drug discovery program exclusively on ethnobotanical information obtained through interaction with traditional healers, and also has policies for collaboration and compensation. [see also Chapter 5 by Steven R. King - *ed.*]

The NCI Plant Collection Program

The NCI plant collections are performed through contracts with organizations possessing the necessary botanical expertise, and having contacts with suitable organizations in the potential source countries. In September, 1986, contracts were awarded to the Missouri Botanical Garden[1] for collections in Africa and Madagascar, to the New York Botanical Garden[2] for collections in Central and South America, and to the University of Illinois at Chicago[3] for collections in southeast Asia. In 1991 these contracts were extended for a further five-year period till 1996.

---

1 Dr. James Miller, Principal Investigator, NCI Plant Collection Contract, Missouri Botanical Garden, P.O. Box 299, St. Louis, MO 63166-0299.

2 Drs. Michael Balick and Douglas Daly, Co-Principal Investigators, NCI Plant Collection Contract, The New York Botanical Garden, Bronx, NY 10458-5126.

3 Dr. Djaja Doel Soejarto, Principal Investigator, NCI Plant Collection Contract, Program for Collaborative Research in the Pharmaceutical Sciences, The University of Illinois at Chicago, 833 South Wood Street, P.O. Box 6998, Chicago, Illinois 60680

Plant collections in Africa have been carried out in Cameroon, the Central African Republic, Gabon, Ghana, Madagascar, and Tanzania. In Central and South America, collections are proceeding in Belize, Bolivia, Colombia, Dominica, the Dominican Republic, Ecuador, Guatemala, Honduras, Martinique, Paraguay, Peru and Puerto Rico, while in southeast Asia collections are being performed in Indonesia (through the Arnold Arboretum at Harvard University[4]), Malaysia, Nepal, Papua New Guinea (through the Bishop Museum[5] in Honolulu), the Philippines, Taiwan and Thailand. In carrying out these collections in over 20 countries, the NCI contractors generally work closely with source country organizations possessing expertise in plant collection and taxonomy, such as botanical institutions, universities, pharmaceutical research institutes, and appropriate government agencies. Scientists from these organizations collaborate in field collection activities and taxonomic identifications, and their knowledge of local species and conditions is indispensable to the success of the NCI collection operations. The organizations also provide facilities for the preparation, packaging, and shipment of the samples to the NCI, and the organizations' staff provide invaluable assistance to the NCI contractors in obtaining the necessary collection and export permits. The collaboration between the source country organizations and the NCI collection contractors has, in turn, provided support for research activities by source country scientists in expanding the inventory of local species and the documentation of their uses. Voucher specimens of each species collected are deposited in the relevant source country national herbariums, thereby expanding the holdings of their flora. In addition, the NCI contractors provide training opportunities for source country personnel through conducting of workshops and presentation of lectures.

The present contracts involve the collection of 1,200 samples of 0.3-1.0 kg (dry weight) each per year, including different plant parts (e.g. bark, leaves, roots, wood, etc.). The contracts specify that collections should include many different species, but that emphasis should be given to the collection of medicinal plants when reliable information on their identity and use is available. Detailed documentation of each sample is required, including taxonomy, plant part, date and site of collection, habitat, and, when available, medicinal uses and methods of preparation used by the traditional healers. The priority given to the collection of medicinal plants and their uses by traditional healers is regarded as important, and collaborations have been established with several organizations involved in the study of traditional medicines.

---

[4] Dr John Burley, The Arnold Arboretum of Harvard University, 22 Divinity Avenue, Cambridge, MA 02138

[5] Dr. Wayne Takeuchi, Botany Department, Bishop Museum, 1525 Bernice S Box 19000 A, Honolulu, HI 96817-0916

Agreements have been signed between the NCI and some of these organizations, and these will be discussed in the following section.

Intellectual Property Rights. NCI Policies for International Collaboration and Compensation

The NCI is very aware of the great value of the natural resources to each country and its peoples participating in the NCI collection programs, and of the significant contributions being made by source country scientists and, in some instances, traditional healers, to the successful execution of these programs. Many of the participating countries and their peoples are very sensitive to the possibility of exploitation of their natural resources by organizations involved in the search for new medicines and agricultural chemicals (e.g. pesticides). Thus, while investigating the potential of plants and other natural sources in drug discovery and development, the NCI also wishes to promote the conservation of biological diversity, and recognizes the need to collaborate with source country organizations and peoples in the investigation of their natural resources. In addition, the NCI is committed to the compensation of source country organizations and peoples in the event that a plant collected in their country yields a drug of commercial value.

The policies for collaboration and compensation formulated by the NCI have been stated in the NCI Letter of Collection (LOC) (see Appendix 1) which is provided to the NCI collection contractors for use in negotiating with source countries and peoples for the collection and screening of their natural resources. Major issues covered by the LOC are:

1) Provision of the results of the testing of their plants and other organisms in the NCI anticancer and anti-AIDS screens[6] to the relevant source country organizations and/or peoples. Organizations are requested to keep the data on active organisms confidential until

---

[6] The anticancer screen is composed of 60 human cancer cell lines representing cancer disease-types, such as breast, colon, central nervous system, leukemia, melanoma, ovarian and renal. Activity is measured by the ability of an extract of a plant or other organism to selectively kill the cells of a particular disease-type (e.g. breast) while not affecting the other cancer cells. The anti-AIDS screen is composed of human lymphocyte cells infected with the AIDS virus. Usually the virus kills the cells in a few days; if, however, addition of an extract of an organism to the infected cells causes them to survive for a longer period (e.g. 5 or 6 days) then the extract might contain some chemical(s) which protect the cells against the viral attack, and the extract is said to be active against the AIDS virus. It is important to note that these tests are carried out *in vitro* (i.e. in the test tube), and observed activity does not mean that the extracts will be active *in vivo* (i.e. in a live animal or human being).

the NCI has had time to assess the potential for development, and the patentability, of novel drugs isolated from such organisms.

2) Invitations to suitably qualified scientists, nominated by the source country organizations or its peoples, to visit the NCI to collaborate in the discovery and development of novel drugs from their organisms, subject to the availability of the necessary space and resources.

3) An undertaking by the NCI to make its best effort to ensure that royalties and other forms of compensation are provided to the source country organization and to individuals of that country, as appropriate, in the event that a drug, isolated from one of its organisms, advances to commercial development. Advanced development and marketing of a drug generally is carried out through establishing a licensing agreement between the NCI and a pharmaceutical company. One of the terms of such a licensing agreement would require the company to provide a level of compensation which would be negotiated in consultation with the source country organization. While the NCI, as a US Government agency, is forbidden by law to guarantee compensation, use of the term "make best effort" implies a strong commitment on the part of the NCI to pursue fair and equitable compensation, and to ensure that the terms of any licensing agreement are fulfilled.

On the basis of consultation with various Source Country representatives, as well as with non-Governmental Organizations concerned with the compensation of Source Country peoples, the NCI has recently modified this term to require direct negotiation of agreement(s) between the successful licensee and the appropriate Source Country Government agency(ies) or other appropriate Source Country organizations. Such agreement(s) will address the concern on the part of the Source Country Government that pertinent agencies, institutions and/or persons receive royalties and other forms of compensation, as appropriate (see appendix 2).

4) A requirement, as part of any licensing agreement, that an organization developing and/or marketing a drug isolated from an organism collected through an NCI contract use the country of origin of the organism as the first source of supply of raw material for production of the drug, subject to the negotiation of a mutually agreeable fair price. Procurement of sufficient raw material for the large-scale production of a drug could involve the sustainable harvest of the wild source organism, or might involve the development of a cultivation program.

The terms of compensation stipulated by the LOC apply to the actual natural drug isolated from the plant or other source organism and to related agents structurally derived from natural drug by chemical or biochemical modification. The level of compensation, however, may vary depending on the relationship of the structurally derived drug to the original isolated natural drug.

To date, agreements based on the LOC have been signed with organizations in seven countries participating in the NCI plant collection program. The agreements are generally made with organizations collaborating with the NCI collection contractors, or which are recommended by the contractors. These include the Centre National de Recherches Pharmaceutiques in Madagascar[7], the Institute of Traditional Medicine in Tanzania[8], the Zimbabwe National Traditional Healers Association coordinated through the University of Zimbabwe[9], the University Centre for Health Sciences of the University of Yaounde in Cameroon[10], the Philippine National Museum[11], the University of Ghana[12], and Federación AWA in Ecuador[13]. Since these agreements have incorporated the terms of compensation as stated in the earlier LOC (point 3 above), the Source Country organizations will be given the option of selecting the new modification requiring direct negotiation of agreement(s) between the successful licensing pharmaceutical company and the relevant Source Country organization(s).

As mentioned earlier, NCI plant collections are proceeding in over 20 tropical and subtropical countries worldwide, and collaborations have been established between the NCI contractors and source country professional institutions. In most cases, source country authorities and institutions have accepted the terms of the LOC without requiring formal agreements, but an increasing interest is now being shown in establishing such agreements. The NCI is very willing to enter into such agreements, and negotiations are currently proceeding with several source country organizations and government agencies. In order to discuss the goals of the program, and explore the scope for collaboration, the NCI periodically invites source country representatives to visit its drug discovery facilities at the Frederick Cancer Research and Development Center

---

[7] Centre National de Recherches Pharmaceutiques, B.P. 702, Route d'Alarobia-Analamahitsy, Antananarivo 101, Madagascar

[8] Institute of Traditional Medicine, Muhimbili Medical Centre, P.O. Box 65001, Dar Es Salaam, Tanzania

[9] Professor G. L. Chavunduka, President, Zimbabwe National Traditional Healers Association, University of Zimbabwe, P.O. Box MP 167, Mount Pleasant, Harare, Zimbabwe

[10] University Centre for Health Sciences, The University of Yaounde, BP292, Yaounde, Cameroon

[11] Philippine National Museum, Executive House Building, P. Burgos St., P.O. Box 2659, Manila, Republic of the Philippines

[12] Vice Chancellor, University of Ghana, P.O. Box 56, Legon, Ghana

[13] President, Federación AWA, c/o Mr. Jaime Levy, Coordinator General, UTEPA, Boyacá 192 y Avenida Universitaria, Casilla Postal 17-21-416, Quito, Ecuador

(FCRDC) in Maryland. Thus far, 28 representatives, mainly scientists, from 19 countries have visited FCRDC, and, in some instances, US contractor facilities, for periods of one to two weeks. These visits have invariably resulted in a better mutual understanding of the goals and concerns of each party, and have expedited the initiation of collection programs or the finalization of agreements.

In general, the available NCI resources restrict collaborations to organizations in those countries participating in the NCI contract collection program, but the NCI is prepared to consider proposals from organizations or groups based in countries or regions not covered by the present collection contracts, or organizations studying organisms (e.g. insects) not included in the present NCI program. Agreements based on the LOC have been signed with the Central Drug Research Institute in Lucknow and the Cancer Research Center in Moscow for the study of medicinal plants from India and Russia, respectively. Medicinal plants from Yunnan Province are being studied in collaboration with the Kunming Institute of Botany in the Peoples' Republic of China. In establishing these collaborations, the NCI undertakes to abide by the same policies of collaboration and compensation as apply to source countries participating in the contract collection program.

The NCI program is focused primarily on the discovery and development of agents for the treatment of cancer and AIDS. From the approximately 114,000 extracts obtained from different parts of about 35,000 plants collected for NCI between 1960 and 1982, only two pure active chemicals were isolated which have resulted in the development of drugs showing efficacy in the treatment of various cancers in human patients. Of these, taxol, isolated from the Pacific Yew tree (*Taxus brevifolia*) has been approved for marketing; two others, topotecan and CPT-11, structurally derived from the natural product, camptothecin (isolated from the Chinese tree,*Camptotheca acuminata*), are being developed by other organizations and are in advanced clinical development. Thus, the chances of developing an effective commercial anticancer drug, such as taxol, are of the order of one in 40,000 to 50,000, based on the number of plant extracts tested. This compares with estimates of one in 10,000 to 20,000 for other diseases. In addition, the time taken to develop the drug to the stage of general use in the treatment of patients can vary considerably, and can be from 10-20 years for anticancer drugs. The experience of Shaman Pharmaceuticals[14] which is basing its drug discovery program exclusively on information obtained through interaction with traditional healers, might result in a more favorable success rate.

---

[14] Shaman Pharmaceuticals, 213 E. Grand Avenue, South San Francisco, CA 94080-4812

Considerable interest has been shown by other research organizations and companies in the testing of materials from the NCI Natural Products Repository (NPR) for activities against diseases related to the NCI mission, including diseases which have an impact on health in developing countries. These diseases include antifungal and parasitic infections, malaria, and tuberculosis. After consulting source country representatives, either directly or through their respective collection contractors, the NCI has formulated a policy for the distribution of extracts to carefully selected organizations. A key factor determining the selection of recipient organizations is the agreement by the organizations to abide by the same policies of compensation and raw material supply as stated in the LOC. Approval for distribution of extracts is granted only after the organization has signed a legally binding material transfer agreement (MTA) with the NCI guaranteeing the rights of source countries to compensation in the event of production and marketing of a drug from an organism collected within their borders; the MTA also requires the recipient to utilize the host (source) country as the first source of supply of raw material for production of the marketed agent. By supplying the extracts to other approved organizations, the NCI is expanding the range of diseases against which they may be tested, and thereby improving the chances of discovering novel drugs from plants and other organisms provided by source countries.

Future Developments

To date, most of the collaborations and agreements established between the NCI and source countries have involved professional organizations with expertise in botany and/or pharmaceutical research. This trend has been dictated largely by the policies of the NCI collection contractors through their collaboration with source country organizations possessing expertise in plant collection and taxonomy. A few agreements have been signed with organizations studying traditional medicine, such as the Institute of Traditional Medicine in Tanzania and the Zimbabwe National Traditional Healers Association, but even these organizations are formally associated with universities.

A notable exception is the recent agreement with the AWA Federation in Ecuador which will permit ethnobotanically-guided collecting by New York Botanical Garden (NYBG) to proceed in AWA Federation territory. NYBG has adopted an ethnobotanical approach in many of its collections for the NCI, and it is anticipated that a number of agreements with indigenous groups in addition to the AWA Federation may be considered in the future. The agreement with the AWA Federation follows the LOC closely in format and detail, except that a Spanish translation accompanies the English version. Thus far, the NCI has found that the format and terms of the LOC have been generally accepted by source country organizations, though the use of the terminology, "will make its best effort" in the clause dealing with royalties and compensation issuing from the sale of commercial drugs developed from source country organisms, has raised questions concerning the NCI's commitment to this issue. As previously indicated, by U.S. law, the NCI cannot be obligated to a given level of royalties in the LOC or any agreement based thereon, since as a US Government Agency, it is not authorized to promise or encumber future intellectual property (patent) rights to any invention of the NCI, except under the terms of a cooperative research and development agreement (CRADA); generally CRADAs are only considered in the case of projects which are in a state of advanced research and development. Explanation of this fact, together with statements of strong support for the policies formulated in the LOC received from all levels of the NCI and the National Institutes of Health, as well as members of the US Congress, generally assures source country representatives of the NCI's total commitment to this issue. However, in response to consultations with various Source Country representatives, as well as with Non-Government Organizations concerned with compensation of Source Country peoples, the NCI has recently modified the clause dealing with compensation issues to require direct negotiation between the successful licensing pharmaceutical company and appropriate Source Country organizations.

It is the intention of the NCI to retain the present format and content of the LOC as long as plants and other organisms are being collected through the current contract mechanism. Once these contracts have ceased to operate, agreements may be amended to reflect a more direct relationship between the source country organization and the NCI. Even under such changed circumstances, however, the NCI regards the policies of collaboration and compensation formulated in the LOC, as a sound basis for any future agreements.

Once a new drug is approved by the NCI for advanced preclinical and clinical development, a separate agreement addressing the specific issues related to the development of that drug may be established between the NCI and the source country organization.

Conclusion

The NCI Letter of Collection has formed the basis for agreements of collaboration and compensation between the NCI and organizations in seven source countries participating in the NCI plant collection program, as well as several other organizations collaborating with the NCI in studies of medicinal plants; negotiations are in progress with several others.

While the majority of the source country organizations entering into these agreements are professional institutions or universities, the NCI regards the terms of the Letter of Collection as being an appropriate basis for agreements with indigenous peoples. The finalization of an agreement between the NCI and the Federación AWA illustrates this point, and the NCI will be very willing to consider agreements with other indigenous groups wishing to participate in the NCI contract collection program subject to their recognition by the source country government. The terms of collaboration, compensation, and use of source country resources for drug discovery and development, as stated in the Letter of Collection, could also form a suitable basis for the negotiation of agreements between indigenous peoples and private sector companies involved in the discovery and development of bioactive agents, including pharmaceuticals and agricultural chemicals.

Appendix 1

DEVELOPMENTAL THERAPEUTICS PROGRAM
DIVISION OF CANCER TREATMENT
NATIONAL CANCER INSTITUTE

Letter of Collection

The Developmental Therapeutics Program (DTP), Division of Cancer Treatment (DCT), National Cancer Institute (NCI) is currently investigating plants, marine macro-organisms and microbes as potential sources of novel anticancer and AIDS-antiviral drugs. The DTP is the drug discovery program of NCI which is an Institute of the National Institutes of Health supported by the United States Government. While investigating the potential of natural products in drug discovery and development, NCI wishes to promote the conservation of biological diversity, and recognizes the need to compensate source country organizations and peoples in the event of commercialization of a drug developed from an organism collected within their borders.

As part of the drug discovery program, DTP has contracts with various organizations for the collection of plants and marine macro-organisms worldwide. DTP has an interest in investigating "name of organisms" from "name of country", and wishes to collaborate with "country organization" in this investigation. Such a collaboration will be within the framework of the collection contract between NCI and "collection contractor".

The role of DTP, DCT, NCI in the collaboration will include the following:

1) DTP will screen the extracts of all "name of organisms" provided from "country" for anticancer and AIDS-antiviral activity, and will provide the

test results to "country organization" as soon as they are available. Such results will be channelled via "collection contractor".

2) The test results will be kept confidential by all parties, with any publication delayed until DTP has an opportunity to file a patent application in the United States of America on any active agents isolated.

3) Any extracts exhibiting significant activity will be further studied by bioassay-guided fractionation in order to isolate the pure compound(s) responsible for the observed activity. Since the relevant bioassays are only available at DTP/NCI, such fractionation will be carried out in DTP/NCI laboratories.

4) Subject to the provision that suitable laboratory space and other necessary resources are available, DTP/NCI agrees to invite a senior technician or scientist designated by "country organization" to work in the laboratories of DTP/NCI or, if the parties agree, in laboratories using technology which would be useful in furthering work under this agreement. The duration of such a visit would not exceed one year except by prior agreement between "country organization" and DTP/NCI. The designated Guest Researcher will be subject to provisions usually governing Guest Researchers at NIH. Salary and other conditions of exchange will be negotiated in good faith.

5) In the event of the isolation of a promising agent from a "name of organism" collected in "country", further development of the agent will be undertaken by DTP/NCI.

6) DTP/NCI will, as appropriate, seek patent protection on all inventions developed under this agreement by NCI employees alone or by NCI and "country organization" employees jointly, and will seek appropriate protection abroad.

7) All licenses granted on any patents arising from this collaboration shall contain a clause referring to this agreement and shall indicate that the licensee has been apprised of this agreement.

8) Should the agent eventually be licensed to a pharmaceutical company for production and marketing, DTP/NCI will make its best effort to ensure that royalties and other forms of compensation shall be provided to the host country organization and to individuals of that country, as appropriate, in an amount to be negotiated with NCI in consultation with the host country organization.

9) Such terms shall apply equally to instances where the invention is the actual isolated natural product, or where the invention is a product structurally based on the isolated natural product (i.e. where the natural product provides the lead for development of the invention), though the percentage of royalties negotiated as payment might vary depending upon the relationship of the marketed drug to the originally isolated natural product.

It is understood that the eventual development of a drug to the stage of marketing is a long-term process which may require 10-15 years.

10) In obtaining licensees, the DTP/NCI will require the applicant for license to seek as its first source of supply the natural products available from "country". If no appropriate licensee is found who will use natural products available from "country", or if "country organization" or its suppliers cannot provide adequate amounts of raw materials at a mutually agreeable fair price, the licensee will be required to pay to "country organization" an amount of money (to be negotiated) to be used for expenses associated with cultivation of medicinal plant species that are endangered by deforestation, or for other appropriate conservation measures.

11) Sections 7-10 shall not apply to organisms which are freely available from different countries (i.e., common weeds, agricultural crops, ornamental plants, fouling organisms) unless information indicating a particular use of the organism (e.g. medicinal, pesticidal) was provided by local residents to guide the collection of such an organism from their country, or unless other justification acceptable to both the "country organization" and DTP/NCI is provided. In the case where an organism is freely available from different countries, but a genotype producing an active agent is found only in "name of country," sections 7-10 shall apply.

12) DTP/NCI will test any pure compounds submitted by "country organization" scientists for antitumor and AIDS-antiviral activity,provided such compounds have not been tested previously in the NCI screens. If significant antitumor or AIDS-antiviral activity is detected, further development of the compound and investigation of patent rights will, as appropriate, be undertaken by DTP/NCI in consultation with "country organization".

Should the agent eventually be licensed to a pharmaceutical company for production and marketing, DTP/NCI will make its best effort to ensure that royalties and other forms of compensation shall be provided to the host country organization and to individuals of that country, as appropriate, in an amount to be negotiated with NCI in consultation with the host country organization.

13) DTP/NCI may send selected samples to other organizations for investigation of their anti-cancer, anti-HIV or other therapeutic potential. Such samples will be restricted to those collected by NCI contractors unless specifically authorized by the country organization. Any organization receiving samples must agree to compensate the source country organization and individuals, as appropriate, in the same fashion as is described in sections 8-10 above, notwithstanding anything to the contrary in section 11.

The role of "country organization" in the collaboration will include the following:

1) "Country organization" will collaborate with "collection contractor" in the collection of "name of organisms", and will work with "collection contractor" to arrange the necessary permits to ensure the timely collection and export of materials to DTP/NCI.

2) Should "country organization" have any knowledge of the medicinal use of any "name of organisms" by the local population or traditional healers, this information will be used to guide the collection of such organisms on a priority basis where possible. Details of the methods of administration (e.g. hot infusion, etc.) used by the traditional healers will be provided where applicable to enable suitable extracts to be made. All such information will be kept confidential by DTP until both parties agree to publication.

The permission of the traditional healer or community will be sought before publication of their information, and proper acknowledgement will be made of their contribution.

3) "Country organization" and "collection contractor" will collaborate in the provision of further quantities of active raw material if required for development studies.

4) In the event of large amounts of raw material being required for production, "country organization" and "collection contractor" will investigate the mass propagation of the material in "country". Consideration should also be given to sustainable harvest of the material while conserving the biological diversity of the region, and involvement of the local population in the planning and implementation stages.

5) "Country organization" scientists and their collaborators may screen additional samples of the same raw materials for other biological activities and develop them for such purposes independently of this agreement.

____
Name (Signature)

____
Name (Print or type)

____
Title

____
Institution or Agency

____________________________	________________
Director, National Cancer Institute	Address
______________	________________
Date	Date

Appendix 2

Modification to clause 8 of the NCI Letter of Collection

8) Should the agent eventually be licensed to a pharmaceutical company for production and marketing, DTP/NCI, will require the successful licensee to negotiate and enter into agreement(s) with the appropriate Source Country Government agency(ies). This agreement(s) will address the concern on the part of the Source Country Government that pertinent agencies, institutions and/or persons receive royalties and other forms of compensation as appropriate.

Chapter
7

Biocultural Diversity Conservation Through The Healing Forest Conservancy

Katy Moran
The Healing Forest Conservancy

In this chapter Katy Moran presents the case for preserving the global stocks of *biocultural* diversity and describes current pilot projects largely framed by indigenous peoples to accomplish this. Every one of the world's major sociopolitical groups has been an aggressive borrower, drawing on the discoveries and ideas of uncountable societies with which it has come into contact across the millennia of its development. In the coming century, as population and consumption pressures on Earth's biocultural resources mount, the survival and well being of all earth citizens will require increasingly clever solutions to prevent its decline. Just as in the past, most of our solutions will derive from the biological diversity and the cultural knowledge found throughout the globe - the very diversity that is now being eroded due to the thoughtless and wasteful practices in vogue today. In the long run, perhaps the most important contribution that IPR will make will be to impart value to the world's biocultural diversity and to increase our inclination to preserve it. The Healing Forest Conservancy is an example of a small but growing number of non-governmental organizations which recognize that the essential conservation objective is not biological or cultural, but biocultural. - ed.

7

Biocultural Diversity Conservation Through The Healing Forest Conservancy

Katy Moran
The Healing Forest Conservancy[1]

The Challenge of Deforestation

Every second of every day, a tropical forest the size of a football field is destroyed with cumulative consequences that cross national borders and affect us all. Deforestation erodes the biological diversity of life, itself, since tropical forests are the habitat of almost half the plant and animal species on our planet. At loss is the diversity of life forms that hold promise for scientists to discover new medicines, crops and industrial applications (Fowler et al. 1988). Forest peoples lose their homelands and humanity loses generations of their traditional knowledge of the use of forest resources. Deforestation diminishes forests' ability to moderate climate and the loss of forest cover exacerbates soil erosion and flooding, increases siltation in rivers and estuaries, and disrupts regional hydrological cycles. A vicious cycle of poverty, destructive population and consumption practices, poor land use and land tenure policies and inappropriate development has doubled the rate of tropical deforestation in the past decade (Moran 1991).

The Value of Biological Diversity

Yet tropical forests represent laboratories of biological resources critical to humanity, particularly medicinal plants. Although the amount and value of this wealth of biological diversity has not been calculated, we do know that one-fourth of the prescription drugs on the market in

---

[1] Katy Moran is Executive Director, The Healing Forest Conservancy, 3521 S Street, NW, Washington, D.C. 20007,USA. The Healing Forest Conservancy is a publicly supported, tax-exempt organization under Section 501 (c) (3) of the Internal Revenue Code.

the U.S. today are plant-derived. It is estimated that in 1990, American consumers spent over $15.5 billion on prescription drugs which contained active ingredients extracted from plants.

The Value of Cultural Diversity

Similarly, peoples who live in or near tropical forests represent libraries of information on the use of plants for medicinal purposes. According to the World Health Organization, 80 % of the population of developing countries, about 3.5 billion people, depend on plant-based traditional medicine for their primary health care. But the traditional knowledge of plant use by the gene-rich developing world is valuable to all of humanity as scientists from the gene-poor industrialized world use it for leads in therapeutic drug discovery and research. Of the 120 active compounds found in plants and used in Western medicine, 74 % have the same therapeutic use as in traditional societies. This knowledge is embedded in forest peoples' cultural systems. Accumulated over millennia, traditional knowledge is as rich and diverse as tropical forests' biological resources, and it is equally as threatened. Since 1900, due to outside encroachment, introduced diseases and loss of habitat, extinction has been the fate of an average of one indigenous culture each year in the Amazon region alone (Cultural Survival 1991).

Conserving Biocultural Diversity

As the medicinal value of this biological and cultural diversity, or "biocultural diversity", becomes more apparent, its conservation for present and future generations worldwide becomes more urgent. Today, there are many non-governmental organizations and private foundations with programs to protect biodiversity. Few, however, explicitly link the long-term survival of indigenous societies in that cause. The non-profit Healing Forest Conservancy (the Conservancy) was founded through a donation from Shaman Pharmaceuticals, Inc., to compensate community and country partners of Shaman in a manner that conserves biocultural diversity. Both for-profit and non-profit interests are uniquely merged through this mutual goal, because Shaman is focused on the discovery and development of novel pharmaceuticals from plants. As the name of the pharmaceutical company implies, Shaman uses the science of ethnobotany, as well as isolation and natural products chemistry, medicine and pharmacology to create a more efficient drug-discovery process. Although the young company has yet to commercialize a product, the use of ethnobotanic leads has brought potential products to clinical trials within a record time frame. After a pharmaceutical product is commercialized, the Conservancy will channel a percentage of product profits to each community and country that Shaman has worked with. Results of the following pilot projects will help to prioritize compensation strategies of the Conservancy.

Currently the Conservancy works globally with other non-profit organizations and tropical forest peoples' organizations to conserve biocultural diversity by focusing on programs that:

- promote sustainable development by local harvesting of natural products in forests which might otherwise be cut for timber or cleared for farmland;
- provide resources to survey, demarcate and deed historic territories to indigenous communities;
- train local people, particularly women, in methods for species collection, identification and inventory of local genetic resources and their uses by merging traditional and non-traditional scientific methods and processes;
- build and strengthen indigenous institutions through education and communication between forest societies and the outside world;
- develop local and regional industries for chemical prospecting through technical training in bioassay, chemical screening, etc.
- link U.S. and international practitioners and policy makers in initiatives that foster the health and welfare of indigenous cultures and tropical forests.

Projects of The Healing Forest Conservancy illustrate ways which non-governmental organizations, industry, and foundations can fruitfully collaborate with indigenous societies with the mutual objective of conserving biocultural diversity. The process enhances the empowerment of indigenous communities to determine the fate of their biocultural diversity.

Medicine Woman

With support in the form of grants, The Healing Forest Conservancy has established an education and training program for women, particularly indigenous women, in developing countries. The program provides small grants for training in technical skills such as biological inventorying, chemical screening or bioassays and ethnobotany to women from societies where the program suits local needs.

Technical Training to Implement the Convention on Biological Diversity. Technical training offers tropical countries the means to implement the Convention on Biological Diversity that emerged from the Earth Summit in Rio in 1992. It also supplies economic incentives for countries to protect their biodiversity by capitalizing on the "green gold" of their biological resources. At the Earth Summit, species inventories were listed in the Biodiversity Convention as the first step to conserve biological diversity, but few countries have completed them. An inventory supplies a catalogue of a country's biological resources;

measures the amount, variation and uniqueness of species; describes how species are distributed and their conservation status; and defines species management options. But most gene-rich tropical countries of the South are burdened with oppressive external debt, impoverished university systems, and few professional taxonomists. They have not been able to collect, identify, inventory, and screen the biological assets housed within their tropical forests and recognized as valuable to the gene-poor countries of the North.

Applying Biological Diversity. The sustainable use of biological resources was also addressed in the Biodiversity Convention and can begin with bioassays or chemical screening of plant species. Bioassays are tests in which organisms or their parts, typically in the form of chemical extracts, are assessed for their effects on diseases. They are a form of inventorying and should be included in the cataloging process. Bioassays are typically carried out in labs of industrialized countries, but increased screening in developing countries offers many benefits. Screening is labor intensive, yet non-invasive, so it can generate jobs and be compatible with local conservation programs. Labs near forests can use fresh samples in the search for chemical activity that may be seasonal. Also, it is more rigorous to study source organisms when they are sporadically variable at different times in different places (US Congress, Office of Technology Assessment 1993).

Applying Cultural Diversity. Rather than random screening of species, organisms can be chosen for bioassays through leads unique to the area and cultures where they are located. Historically, traditional communities have utilized the relationship of local flora and epidemiology as traditional healers have based the selection of their medicinal plant use on observation of the therapeutic effects of local plants on humans. For pharmaceuticals, concentrating on the traditional use of plants focuses leads for screening and results in a more timely and less expensive drug discovery process. Likewise, leads from the traditional process of plant preparation for healing provide clues to the type of chemical compounds in plants under investigation. Combining industrialized countries' technology with traditional knowledge of the use of local species -- merging ancient and modern knowledge systems -- offers a powerful methodology for more efficient drug discovery and a pragmatic reason for countries to protect their biodiversity.

Benefits of Applied Biocultural Diversity for Developing Countries. Local capacity-building, through training and education for skills in technical jobs, supplies income-producing opportunities to communities that are best-located to protect species. More importantly, if training, education, and employment opportunities are available to women, ecological impacts can be magnified. Data exist to demonstrate that women who have options between having a job or having another child typically choose the former, effectively lessening population pressures on natural resources. Yet few programs offer this opportunity specifically to women.

Regional medical needs can be addressed by assuring the continuity of plant resources that provide health care through traditional medicines, and plant reserves where future healers can be trained (Balick and Mendelsohn 1992). National governments of developing countries can benefit from a strengthened infrastructure for science and commerce, yielding jobs and taxes (Clark and Juma 1991). Also, fees can be charged for "chemical prospecting" allowing debt-ridden nations to forgo short-term profits from logging, cattle-grazing, and monoculture development projects that destroy forests. Chemical screening of plants adds value to genetic material and can result in the establishment of working links with industries and universities in industrialized countries that have complex laboratories currently better equipped to develop and market new therapeutic drugs. Proprietary arrangements can ensure that compensation from commercialization of natural compounds or synthesized chemicals revert fairly to the peoples and nations of original production.

Terra Nova

The government of Belize has designated a 7,000 acre tract of land, named Terra Nova, to establish what many believe to be the world's first ethnobiomedical plant reserve. The land, located in the Cayo District of Belize, has terrain ideal for many types of Maya medicinal plants. It is also a nursery for "orphaned" species -- medicinal plants integral to the survival of traditional healing in Central America that have been rescued from bulldozers and transplanted to a safe location. To halt current poaching and logging near Terra Nova, The Healing Forest Conservancy has supported surveying, demarcating and deeding the land. Title for Terra Nova has been deeded to The Belize Association of Traditional Healers, following an indigenous pattern of communally owned and managed resources. The Association holds monthly public education meetings for local villagers where traditional healers discuss medicinal plants and traditional remedies for a variety of common ailments.

Future plans, supported by the Conservancy and the New York Botanical Garden's Institute of Economic Botany, include making Terra Nova a self-supporting extractive reserve through a factory of herbal remedies using Maya medicine. Included in the plan is a clinic with a sliding fee scale to help meet health needs of nearby villagers whose primary health care is supplied by traditional Maya medicinals. Today, Terra Nova offers a means for The Traditional Healers Association to train and pass on the healing forest legacy to future generations of practitioners in a reserve that unites traditional peoples' use of plants with their sustainable extraction.

Usko-Ayar Amazonian School Of Painting

Strengthening Cultural Identity. The Usko-Ayar Amazonian School of Painting in Pucallpa, Peru, is much more than an art school. While learning to paint local scenes of the forest, students also discover the names and uses of rain forest plants by recording the myths and traditional plant knowledge of their elders in painted form. Many students become accomplished artists as they enrich their understanding of the natural world of the Amazon while deepening their cultural identity.

Usko-Ayar, meaning "Spiritual Prince" in Quechua, offers classes free of charge and provides art supplies for promising students. Since the non-profit school was founded in 1988, it has taught more than 600 children from working-class families in rural areas of the Ucayali River in the Peruvian Amazon. Paintings from the school have earned acclaim at international art exhibits, particularly the collection of the works of Pablo Amaringo, the former shaman who founded the school. Amaringo, who has Lamista, Cocama, and Piro Indian ancestors, was awarded the United Nations Global 500 Award in recognition of his protection of the environment through the school's work.

Sustainable Development Utilizing Biocultural Resources. The Healing Forest Conservancy held an exhibit and sale of Usko-Ayar paintings with Shaman Pharmaceuticals and raised enough funds to purchase a boat for the school to expand. Using a floating art school, Usko-Ayar can now reach Peruvian children who live along less accessible river communities. Also, Shaman displays and sells Usko-Ayar paintings at corporate headquarters in San Francisco and, through the Conservancy, sends proceeds back to the students and the school.

The Richard Evans Schultes Award

Ethnobotany And Deforestation. To foster and encourage professionalism in the expanding applications of ethnobotany, The Healing Forest Conservancy will present an annual award to a scientist, practitioner, or organization, indigenous or non-indigenous, that has made an outstanding contribution to ethnobotany or to indigenous peoples issues related to ethnobotany. Ethnobotany, literally "people botany", focuses on the relationship between humans and their plant resources (Frake 1962). It is an interdisciplinary science drawing on anthropology, botany, ecology, economics, medicine, and other disciplines. Increased awareness of ethnobotany mirrors increasing popular concerns about deforestation

(Moran 1992). Today, scientists and environmentalists use ethnobotanical data to supply evidence that forests sustain a cornucopia of food, fodder, fiber, fuel, and other forest products that offer economic reasons to halt deforestation (Phillips and Gentry 1993). In addition, advances in biotechnology have renewed interest in plant-derived pharmaceuticals and other promising industrial applications from plant chemical compounds.

The annual award of the Conservancy is in the name of Richard Evans Schultes, widely recognized as "the father of ethnobotany". This distinction was bestowed on Schultes in 1984 when he received the annual Gold Medal of the World Wildlife Fund from the organization's then-president, Prince Philip of the United Kingdom. Professor Schultes has received numerous other awards, including the Tyler Prize for Environmental Achievement and the Linnean Gold Medal. He also was awarded the Cross of Boyaca, the highest award of Colombia, where Schultes conducted much of his research. A two million acre portion of Colombia's Amazon forest was also named "Sector Schultes" in his honor. Schultes earned his Ph.D. in biology from Harvard, where he now serves as Professor Emeritus, and is an internationally renowned specialist in the botany of rubber trees, medicinal plants and hallucinogens. He has published over 400 technical papers and many books, including The Healing Forest (Schultes and Raffauf 1990), after which The Healing Forest Conservancy was named. Schultes' deep respect for the Indians of the Northwest Amazon is legendary, but best related in his own words:

> The accomplishments of aboriginal people in learning plant properties must be a result of a long and intimate association with, and utter dependence on, their ambient vegetation. This native knowledge warrants careful and critical attention on the part of modern scientific efforts....If phytochemists must randomly investigate the constituents of biological effects of 80,000 species of Amazon plants, the task may never be finished. Concentrating first on those species that people have lived and experimented with for millennia offers a short-cut to the discovery of new medically or industrially useful compounds (Schultes 1988 :11).

Calvin Sperling Recipient of 1993 Richard Evans Schultes Award. Richard Schultes' distinguished academic and applied accomplishments offer an ideal that all ethnobotanists should be encouraged to follow. Consequently, the first annual Richard Evans Schultes Award was presented during the June, 1993 Society for Economic Botany meeting, of which Schultes is a founding member. Calvin R. Sperling, Ph.D., of the National Germplasm Resources Laboratory at the U.S. Department of Agriculture was recognized for his comprehensive work as a field ethnobotanist in the preservation of genetic resources and the ethnobotany of economic plants. The Schultes award featured a $5,000 cash prize donated by Conservation International, a non-profit organization focused on the conservation of global biological diversity and the welfare of tropical forest peoples.

Nominations for the 1994 award are now open. Balance of the award in geographic location, gender and field of study is encouraged. The International Selection Committee is chaired by Michael J. Balick, Ph.D., Philecology Curator of Economic Botany and Director of the New York Botanical Garden Institute of Economic Botany. The Society for Economic Botany was founded in 1959 as an international scientific organization to further ethnobotanic research and to disseminate research results through meetings and publications. Its international journal, "Economic Botany" publishes original research, review papers, historical studies and book reviews.

Conclusions

The Healing Forest Conservancy operates on the premise that loss or homogenization of life forms and cultural systems is a trend we must resist. Biocultural diversity enhances the sustainability of both natural and social systems because, when necessary, it supplies a greater range of options for adaptation -- a cushion against disaster in the face of sudden or irreversible change. By spreading risk, it equips natural and social systems with alternatives for continuing survival if a component of a system fails. Biocultural diversity is valuable because it retains options and possible solutions to crises not yet envisioned, and answers to questions not yet asked. It is in the best interest of The Healing Forest Conservancy, as well as all peoples and all nations, to regain, protect and nurture existing biological and human resource systems while they are still useful, still replicable and still recoverable.

Bibliography

Balick, Michael J. and Robert Mendelsohn
1992 Assessing the Economic Value of Traditional Medicines from Tropical Rain Forests. Conservation Biology 6,1: 128-130.

Clark, Norman and Calestous Juma
1991 Biotechnology for Sustainable Development. Nairobi: ACTS Press.

Cultural Survival
1991 Intellectual Property Rights: The Politics of Ownership. Cultural Survival Quarterly . Summer 15,3.

Fowler, Cary and Eva Lachkovics, Pat Mooney and Hope Shand
1988 The Laws of Life. Development Dialogue 1-2. Uppsala: Dag Hammerskjold Foundation.

Frake, Charles O,
1962 The Ethnographic Study of Cognitive Systems. Anthropology and Human Behavior. (Thomas Gladwin and William C. Sturtevant, eds.). Washington, D.C.: Anthropological Society of Washington.

Moran, Katy
1991 Debt-for-Nature Swaps: US Policy Issues and Options. Renewable Resources Journal 9,1: 19-24.

1992 Ethnobiology and US Policy. Sustainable Harvest and Marketing of Rainforest Products. (Mark Plotkin and Lisa Famolare, eds.). Washington, DC :Island Press. Pp. 289-301.

Phillips, Oliver and Alwyn H. Gentry
1993 The Useful Plants of Tambopata, Peru: I. Statistical Hypotheses Tests with a New Quantitative Technique. Economic Botany 47,1: 15-32.

Schultes, Richard Evans
1988 Primitive Plant Lore and Modern Conservation. Orion Nature Quarterly 7,3: 8-15.

Schultes, Richard Evans and Robert F. Raffauf
1990 The Healing Forest: Medicinal and Toxic Plants of the Northwest Amazonia. Portland: Dioscorides Press.

US Congress, Office of Technology Assessment
1993 Pharmaceutical Research and Development: Costs, Risks and Rewards. Washington, DC: US Government Printing Office.

Chapter
8

Buying Secrets: Federal Government Procurement of Intellectual Cultural Property

David Ruppert
National Park Service

As tribal groups in the United States were removed from desirable lands and pushed onto small reservations, countless sites providing spiritual anchorage to Indian people fell into the hands of strangers. In western states, especially, many such sites lie inside national parks, national and state forests, and other public lands which, themselves, are under intense pressures for expanded commercial or tourist exploitation. Critically important sacred sites are in jeopardy, but protecting them is not easy. In the chapter to follow, David Ruppert analyzes the agonizing conundrums that IPR negotiations between indigenous communities and federal officials encounter, arising especially from legal constraints embedded in federal law. - ed.

8

Buying Secrets: Federal Government Procurement of Intellectual Cultural Property

David Ruppert
National Park Service

Introduction

National Parks throughout the country contain places or resources of cultural importance to contemporary cultural groups. Although virtually all parks in the West can trace historical links to American Indian occupancy or use, many parks today remain important to contemporary tribal communities. American Indian communities in the western United States have been particularly vocal in expressing their traditional cultural ties to those parks which, at the time of initial contact with European and Euro-American immigrants, were once part of their traditional territories. Today, park lands in many states are routinely used by members of these communities for traditional cultural purposes. For years the Park Service, and Congress, have recognized that the national parks must become aware of the culturally important sites located within their boundaries in order to plan appropriate park development.

Park Service efforts to identify and learn more about these areas of cultural significance have taken the form of a program of funded ethnographic research conducted in collaboration with tribal communities having close cultural affiliation with specific parks.[1] Research projects sponsored by the agency seek to identify what the Park Service

---

[1] The Ethnographic Program Office was established in the Rocky Mountain Region in August of 1991. This program is guided by National Park Service (NPS) Cultural Resource Management Guidelines, 1985 (NPS - 28), NPS Native American Relationships Management Policy (Federal Register, Tuesday, September 22, 1987; pp. 35674-78, NPS). Legislation providing authority for the program include the Native American Indian Religious Freedom Act of 1978 (PL 95-341), The National Historic Preservation Act 1966, amended (PL 96-515), Regulations of the Advisory Council on Historic Preservation (39 CFR 800), the Archeological Resource Protection Act of 1979 (PL 96-95), and the Native American Graves Protection and Repatriation Act of 1990 (PL 101-601).

refers to as "ethnographic resources." These resources often involve specific geographic locations, animal or plant materials, or mineral deposits important in the cultural life of local tribal communities. The research to identify and understand these resources usually entails interviewing tribal members having specific knowledge of the traditional use and importance accorded to places or physical substances located in park areas. This knowledge is, of course, a type of "intellectual property" of the tribal groups concerned.

The process of collecting information on these ethnographic resources has brought the agency face-to-face with the issues of ownership and control of this intellectual "cultural" property. In many cases, the agency's research efforts to collect indigenous cultural knowledge center on topics particularly sensitive to American Indian communities, such as places or substances located in parks and used for religious or ceremonial purposes. Due to the sensitivity of this type of information, some tribal communities have declined to provide information or permit research to take place among community members, despite the fact that the vulnerability of the sites to inadvertent disruption continues. Other tribal groups have agreed to share this sensitive information, but look for assistance from the agency in finding ways to protect it from general public access. These dilemmas, and the difficulties of responding to them within the framework of United States law, are illustrated in the following case, involving the ethnographic resources of Glacier National Park in northern Montana.

Glacier National Park Project

Like other federal land managing agencies, the National Park Service constructs "land use plans" or "resource management plans." These documents are the focus of much attention in most agencies since they are often the product of massive data collection and environmental analyses, take a long time to complete, and require the expenditure of sizable amounts of money. These plans provide park superintendents, forest managers, and other federal administrators with overall long-term resource management objectives - the "vision" of what a park, forest, or a specific natural resource should be in the future.[2] As such, these plans

---

[2] There exists a long history of legislative authorities which gave rise to present NPS plans. Most recent authority to plan in parks stems from Public Law 95-625, the National Parks and Recreation Act of 1978, which requires the preparation and timely revision of general management plans for each unit of the National Park System. The purpose of each NPS area is usually defined in its enabling law, presidential proclamation, or executive order and documented in the "Statement for Management." Planning is to achieve the purpose of the park by providing specific guidance for preservation, use, and development. (National Park Service, 1982; U.S. Department of the Interior, 1991).

become important guidelines for decision-making, helping to determine if a specific decision will further the long-term goals of the agency.

Early in the planning process ethnographic resources were judged to be potentially very important in Glacier National Park since the park's eastern side borders the Blackfeet Indian Reservation. It was widely acknowledged by park personnel, but not well documented, that contemporary members of the Blackfeet Tribe use park resources for traditional purposes. Further, the Kootenai and Salish have strong historical and contemporary ties to park lands near the Flathead Valley on the park's western edge. However, little or no documentation existed on contemporary uses of park resources by these communities. In order to fill this gap in knowledge the park contracted with a university-based anthropologist with many years experience in the region to work with the Blackfeet, the Kootenai and the Salish.

As a matter of policy, the NPS requires that the contractor receive formal permission from the tribal council, or its official representatives, to conduct research among the members of the community under study. In an effort to secure this permission a meeting between tribal representatives, the contractor and park officials was held at the park in November of 1992 to discuss all aspects of the research project. At this meeting the tribal representatives demonstrated a clear understanding of the project goals and the reasons the NPS was seeking the cultural information to help in the planning process. Tribal representatives and park personnel both felt it was important to find new ways to increase tribal participation in the planning process and to identify and protect ethnographic resources within the park.

Strong feelings were expressed at this meeting about the type of data being asked for in the project. Information about sacred sites, vision questing, and the use of plants and minerals for ceremonial purposes was described as highly sensitive; in fact, some tribal restrictions forbid sharing this information even with other tribal members, much less with outsiders. A general concern focused on the potential misuse of this information by government personnel who would not understand its meaning to Indian peoples. There was also the concern that, once gathered by the NPS, such sensitive information could not be kept out of the public domain and could not be kept confidential.[3] Another feeling among tribal representatives was that

---

[3] The issue of confidentiality of culturally sensitive information has been the subject of recent and proposed legislation. The October, 1992, amendment to the National Historical Preservation Act (P.L. 102-575, Section 304) authorizes the Secretary of the Interior to exempt certain types of information from Freedom of Information Act requests. Culturally sensitive information could fit the definition of protected data under this amendment. In addition, the recently introduced bill to amend the Native American Religious Freedom Act of 1978 (Senate Bill 1021: the "Native American Free Exercise

researchers had often come to the tribes asking for cultural information and that nothing had been returned; non-Indian people had made careers out of cultural information that was central to tribal life while the tribes benefited little or not at all from their research. These discussions resulted in requests that the park and the contractor recognize the intellectual property rights of the tribe to information collected through interviews with tribal members.[4]

A Memorandum of Understanding (MOU)

It was decided by all parties that the best vehicle to use to recognize these property rights was a Memorandum of Understanding (MOU), a document that itemizes points of agreement and legally binds all parties to specific actions or responsibilities. An MOU is a flexible document in that stipulations can address specific or broad contexts and are openly negotiated between all parties involved.[5] Consequently, I developed a draft MOU attempting to define a workable approach for five problem areas. First, it defined the concept of "ethnographic resource"[6] and the types of information related to these resources which the park needed for its planning process. Second, it specified the kind of information or data which would qualify to be protected by tribal rights to intellectual property. This information was termed "new data" resulting from interviews detailing cultural information not found in other documented sources (existing published and unpublished documents found in libraries, archives or private collections). Third, the MOU placed stipulations on the use of this "new data" by the park for planning, decision-making, and public education purposes. These stipulations also specified the tribes' right to recall or deny the use of this "new data" by the park if the use to which they were put was considered inappropriate by the tribe. Fourth, the agreement also outlined the tribes' right to grant or deny permission for the publication of "new data." And

---

of Religion Act" introduced May 25, 1993) also contains explicit language protecting culturally sensitive information from public disclosure.

4 As defined in this paper, intellectual property rights are those rights held by an ethnic community affecting the use and control of traditional information (corporately held information relating to beliefs, values, and/or traditional behavior) which define that community as a distinct cultural group. "Rights" refers to the cultural group's recognized authority to control the use and disposition of this traditional cultural information by non-group members.

5 Such documents may become more common as negotiations and the need for signed agreements find their way into the "professional ethic" of anthropological research (Posey, 1990).

6 An ethnographic resource is any natural or cultural resource, landscape or natural feature linked by an ethnic community to the traditional practices, values, beliefs, history and/or ethnic identity of that community

fifth, the agreement defined a process of dispute resolution. This process was to be followed by the park and the tribes should disagreements arise over the adherence (or lack thereof) to the various stipulations agreed to in the MOU.[7]

Unfortunately, when the draft MOU was reviewed by the agency's legal staff, a number of conflicts with operative U.S. statutes turned up, posing large obstacles to establishing a formal means of recognizing these property rights. While our efforts had led to a greater understanding by agency personnel of the concerned tribes' desire to maintain as much control as possible over sensitive cultural knowledge they also led to a greater understanding of the legal and regulatory climate within which federal agencies must operate when issues related to intellectual property rights emerge. The remainder of this paper provides a brief description of the federal laws, regulations and agency policies which constrain agency and tribal officials alike when considering the ownership of intellectual property, and what avenues may be worthwhile pursuing if IPR agreements are to succeed.

Procurement Laws and Federal Property

The initial draft of the MOU was sent to the tribes participating in the project, and to legal review within the Department of the Interior. The Interior Department review resulted in a substantially changed document. It was the solicitor's opinion that the federal government could not recognize the intellectual property rights in this instance. Since the ethnographic information was to be collected through a research contract, the information resulting from the research falls under federal property procurement laws. Generally, information purchased under the authority of these laws becomes the property of the federal government and property rights cannot be granted to another party without explicit authority to do so.[8]

---

[7] This draft MOU was considered to be unenforceable by the Interior Department Solicitor's Office since it was that office's legal opinion that intellectual property rights could not be recognized in this case. A copy of this draft MOU can be obtained by writing the author at the following address: National Park Service, P.O. Box 25287, Denver, CO 80225.

[8] The Federal Acquisition Regulations (FAR) recognize that the Government may acquire information or data that was not compiled or produced at Government expense. In this regard, the Government may acquire less than full rights in the data and certain restrictions may be placed upon its use. However, the Government normally acquires full rights in any information or data it compiles or produces at taxpayer expense. In this regard, the information becomes part of the public domain, available to anyone. The legal theory supporting this position is that taxpayers should have access to that which they paid to obtain (see FAR 27.4).

With the solicitor we suggested that "new" ethnographic data be collected and that at the end of the research project the primary information (field notes, tapes, etc.) be formally returned to the tribe of origin.[9] It was suggested that official transfer of research data could take place in a formal and culturally appropriate ceremony. Although this appeared to be an appealing suggestion for a number of reasons, it also was rejected in light of the fact that the National Park Service did not have explicit authority under law or regulation to expend appropriated funds to acquire information and then give the product of the contract to the tribe. Since the data collected becomes public property, it cannot be given to any private party without the legal authority to do so. The authority to transfer property is normally provided by law. Consequently, the authority to give ethnographic information collected through contract back to the tribe of origin would have to be granted by Congress in new legislation. New legislation can often be difficult to obtain since it may require both broad political and financial support to initiate and follow through to passage.[10]

Of course, there are provisions for selling or transferring the ownership of excess government property (e.g. surplus automobiles or office equipment) to private entities. Such property must be declared to have no real economic value to the government and can be sold through an auction. There is legal authority to transfer ownership of animal resources to state and local governments, and also private institutions, with a preference given to distributing excess wildlife to Indian tribes. The recipient of these animal resources normally is required to pay the

---

9 The rights of the researcher regarding the use of these data was not discussed at this time. However, it was envisioned that the researcher would have the same access to the data as would the Park Service; through permission from the tribe to use the data and/or publish them.

10 Laws designed to protect American Indian cultural heritage are not impossible, of course, to get through Congress as is evidenced by the passage of the Native American Religious Freedom Act of 1978 (P.L 95-341) and its amendments, now under consideration by Congress, and the more recent Native American Graves Protection and Repatriation Act of 1990 (P.L. 101-601). President Clinton signed into law the "Religious Freedom Restoration Act of 1993" on November 16, 1993 (P.L. 103-141). This statute does not address the issue of rights to, or control over, cultural information. More significant is the proposed "Native American Free Exercise of Religion Act" which was introduced in the 103rd Congress as Senate Bill 1021. This proposed legislation recognizes the need to protect from public scrutiny sensitive religious or cultural information related to American Indian religious sites or activities. The bill is silent on property rights to this type of information, but it does allow federal agencies to deny Freedom of Information Act requests to make it public. If passed, the bill would also give authority to federal land managers to periodically close portions of federal lands to public use or visitation out of respect for American Indian religious beliefs or practices.

administrative costs of animal capture, transport and veterinarian care.[11] There are, however, no existing authorities in law or policy which allow the transfer of ownership in the type of property (intellectual) collected during the proposed research project.

As a consequence of this legal review the MOU was redrafted to reflect the solicitor's opinion that the National Park Service would not recognize the intellectual property rights of the tribes involved in the proposed research. This newly worded agreement was sent, along with three options, to tribal representatives for consideration. These options included:

1. Business As Usual Option: The new MOU could be signed without federal guarantees of tribal intellectual property rights. Under this option research would be conducted with tribal permission with the additional understanding that under federal procurement law all rights to information were retained by the federal government and in the public domain.

2. Tribally-Managed and Funded Research: The research project would go forward and the National Park Service would assist the tribes in procuring independent funding to collect "new" information defined in the original research design. The advantage of this option is that if data were collected with funding independent of government sources the tribe would retain control over the information. After the data were collected and analyzed, the park and tribes would remain free to enter into an agreement to use this new ethnographic information for specific purposes. The arrangement between the park and the tribes would take the form of a licensing agreement under which the park would pay the tribes for the use of ethnographic information for specified purposes. Regardless of the park's use of the information, the tribes would remain owners of the information collected and retain the power to determine how it should or could be used.

3. No Tribal Permission Option: Under the third option the tribes would simply not allow the research to include the interviewing of tribal members.

---

[11] The reader is referred to the Federal Register for an explanation of the disposal of live elk, buffalo and bears in Yellowstone National Park, and live buffalo in Wind Cave National Park (36 CFR Pt.10). Badlands National Park distributes excess buffalo to nearby American Indian communities under a Cooperative Agreement. Such agreements are permitted under National Park Service Management Policies of 1988 (Chapter 4). Agency Management Policies indicate that under such agreements preference can be given to native Americans. It should also be noted that although the federal government treats these surplus animals as federal property they legally cannot be described as "owned" by the government.

None of the tribes elected the second option. The Blackfeet Tribal Council chose the first option and agreed to sign the MOU allowing the research to include the collection of "new" data though the interviews with knowledgeable tribal members. The Confederated Kootenai and Salish Tribes rejected the first two options. After the Kootenai Culture Committee members conferred with the tribal council the Confederated Tribes chose the third option - not allowing the interviewing of tribal members.

The Confederated Kootenai and Salish Tribes had been the first to bring up the issue of Intellectual Property Rights and felt that research should not be conducted without a guarantee of these rights. They rejected the second option to fund, manage, and conduct the research themselves. Independent funding meant grant proposal preparation, a good deal of in-house data collection and/or contract management, maintenance of budgets, and report writing. They saw no advantage in taking on these responsibilities and essentially doing the federal government's work for federal purposes. In addition, they reasoned that federal government research priorities should not determine the priorities of the Culture Committee. Although under the second option the tribe would be free to charge the National Park Service a fee for the use of traditional information, there was no up-front guarantee that the federal government would find a use for the information once it was collected by the tribes. Without a guarantee of use fees, there was no sure way for the tribe to offset the costs it may incur in collecting and organizing the data.

However, the Kootenai and Salish agreed to consider a compromise on the research. Much of the planned research involved the collecting and collating of existing data (published and unpublished works in private collections, archives and libraries). The researcher would review this documentation and provide the park a summary of ethnohistoric references to American Indian uses of the park areas or resources. Representatives of the Confederated Tribes agreed that such a summary was useful for park purposes but felt that some earlier works misrepresented traditional tribal beliefs and values. The Tribes felt it was possible to become involved in the research for the purposes of reviewing the summarization of earlier work and commenting on its accuracy. Consequently, the MOU was rewritten to limit the research on Kootenai and Salish issues to already existing documentation. The Park Service offered to contribute funding for the tribes to review this summary of earlier work and to provide commentary on the sources and the contents of earlier ethnographies. The process under which such a review would take place had yet to be determined at the time this article was prepared.

Remaining Questions

The case discussed here certainly does not offer concrete answers to the question, "How does a federal agency recognize the intellectual property rights of an indigenous people?" On the contrary, it points out the difficulty of recognizing such rights when federal procurement laws are used to conduct research. But the case may provide a greater understanding of the legal and regulatory context within which contract ethnographic research work is typically conducted by federal agencies. Within this context it is clear that a strict reading of federal procurement statutes poses difficulties in terms of "ownership" of research products for those who wish to find a way to honor the intellectual property rights of an indigenous people. In the remainder of this paper I want to suggest some aspects of the problem, and possibly fruitful avenues to explore, that might prove useful in future efforts to recognize the intellectual property rights of indigenous peoples.

One aspect concerns how government property is disposed of. There exist regularized mechanisms to "dispose" of government property under certain conditions. Perhaps the concept of "disposal" of property can be broadened to include intellectual property in a case like the one presented here. Formally, "disposing" of property could include culturally appropriate ceremonies marking the return of documented knowledge to the people or peoples who provided it to the agency for specific purposes.

Another avenue to pursue may be the distinction between federal grants and federal procurement contracts related to acquisition of intellectual property. A "grant" is a kind of contract, but there are distinctions. The essential difference lies in the relationship between the government and the recipient of a grant. Contracts are usually highly specific and rigid in their design and administration; grants are more loosely structured and are dominated by a grantee's goals and the need for a grantee's autonomy. A contractor is expected to be motivated by a desire for a reasonable profit; a grantee normally is not primarily motivated by profit. Grants carry all of the elements of a procurement contract, but unlike a contract they are issued through "cooperative agreements" with specific institutions and can be very broad in scope as to goals and purpose. (Gabig, 1986)[12] The extent these distinctions

---

[12] Grants can be issued through the establishment of "cooperative agreements" between governments and other entities. The reader is referred to the Federal Grant and Cooperative Agreement Act of 1977. Gabig (1986) provides a discussion of the differences between grants and procurement contracts. He also provides a discussion of the effects the Freedom of Information Act (FOIA) has on the protection of information in the possession of federal agencies. FOIA requests may well force agencies to release sensitive cultural information to the public if steps are not taken to ensure that the information meets one of FOIA's exemptions. Patents, copyrights and trade secrets as

affect control or ultimate ownership of information collected in research is unknown. Cooperative agreements made directly with tribal groups to administer and conduct ethnographic research, for federal as well as tribal purposes, may be one approach to the ownership and control of indigenous knowledge within the context of federal procurement.

Also, one must be clear about what is being "procured" in research contracts or grants. Are a researcher's field notes the object of procurement, or is a report, summary, or analysis the object of the purchase? Can a contract document explicitly exclude sensitive raw data from procurement and only specify as a deliverable to the government a product which is derived from these data? If this were possible under federal procurement law, could these sensitive data be retained by, or returned to, the community of origin without running afoul of federal purchasing laws?

Another question concerns the individual researcher's rights regarding the "ownership" or control of field notes and the data they contain. How do these researcher ownership issues mesh with the ownership rights claimed by indigenous groups or even individuals? Normally, when natural research projects are conducted within a park, contracts often require that copies of original field notes be deposited in the park archives. Is such disposition of field notes reasonable for ethnographic work in light of discussions regarding contemporary intellectual property rights sensitivities?

Finally, within the context of American Indian tribal communities, are the rights of ownership to intellectual property an issue of corporate or individual rights? The Memorandum of Understanding, the vehicle used in the case presented here, may be appropriate under conditions where an entire community (or their representatives) claim rights to own or control cultural data, but it may not be the most appropriate vehicle when claims to rights over information is an individual matter - where individuals and not groups are recognized as the legitimate owners of traditional cultural information. This may be the case when specific knowledge concerning religious matters is under the control of individual tribal specialists and these individual ownership rights are recognized by tradition. Questions of individual vs. corporate or group ownership rights are also discussed by Pinel and Evans in Chapter 3 of this sourcebook. The problem of collective vs. individual rights is discussed in more detail elsewhere by Brush (1993).

These questions and others emerged in discussions with the Blackfeet and the Confederated Salish and Kootenai tribal representatives and they are simply reported here to shed additional light on the case discussed. Few specific guides for action can be derived from the above described case other than the need to be flexible in addressing the

---

they apply to information collected from grant activities are also briefly discussed by Gabig.

issue if a solution can be found under existing federal procurement laws. The solicitors who reviewed the original MOU noted that in the absence of legal authorities for agencies to recognize American Indian intellectual property rights perhaps it is time to consider new legislation addressing these rights. An important side benefit in considering new legislation would be to provide an open forum for discussion of this important issue. The more long-lasting benefit would be a consistent set of guidelines for federal agencies and tribal groups, guidelines that not only provide for the recognition of intellectual property rights of indigenous people, but also enlarge the foundation upon which federal agencies and tribal communities can work cooperatively to protect sites and other resources of traditional cultural importance.

Bibliography

Brush, Stephen B.
1993 Indigenous Knowledge of Biological Resources and Intellectual Property Rights: The Role of Anthropology. American Anthropologist 95,3: 653-686.

Gabig, Jerome S.
1986 Federal Research Grants: Who Owns the Intellectual Property? Public Contract Law Journal 6,1: 187-212.

Posey, Darrell A.
1990 Intellectual Property Rights and Just Compensation for Indigenous Knowledge. In, Anthropology Today, August, vol. 6, 4.

U.S. Department of the Interior
1991 The National Parks: Shaping the System. Washington, D.C.: National Park Service.

Appendix I

Review Draft MEMORANDUM OF UNDERSTANDING REGARDING PROPOSED ETHNOGRAPHIC RESEARCH IN GLACIER NATIONAL PARK (CONTRACT #1443-RP-1200-92-021)

among The National Park Service, Glacier National Park, the Confederated Salish and Kootenai Tribes of the Flathead Nation, and the Blackfeet Tribe.

Whereas, the National Park Service, Glacier National Park intends to conduct ethnographic research (known here as the Research Contract) to identify places and/or natural and cultural resources within in or near the park having cultural importance to the Blackfeet, Kootenai and Salish tribal communities (known here as the Tribes); and

Whereas, the National Park Service, Glacier National Park, wishes to coordinate all Research Contract activities with official representatives of these Tribes; and

Whereas, Native American ethnographic resources within Glacier National Park of the aforementioned Tribes may have historical and scientific value with the potential to contribute important information to the disciplines of history, archeology, cultural anthropology, and medicine in a manner that can improve the quality of life and enrich our understanding of human society. Any action potentially having these results would be done only with concurrence of the signatories to this agreement; and

Whereas, The American Indian Religious Freedom Act (P.L. 95-341) recognizes that traditional American Indian religions are an integral part of Indian life, and that they are indispensable and irreplaceable, and that infringements on the practice of these religions has occurred from the enforcement of laws and regulations which have not taken into account traditional Native American religious beliefs and practices.

Whereas, it is the intent of the parties to avoid any perceived or real negative impact to the traditional cultural values or activities of the aforementioned Tribes.

Whereas, it is the policy of the National Park Service (cf. Federal Register, Vol. 52, No. 183, September 22, 1987) to ensure that park plans and programs do not unreasonably interfere with Native American use of traditional areas or sacred resources, that National Park Service managers maintain effective consulting relationships with potentially affected Native American groups, and that NPS management decisions will fully consider the concerns of potentially affected Native American tribes or groups.

Whereas, it is the intent of the National Park Service to use ethnographic information gathered through the Research Contract to better inform Glacier National Park decision-making procedures related to all resource management activities, to all long-term resource management planning, and to public education and interpretation programs. Any such action as this would only be done with concurrence of signatories to this agreement.

NOW, THEREFORE: The National Park Service, Glacier National Park, and the aforementioned Tribes agree that ethnographic data collection under the Research Contract will take place and all Research Contract activities will comply with the stipulations set forth in this agreement.

For the purposes of this Memorandum of Understanding (MOU), the following definitions shall apply:

1. "New Data" means any ethnographic information collected through research procedures conducted during the course the Research Contract (including, but not limited to structured or unstructered interviews, survey instruments, participant observation, video and audio taping, photography) and not previously recorded or otherwise documented. "New Data" does not include undocumented existing ethnographic data found in personal notes, recording, collections, and archives collected in activities not related to the Research Contract.

2. "Researcher" means the person or persons designated to the terms of the Research Contract to conduct data collection and analysis.

3. "Tribes" means the American Indian communities represented by their official elected tribal governing bodies and subject to the terms and conditions of this agreement.

4. "Tribal Representatives" means any individual or individuals, or any organization officially designated by the Tribal Council of each of the Tribes to represent the respective Tribes in matters related to this Research Contract.

5. "Research Contract" means the terms and agreements set forth in National Park Service Contract # 1443-RP-1200-92-021.

6. "Traditional Practices" means behavior of individuals or groups derived from cultural rules, tenets, norms, or beliefs. These behaviors (either individual or group) are part of a distinct ethnic group's cultural complex with a demonstrated continuity through time.

7. "Ethnographic Data" means information collected during the course of the Research Contract which pertains to the traditional cultural beliefs and practices of the cultural groups under study.

Research Contract Stipulations

1. The National Park Service shall provide a professional cultural anthropologist at the regional office level to serve as the Contracting Officer's Representative (known here as COR) to manage the Research Contract.

2. The National Park Service, through the COR, will consult with representatives of the Tribes on all matters related to the Research Contract.

3. The individual responsible for executing the Research Contract activities (known here as the Researcher) will coordinate all planned data collection activities with the Tribes and with the COR.

4. Members of the Tribes and the Tribes, as the principle parties providing non-documented, non-published ethnographic information (known here as New Data) to the Researcher or his agents through interviews, survey instruments, or participant observation, retain intellectual property rights to this information. The individual Tribes shall determine the disposition (storage and manner of use) of any New Data resulting from the Research Contract.

To the extent possible under law and regulation any information resulting from Research Contract activities and acknowledged by the Tribes to be owned by the National Park Service will not be made available for public access or review. However, it is understood by all parties to this agreement that any data owned by the National Park Service may be subject to public access.

5. The National Park Service agrees to use any and all New Data resulting from the Research Contract only after consulting with and gaining permission from official representatives of the Tribes. These uses include, but are not limited to, resource management planning, interpretation planning, public education programs, cultural and natural resource activities, and general activities related to NPS operations.

6. Original field notes, photos, videos, and sound recordings of New Data will reside with designated offices of appropriate Tribes. Copies of these materials will reside in the archives of Glacier National Park and/or any other National Park facility only if so permitted under terms agreed to by the Tribes participating in the Research Contract. Any and all uses of these materials will not be permitted without the explicit permission of the affected Tribes.

7. The Tribes agree to allow summaries and/or general descriptions of New Data resulting from the Research Contract to reside in the archives of Glacier National Park and other National Park facility to be used for purposes including, but not limited to, resource management planning, interpretation of cultural and natural resources, public education programs and general publications on NPS resources. The form and content of these general summaries of New Data will be determined only through a full review by the Tribes. The NPS and the Research agree to adhere to all reasonable stipulations placed on the form, content and use of these general summaries.

Dispute Resolution

All disputes regarding the collection, disposition and use of New Data resulting from the activities of the Research Contract shall be resolved in accordance with the procedures set forth in this agreement; such disputes shall not interfere with the stipulations set forth above.

1. In the event that any Tribe(s), as party to this agreement, find(s) conflict with the fulfillment of the stipulations set forth in this agreement or with specific aspects of the execution of the Research Contract the Tribe(s) shall give written notice of such claims to the Superintendent of Glacier National Park.

2. The Superintendent of Glacier National Park, or his designee, shall convene a meeting with the disputing parties within 15 days of receiving the notice. The disputing parties shall attempt to reach a mutually acceptable resolution within 7 days.

3. If the disputing parties cannot agree within 7 days they shall agree to designate a third part to mediate the dispute. If a third party cannot be agreed upon within a 7 day period the Superintendent of Glacier National Park shall appoint one to serve in that capacity.

4. The disputing parties shall attempt to reach a resolution with the assistance of the third party.

5. If a resolution cannot be reached within 30 calendar days of the designation of the third party, the third party shall resolve the dispute.

Term and Amendment

1. From the date of the last signature, this MOU shall remain in effect for a period not to exceed 5 years. Before the end of this 5 year period any party to this agreement may terminate its participation in the agreement.

2. Any signatory party may terminate its participation in this MOU upon 30 days written notice to the other signatories.

Additional Parties

Tribes, in addition to those listed below, may execute this MOU at a later time, if they express a desire to do so.

Multiple Counterparts

This document may be executed in multiple counterparts, and when taken together, shall be deemed as one instrument.

NATIONAL PARK SERVICE

By:____________________ Date: Title:

BLACKFEET TRIBE

By: ____________________ Date: Title:

CONFEDERATED TRIBES OF SALISH AND KOOTENAI NATION

By: ____________________ Date: Title:

Part Two

Conceptual and Political Challenges to IPR

Chapter
9

A Non-Market Approach to Protecting Biological Resources

Stephen B. Brush
University of California, Davis

To argue that indigenous intellectual property rights should be recognized in national and international law because it is a good or just idea is not sufficient, and may be naive. In a practical world, the political, economic and judicial consequences inevitably shape, and often determine, what is achievable. For indigenous societies, rights over the control of, and commercialization of, plant varieties is a central issue, because that is where the greatest commercial pressure and potential is. Steven Brush, in this chapter, finds IPR to be an unpromising avenue to protecting these rights. He concludes, "Simply put, few states will be willing to impose the costs and inefficiencies of monopolies for the rights of minority populations." Brush argues that, with respect to plant varieties, indigenous leaders and their allies may find more success under a rapidly broadening international legal concept, farmers' rights. - ed.

9

A Non-Market Approach to Protecting Biological Resources

Stephen B. Brush
University of California

The conclusion of this paper is that intellectual property rights, as conventionally defined, are inappropriate to protecting the biological resources of indigenous people[1]. This conclusion does not mean that we abandon the search for a method to recognize and reward indigenous people for their biological resources. However, applying the customary tools of intellectual property (patents, copyrights, trademarks, trade secrets, and plant variety protection) to indigenous knowledge is likely to do more harm than good, both to indigenous groups and to others[2]. While conventional intellectual property rights are unacceptable, other means can recognize the contributions of indigenous people and their biological resources.

To understand why intellectual property is inappropriate for indigenous knowledge, consider the monopolistic and exclusionary nature of intellectual property and the collective nature of indigenous knowledge (Benko 1987; Weil & Snapper 1990). Intellectual property rights were invented in the early development of European capitalism and are clearly linked to the rise of both industrial capitalism and the nation state (Machlup & Penrose 1950). The essence of intellectual property is to create a state sponsored monopoly over ideas, things that are impossible to monopolize without sovereign protection. The usual elements of the concept of property as applied to material things -- occupation, possession, control, appropriation, restitution, and so forth -- are largely inapplicable to creations of the intellect, especially without direct state intervention. This intervention has always come with a high cost -- the need to label ideas, application for protection, monitoring for possible infringement, expert witnesses, and lawsuits. Moreover, the

---

1 Indigenous people are defined as people living in tribal societies and people of aboriginal cultures in nation states. Indigenous people are often minority cultures in nations dominated by a national culture that is not aboriginal or is constituted by one culture. This definition thus includes both tribal and peasant peoples. Domination is usually by political and military means, and it includes linguistic, religious and economic subjugation.

2 For reviews of intellectual property see Benko (1987) and Penrose (1950). For the protection of biological (plant) material see Caldwell and Schillinger (1989).

benefits of owning intellectual property are disputed and who benefits often seems arbitrary (Penrose 1951; Benko 1987).

Intellectual property can only be guaranteed by the power of the state. Monopolies are normally antithetical to economic health of capitalist societies because they perpetuate economic inequality, raise cost to everyone else, and lead to inefficient allocation of resources. Two general arguments, however, have been used to defend the monopoly of intellectual property: natural rights and economic benefits (Penrose 1951). The natural rights argument rests on two notions:

1. Individuals have a natural property right to their own ideas, which society is morally obligated to recognize.

2. Justice requires that individuals who provide knowledge be compensated for this service, just as all labor deserves compensation.

Neither of these notions has survived into the 20th century as a rationale for monopoly rights because of the contingencies that are always attached to intellectual property. These contingencies include restrictions on who can claim rights (e.g. first to file), whether an invention is judged useful and non-obvious, and the fact that rights are only recognized for a limited time. Like all property, intellectual property is a social invention rather than a natural right (Levin et al. 1987).

The second main argument for monopolizing ideas is economic, that it stimulates innovation by guaranteeing profits to creative individuals (Robinson 1956). Utility has become the prevailing rationale for intellectual property rights. A recent twist on the utility argument is that intellectual property might serve conservation needs by giving incentives to persons to preserve biological or other environmental resources (McNeely 1988; Sedjo 1992). Recent proposals for extending intellectual property to indigenous knowledge rest on a two part syllogism between Western and non-Western knowledge. First, as demonstrated by cognitive anthropology, a fundamental structural similarity exists between the two types of knowledge. For example, Berlin et al. (1974) show that Mayan plant knowledge is organized into a taxonomic system that is similar to the Western scientific system using Linnean classification. Second, folk knowledge and scientific knowledge can be valuable in the same ways, especially regarding the conservation of biological resources. Many ethnobotanists argue that indigenous people are equally effective at maintaining biological resources as nature preserves and gene banks (Redford & Padoch 1992; Oldfield & Alcorn 1987).

Advocates for indigenous intellectual property have emphasized the rights rationale (e.g. Posey 1990; Mooney 1980 & 1983; Fowler & Mooney 1990). However, since the natural rights argument is no longer used to justify intellectual property, we must wonder whether similar arguments will carry weight for indigenous intellectual property. I would guess not. Simply put, few states will be willing to impose the costs and inefficiencies of monopolies for the rights of minority populations.

This throws the debate onto the economic benefit or utility side. There is a compelling argument to be made for protecting indigenous knowledge as a means to conserve biological diversity. The case for conserving crop genetic resources is particularly strong (Brush 1991 & 1992; Oldfield and Alcorn 1987).

Many policy makers and scientists now accept the idea of *in situ* or habitat conservation for biological resources (WRI 1992). *In situ* conservation of crop germplasm is now promoted along with other strategies to save biological diversity of the tropics (Brush 1991). If *in situ* conservation is going to work, farmers must have incentives for saving genetic resources that they might otherwise discard. Since crop germplasm has been treated as a public good, public investment has been the means to achieve conservation. However, virtually no public programs have been organized to promote *in situ* conservation of crop resources, and farmers have not received direct benefit from their conservation efforts.

The question is whether intellectual property monopolies will promote *in situ* conservation. Commoditization via intellectual property might complement public programs to save biological resources in gene banks. By defining biological resources as a private rather than a public good, farmers may reap benefits from saving biological diversity and offset the individual loss suffered from conserving an older crop variety (Sedjo 1988).

At first glance, the conditions for this would seem propitious. The value of biological resources is recognized, as is the role of farmers and indigenous plant specialists in creating and conserving these resources. A multi-billion dollar industry in agricultural seeds uses germplasm resources from traditional agriculture, and intellectual property, or breeders' rights,[3] is accepted by that industry (Barton & Christensen 1988).

---

[3] Breeders' rights are intellectual property rights granted to plant sceintists who create new genotypes through breeding or other non-obvious techniques. Plant variety protection is the most common form of breeders' rights (Mastenbroek 1988; Jondle 1989), but utility patents and trade secrets are also used.

Obstacles

The direct use of intellectual property by indigenous people who maintain crop genetic resources must, however, confront five major obstacles:

1) General and collective knowledge is not protected under existing intellectual property regimes. In fact, histories of collective invention in industrial societies are noteworthy for the absence of intellectual property mechanisms (Allen 1983). Collective endeavors might be profoundly unsettled by commoditization, since it introduces division of profits into social relations.

2) Membership in and boundaries between indigenous groups are ambiguous. Most crop germplasm resources are maintained by peasants, and it is often futile to distinguish between indigenous and non-indigenous status. Does a Mayan speaking peasant belonging to a corporate community in Chiapas, Mexico have more rights to intellectual property than a Spanish speaking peasant in an open community? This question can be asked in most societies where valuable crop genetic resources exist.

3) The distribution of knowledge and biological resources within and between groups is very uneven. If the goal is to achieve conservation, then rights to a person or group with more resources might be justified, but this will create a new inequity.

4) Intellectual property has always depended on sovereign power and more recently nation upon state power, a power not generally used in favor of indigenous people (Bodley 1990). No immediate benefit to the general populace will be secured by granting intellectual property right to indigenous groups, and additional costs will be unpopular among other farmers and consumers .

5) The market for biological resources is undeveloped and may not exist at all. In fact crop germplasm resources are underutilized since breeders prefer to work with well known elite lines rather than unknown material from farmers' fields (Peeters and Galwey 1988; Marshall 1989). Intellectual property can increase the scarcity of biological resources but not the demand. There are large stockpiles of biological resources in the public domain. These stockpiles are probably sufficient to deflate any market for biological resources. The large number of potential suppliers of biological resources will have the same deflating effect.

Negative Effects

Three negative effects are likely to follow attempts to commoditize crop biological resources and ethnobiological knowledge via intellectual property rights:

1. raise the price of food and drugs to defray the transaction costs of intellectual property;

2. arbitrarily benefit certain groups and disenfranchise others; and

3. increase the power of national bureaucracies that enforce monopolies.

These problems make it unlikely that the market approach of intellectual property will fail to meet either equity or conservation goals.

Farmers and users of biological resources will try to break intellectual property cartels, leading to high enforcement costs to limit the flow of biological materials and to boom and bust economic cycles. For example, by the late 1960s, *Dioscorea* was economically the most important pharmacological plant in the world because of steroids derived from it (Prescott-Allen & Prescott-Allen, 1986). Mexico had secured a monopoly on this product by protecting the processing of the plant as a trade secret. In 1975, Mexico formed a state company to market steroids from *Dioscorea*, partly to benefit peasant collectors who supplied the raw plant material. As the Mexican state company raised prices for steroids, drug companies quickly turned to other sources. Between 1963 and 1976, Mexican steroid production fell from 75% to 25% of the world supply, and international competition has lowered the price of steroids below their 1975 level, leaving Mexican peasants with less return than ever.

The ability of one group to gain a monopoly over biological resources will lead to competition between groups and to economic inequities between groups with and without monopolies. Communities or groups that secure rights will logically want to exclude others, adding to the power of state bureaucracies to supervise these rights. Arbitrary distinctions in granting rights are inevitable since biological resources, knowledge and cultural identity are fluid. An example of this fluidity is the drug resperine from the root of *Rauvolfia serpentina*. Resperine, used to treat high blood pressure, insomnia and some mental disorders, is frequently listed as a leading drug that owes its origin to indigenous knowledge; it has a world market value of $42 million (Posey 1990). Today *Rauvolfia* is grown throughout India, Burma, Andaman Islands, Thailand, Vietnam, Java, Sumatra and Malaysia. In India alone, the drug is in the ethnomedicinal lexicons of several languages: Hindi, Sanscrit, Bengali, and Telegu (Lall Dey 1973).

National elites will claim sovereign power over biological resources and appropriate financial benefits of their conservation. An example of this problem might be seen in the case of wheat germplasm from eastern Turkey. In the 1950s and 1960s, the most widespread wheat variety in North America was “Turkey Red”. This variety was popular because of disease resistance found in collections made by J. Harlan in 1948 and transferred into "Turkey Red". The disease resistance in this case was discovered among wheat varieties obtained from Kurdish farmers who had migrated across the Turkish border from Iraq (Calvin Sperling, personal communication). Neither Turkey nor Iraq recognize the rights of Kurds to cultural autonomy, and it is unlikely that either country would guarantee rights of Kurdish farmers to intellectual property.

A Non-Market Approach

The obstacles and negative effects described above require an alternative approach to defining property rights over biological resources. One such approach is "Farmers' Rights" that has been developed by the FAO to create an international fund for conservation of crop genetic resources(FAO 1989; Brush 1992; Fowler and Mooney 1990). This approach is anticipated in the Biodiversity Treaty drafted for the United Nations Convention of the Environment and Development (UNCED) in 1992 (Reid, et al. 1993). Farmers’ rights differ from conventional intellectual property protection since their object is conservation rather than commoditization of biological resources The FAO (1989: 3, n.1) defines these as:

> ...rights arising from the past, present and future contributions of farmers in conserving, improving, and making available plant genetic resources, particularly those in centres of origin/diversity. These rights are vested in the International Community, as trustee for present and future generations of farmers, for the purpose of ensuring full benefits to farmers, and supporting the continuation of their contributions...

Farmers’ rights require the creation of an international fund to be used to support *in situ* conservation and to the general benefit of people who produce crop genetic resources. Activities that might be supported under this fund include securing land and water rights for farming communities that produce genetic resources, community development in these communities, support for research to increase productivity and income without substituting new varieties for local ones and marketing of special products made with local varieties. Farmers’ rights use the language of intellectual property rights, but they are fundamentally different from breeders' rights and other forms of intellectual property. Breeders' rights are assigned to individuals or legal persons for specific creations and for a limited period of time (Mastenbroek 1988; Caldwell & Schillinger 1989). Breeders' rights rely on enactment and enforcement of legislation at the national level. Farmers' rights are international in scope and do not require formal legal enactment other than multilateral agreement. Farmers' rights are group rights, assigned to the collective interests of those who have nurtured crop germplasm. These rights are not assigned to specific varieties, types of plants, or to specific farmers. Monopoly profits are not involved in farmers' rights, and their purpose is to encourage farmers to nurture and conserve and to utilize and improve genetic resources. Farmers' rights do not imply direct compensation or bilateral reciprocity, such as selling a license for exclusive rights to collect and use crop germplasm. While the value of breeders' rights is determined by the market, farmers' rights must be valued by non-market mechanisms such as a direct levy on users of crop genetic resources in developed countries or a national assessment based on UN funding formulas.

Farmers' rights provide a viable alternative to conventional intellectual property rights, and they are preferable to such steps as patenting and licensing genetic resources. Extending farmers' rights is, however, not without pitfalls. Perhaps the major pitfall is that the doctrine will be used to demand compensation that will benefit the elite of countries with genetic resources, bypassing the groups that nurture these resources and who must be brought into the conservation effort. If this happens, the doctrine may be discredited in both developed countries and among the farmers who continue to grow traditional crops. Another pitfall is that a policy of farmers' rights will result in some of the costs and inefficiencies that characterize intellectual property in developed countries, especially bureaucracy and litigation. Of particular concern is the possibility that demands for farmers' rights will be met with counter-demands in developed countries that technology and information transfer be restricted. Expectations that donations to an international farmers' rights fund be rewarded with *quid pro quo* rights to unimproved germplasm are also troublesome. Indirect compensation through an international fund is not likely to persuade countries to relinquish national sovereignty over genetic resources. Mutual coercion between less developed and developed countries over the issue of farmers' rights and technical assistance seems destined to be harmful to interests of farmers and consumers in both.

Proponents of intellectual property rights for indigenous knowledge seek to expand capitalism and market relations to control the exchange of biological resources such as seeds. Overturning the historic practice of free exchange and common heritage for biological resources is a heavy cost to pay for benefits that are uncertain and poorly distributed. Farmers rights offer a path away from the quagmire of state sponsored monopolies, litigation, and competition. They also offer a model for protecting other forms of indigenous knowledge and biological resources without resorting to direct marketing.

Bibliography

Allen, R. C..
1983 Collective Invention. Journal of Economic Behavior and Organization 4: 1-24.

Barton, J. H. and E. Christensen
1988 Diversity Compensation Systems: Ways to Compensate Developing Nations for Providing Genetic Materials. In. Seeds and Sovereignty (J. R. Kloppenburg, ed.). Durham, NC: Duke University Press. Pp. 338-355.

Benko, R. P.
1987 Protecting Intellectual Property Rights: Issues and Controversies. Washington, D.C.:, American Enterprise Institute for Public Policy Research.

Berlin, B.
1992 Ethnobiological Classification: Principles of Categorization. Princeton, NJ: Princeton University Press.

Berlin, B., D. Breedlove and P. Raven
1974 Principles of Tzeltal Plant Classification: An Introduction to the Botanical Ethnography of a Mayan-Speaking Community in Highland Chiapas. New York: Academic Press.

Bodley, J. H.
1990 Victims of Progress (3rd Edition). Mountain View, CA: Mayfield Publishing Co.

Brush, S. B.
1991 A Farmer-Based Approach to Conserving Crop Germplasm. Economic Botany 45: 153-166.

1992 Farmers' Rights and Genetic Conservation in Traditional Farming Systems. World Development 20: 1617-1630.

Caldwell, B. E. and J. A. Schillinger, eds.
1989 Intellectual Property Rights Associated with Plants. Crop Science Society of America, American Society of Agronomy, Soil Science Society of America, ASA Special Publication No. 52.

Food and Agricultural Organization (FAO)
1989 Report of the Commission on Plant Genetic Resources, Rome.

Fowler, C. and P. Mooney
1990. Shattering: Food, Politics and the Loss of Genetic Diversity. Tucson: University of Arizona Press.

Jondle, R. J.
1989 Overview and Status of Plant Proprietary Rights. In, Intellectual Property Rights Associated with Plants (B. E. Caldwell and J. A. Schillinger, eds.). Crop Science Society of America, American Society of Agronomy, Soil Science Society of America, ASA Special Publication No. 52. Pp. 5-16.

Lall Dey, K.
1973 The Indigenous Drugs of India. New Dehli: Papa (1894) Primlane The Chronica Botanica.

Levin, R. C., A. K. Klevorkick, R. R. Nelson and S. G. Winter
1987 Appropriating the Returns from Industrial Research and Development. Brookings Papers on Economic Activity 3: 783-820.

McNeely, J. A.
1988 Economics and Biological Diversity: Developing and Using Economic Incentives to Conserve Biological Resources, Gland, Switzerland: International Union for the Conservation of Nature and Natural Resources.

Machlup, F. and E. Penrose
1950 The Patent Controversy in the Nineteenth Century. The Journal of Economic History 10: 1-29.

Mastenbroek, C.
1988 Plant Breeders' Rights, an Equitable Legal System for New Plant Cultivars, Experimental Agriculture 24: 15-30.

Marshall, D. R.
1989 Limitations to the Use of Germplasm Collections. In, The Use of Plant Genetic Resources (A. H. D. Brown, O. H.. Frankel, D. R. Marshall, and J. T. Williams, eds.). Cambridge: Cambridge University Press. Pp. 105-120.

Mooney, P. R.
1980 Seeds of the Earth: A Private or Public Resource. London, UK: International Coalition for Development Action.

1983 The Law of the Seed: Another Development and Plant Genetic Resources. Development Dialogue 1983: 1-2. Uppsala: Dag Hammarskjöld Foundation.

Oldfield, M. and J. Alcorn
1987 Conservation of Traditional Agroecosystems. BioScience 37: 199-208.

Peeters, J. P. and N. W. Galwey
1988 Germplasm Collections and Breeding Needs in Europe. Economic Botany 42: 503-521.

Penrose, E. T.
1951 The Economics of the International Patent System. Baltimore, MD: The Johns Hopkins University Press.

Prescott-Allen, C. and R. Prescott-Allen
1986 The First Resource: Wild Species in the North American Economy. New Haven: Yale University Press.

Posey, D.
1990 Intellectual Property Rights and Just Compensation for Indigenous Knowledge. Anthropology Today 6: 13-16.

Redford, K. H. and C. Padoch, eds.
1992 Conservation of Neotropical Forests: Working from Traditional Resource Use. New York: Columbia University Press.

Reid, W. V., S. A. Laird, C. A. Meyer, R. Gámez, A. Sittenfled, D. H. Janzen, M. A. Gollin, and C. Juma
1993 Biodiversity Prospecting: Using Genetic Resources for Sustainable Development. Washington, D.C.: World Resources Institute (and others).

Robinson, J.
1956 The Accumulation of Capital. London: Macmillan & Co Ltd.

Sedjo, R. A.
1988 Property rights and the protection of plant genetic resources. In, Seeds and Sovereignty (J. R. Kloppenburg Jr., ed.) Durham, NC: Duke University Press. Pp. 293-314.

1992 Property Rights, Genetic Resources, and Biotechnological Change. Journal of Law and Economics 35: 199-213.

Weil, V. and J. Snapper, eds.
1990 Owning Scientific and Technical Information. New Brunswick, NJ: Rutgers University Press.

World Resources Institute (WRI)
1992 Global Biodiversity Strategy: Guidelines for Action to Save, Study, and Use Earth's Biotic Wealth Sustainably and Equitably. Washington, DC: World Resources Institute.

Chapter
10

Natural Products and the Commercialization of Traditional Knowledge

Sarah Laird
Green College, Oxford University

The past several years have seen a remarkable change with respect to the principle of compensation to host countries of origin for plants and extracts gathered by transnational pharmaceutical companies seeking new drug compounds. More slowly, the rights and compensation of originating indigenous societies, is gaining acceptance when those plants and extracts are found with the assistance of indigenous knowledge, or obtained in commercial quantities from areas occupied by indigenous people. In this chapter Sarah Laird describes three scenarios in which traditional knowledge is transferred to commercial interests, and the types of benefits and control over this process retained by the communities. - ed.

10
Natural Products and the Commercialization of Traditional Knowledge

Sarah Laird
Green College, Oxford University

Over the past decade, pharmaceutical, biotech, and personal care companies have shown an increased interest in natural products as a source of new ingredients for existing products or leads for the development of new products. While some have argued that this is a passing fad, it is in fact the most recent cycle in a long history of research into natural products and traditional knowledge that has yielded important medicines, crop varieties, and systems of resource management. Fashions in scientific and consumer tastes drive these developments, but it is a mistake to assume that these fashions are a matter of whim and that each cycle begins and ends at more or less the same level of understanding and interest.

The resurgence of interest in natural products on the part of the pharmaceutical industry, for example, was not triggered by PR departments intent on marketing "green" medicines to consumers, but rather by the development of sophisticated receptor and enzyme-binding screens that made rapid and cost-effective screening of plants possible.[1] These technologies have allowed researchers to screen thousands of compounds a year and have led many companies to look to the natural world, particularly species-rich tropical countries, for a source of these compounds.[2]

---

[1] Numerous pharmaceutical companies, including Merck Sharp and Dohme, Briston-Myers Squibb, SmithKline Beecham, Glaxo Group Research, Eli Lilly, and Pfizer have natural product screening programs that include plants, microbes, and marine organisms. The sources of their materials are a variety of research institutes, botanical gardens, and independent collectors. For more information, see the World Resources Institute publication, Biodiversity Prospecting (Reid et al. 1993) which includes the table "A Sample of Companies Active in Plant and other Natural Product Collection and Screening" (pp. 8-13).

[2] It is estimated that only about one in 10,000 chemical substances screened will produce a valuable lead in the pharmaceutical and biotech industries (McChesney 1992:5). This has mistakenly led some to assume that only one in 10,000 species have commercial potential in these industries, but this is not the case. Each plant or plant extract may contain hundreds of compounds. Moreover, each screen has highly specific biochemical targets and does not determine all the possibilities for a particular compound.

The interest in traditional knowledge as a starting point for new product development tends to parallel interest in natural products and - too - is not a trendy new concept. In the pharmaceutical arena (arguably the most "high-tech" and time and money consuming of them all), of the 119 drugs of known chemical structure still extracted from higher plants and in use today, over 74% were discovered by chemists attempting to identify the chemical substances in plants that were responsible for their use in traditional herbal medicine (Farnsworth 1990: 6). Many researchers believe that traditional knowledge can provide an important lead for companies searching for new natural products.[3] Ethnobotanical data, however, do not form the basis of most industry R&D programs, and a distinction must be made between collections of biochemical and intellectual resources. In many cases, nonetheless, traditional knowledge is supplied by collectors along with taxonomic and ecological data.[4]

The most striking difference between this cycle of natural products research and those of the past, however, has not been in the scientific, but in the ethical, legal and policy arenas. Over the past two decades, increasing attention has been paid to the need for biodiversity-rich regions, and traditional communities and individuals, to control and receive benefits from the commercialization of their biological, genetic and intellectual resources. Institutions and companies which ten years ago would have been unlikely to recognize this issue as legitimate or constructive, now publicly voice support for the notion that commercial-

---

[3] Michael Balick, Director of The New York Botanical Garden's Institute of Economic Botany supports the use of what he calls the "ethnobotanical filter" of indigenous knowledge of medicinal plants. A preliminary test of plants he collected in Honduras and Belize in an NCI *in vitro* anti-HIV screen showed that of the 18 species collected randomly only 6% showed activity, while 25% of the 20 ethnobotanically collected species showed activity (Balick 1990:28). Paul Cox of the Department of Botany and Range Science at Brigham Young University conducted a study that similarly showed promising leads from traditional medicine: 86% of the plant species used in Samoan traditional medicine showed pharmacological activity in broad *in vitro* and *in vivo* screens (Cox 1990:43).

[4] Recently Merck Sharp and Dohme Research Laboratories, which has collecting agreements with INBio and The New York Botanical Garden, has been speaking with ethnobotanists about potential R&D collaborations. Many other companies, like SmithKline Beecham, Glaxo, Bristol-Myers Squibb and the NCI collection receive ethnobotanical data as part of their collections. Biotics, which supplies ethnobotanical data to SmithKline Beecham, collects "common knowledge" from markets or provides SmithKline with the results of literature searches on natural products databases. The University of Illinois at Chicago provides detailed ethnobotanical information to companies through its database NAPRALERT and, as with the Missouri and New York Botanical Gardens, provide the National Cancer Institute with ethnobotanical data on the samples they collect.

ization cannot take place without the return of benefits and sustainable use of the resources in question.[5]

But underlying the public discourse, and often outside the realm of the international policy debate, the working values of traditional knowledge and stewardship of forest resources are being set at points of exchange and in the process by which knowledge is transferred from a community to the business sector. The nature of these transactions can provide us with some insight into what is traded, the extent of local peoples' control over this process and the benefits that accrue to these peoples from the commercialization of their intellectual and biological resources. Following is a brief discussion of three scenarios in which traditional knowledge and the fruits of stewardship are transferred to industry: the collection of biochemical and genetic resources from communally-held lands and indigenous reserves; academic ethnobotanical surveys; and commercial collections of materials and knowledge by middlemen or industry representatives.

---

5 Rosemary Hennings, spokeswoman for Wellcome plc in the United Kingdom dramatically illustrated the change in attitude last June when responding to a question about the Biodiversity Convention. Wellcome, which was founded on the fortunes of a pharmacist who developed the muscle relaxant d-tubocurarine from Amazonian curare (for which no contract or mechanism to return benefits to local communities that used the plant as an arrow poison was in place), is not currently researching plants. "But were we to do so, we would of course pay royalties. We would never expect to get something for nothing," she said (Vromen, 1992).

Lynn Caporale, Senior Advisor of Scientific Liaison at Merck Sharp and Dohme Research Laboratories notes of their agreement with INBio: "On our side it was undertaken as a way to obtain diverse samples for screening to help us in our work of discovering new treatments for serious diseases. Costa Rica has created in INBio a mechanism by which our need for diverse identified samples can be used to support local needs for conservation and sustainable development" (Caporale 1992:6).

Eli Lilly and Company and Shaman Pharmaceuticals, Inc. announced an agreement in October 1992 to "jointly develop certain antifungal drugs drawn from the knowledge of native healers." In return for an option to obtain exclusive worldwide marketing rights to products identified, isolated and initially screened by Shaman, Lilly made a $4 million equity investment in Shaman. Shaman has formed a nonprofit arm called the Healing Forest Conservancy which will return a portion of its profits to peoples and countries where they work. Dr. Mel Perelman, president of Lilly Research Laboratories, said that "Lilly has selected Shaman as a partner in our natural products research program because of its technique for identifying and screening pharmacologically active compounds and its corporate responsibility in conserving the environment" (Lilly 1992:2-3; Wall Street Journal 1992:B1,7).

The Collection of Biochemical and Genetic Resources from Communally-held Lands and Indigenous Reserves

In these cases, ethnobotanical information is not recorded, as such, but collectors work in areas not only under the control of communities that should be informed of collections, but in forests or areas which have long been managed by these groups, and so are not "pristine" wildlands. In general, it is rare that collections of biological and genetic resources are made in a social or cultural vacuum. Rarely will an area be so deprived of a cultural history or contact with peoples living in and around it, and biological and intellectual resources be so generalized, that local peoples have no distinctive claim to them.

Even random collections in such areas will not produce a truly "random" ecological sample, as communities have long promoted or selected for desirable species.[6] In these cases collectors often have limited contact with communities, but not only should communities provide informed consent for such collections - that is with full knowledge of the potential commercial applications of this research and the right of refusal - they should also be granted some type of control over the commercialization of these products and receive benefits from revenues produced from their sale.

The Kuna Indians in Panama, for example, have established a program to manage their forest reserve and the activities of scientists within this reserve. In 1988 they published the manual *Research Program: Scientific Monitoring and Cooperation*, which provides guidelines for researchers and establishes practices for the return of appropriate benefits such as copies of reports (in Spanish), photographic materials, plant and animal specimens, the training of Kuna researchers and the hiring of Kuna guides and informants (Chapin 1991:7).

Academic Ethnobotanical Surveys

Academic research does not provide - in and of itself - a direct link between traditional knowledge and the commercial development or improvement of natural products. However, when academic research is published, recorded knowledge becomes a part of the public domain and communities lose the ability to control and monitor its commercial use.

---

[6] Samples are collected by random or rational methods. Random collections contain taxonomically diverse samples from a given area. Rational methods include taxonomic collection of species within a genus shown to have exhibited promising bioactive compounds, ecological collection of samples that provide information on potential chemical activity based on observed ecological relationships between plants, insects and other animals, and ethnobiological collections that provide information on the uses of plants, insects, animals, etc. in traditional communities.

Academic literature is commonly consulted by industry researchers, and ethnobotanical information can quietly make its way into the R&D efforts of commercial enterprises. The infamous case of the rosy periwinkle, *Catharanthus roseus*, for example, did not grow out of ethnobotanical surveys conducted by Eli Lilly staff in Madagascar (from where the plant originates), nor even in the Philippines, where its recorded use first interested researchers at Eli Lilly Company. *Catharanthus roseus* was first investigated because researchers in laboratories in North America, conducting a literature search for plants from the Australasian area with "folkloric usage of believable quality and the reported presence of certain types of plant ingredients" read of its traditional use in the Philippines as an insulin substitute (Svoboda 1992:1). The free exchange of information is critical to the development of valuable new products like vincristine and vinblastine. This exchange should not be excessively restricted, but mechanisms should be developed to balance the global goods resulting from free exchange with the need to ensure that communities have a voice in how their knowledge is published and subsequently used.

Because cultural diversity is considered more endangered than biological diversity, it is often suggested that traditional knowledge be recorded as quickly as possible through ethnobotanical studies. But the need to record knowledge must be balanced with the need to make sure that these records actually benefit the communities that provide the knowledge (as with the current Human Genome Diversity Project). This means that communities must be informed of the potential commercial applications of research, and are afforded some control over, and receive some type of benefit from, its commercial use.

The conflict between the need to record knowledge and the need to create mechanisms by which the use of that knowledge is controlled by communities for their own benefit creates conceptual and practical problems. For example, at the March, 1991 U.S. National Institute of Health workshop *Drug Development, Biological Diversity and Economic Growth*, participants recommended in conclusion that "intellectual property rights should be extended in some form to traditional knowledge, and mechanisms to provide the appropriate protection and compensation are urgently needed," and later that "an immediate priority is the completion of species and traditional knowledge inventories, which should include information dissemination. These inventories need to be developed using electronic databases with wide access" (Schweitzer et al. 1991:1294-1298). But, if traditional knowledge is inventoried like species and then disseminated widely, there is little likelihood that communities will retain any significant control over its commercial application.

While publication provides an indirect link between academic research and commercial product development, there are often direct links between academics and commercial interests. The bulk of collectors to date are academics with contracts from industry. These contracts make it possible for researchers to continue with their chronically under-funded botanical, pharmacological or other academic research. But a practical distinction between collections for academic and those for commercial ends must be made clear to the communities with which researchers work.[7]

Commercial Collections of Knowledge and Samples by Middlemen or Company Collectors

These collections are the most obvious transactions by which knowledge and biological resources are supplied to commercial interests. Collectors range from individuals who collect for "spot" payments to university-based plant-collection programs, to botanical gardens supplementing their field-research budgets, to private, for-profit brokers, to private and public research institutes based in developing countries. While the majority of collectors operate out of non-profit academic or research institutions, they form the link between the communities with which they work and the commercial interests on whose behalf they collect. As a result, their relationship with communities is no longer purely one of scientific collaboration, but of commercial partnership. At this stage, collectors are by no means getting "rich", but they can ensure that as part of their collections they provide immediate compensation, such as health care, education, and training; they can also ensure that collaborating communities are written in to any legal document which they sign with their commercial partners, or are otherwise ensured benefits from the future development of commercial products.

Some companies, such as Shaman Pharmaceuticals and the Body Shop, develop relationships with the communities with which they work, and negotiate directly for the terms of these relationships. Shaman Pharmaceuticals, for example, recently signed an agreement with 120 delegates to the Aguaruna Indian Federation for a collaboration involving the sourcing of a promising product. During its collections, Shaman's policy is to provide "immediate reciprocity", such as health care and education (King, pers. comm., 1993). The Body Shop is in the process of developing a "model" agreement with the Kayapo Indians in Brazil for ethnobotanical research leading to the development of new ingredients for their products (Body Shop, 1993). In these cases, there

---

[7] "Practical distinction" means informing communities of the nature of the commercial contract collectors have with a company, the way in which knowledge will be used for commercial product development, who will have access to this knowledge, and in some cases the signing of separate agreements or letters of intent that outline the issues involved in commercial collections that will not be included in most academic research agreements (such as patents, royalties, future supplies of raw materials, advance payments from companies and the disbursement of commercial revenues.

also exists the perceived underlying benefits that result from making existing markets work more equitably for the benefit of local people.

But the majority of companies will be loathe to become involved in direct negotiations with communities, seeing it as extrinsic to their area of expertise. While companies should be encouraged to develop policies that dictate principles and criteria for their collection of materials from the tropics, it is unlikely that most will devise region or community-specific policies and guidelines that would have a direct bearing on negotiations with local peoples.[8] In the vast majority of cases, these negotiations will be left in the hands of collectors. It is important, therefore, that separate written agreements be developed by collectors and communities that outline the nature of their commercial relationship and detail the types of benefits that will be channelled, via the collector, to communities immediately and in the long term should a valuable product be developed from their knowledge or resources.

Relationships and transactions between communities and collectors will always be complex and case-specific. Not only must the diversity in cultural concepts of property and knowledge be considered, but the many different ways in which knowledge manifests itself, comes to be traded, and is ultimately incorporated into the process by which a new product is commercialized. It must also be recognized that the pharmaceutical, biotech, agricultural, and personal care industries draw on genetic, biochemical and traditional intellectual resources in distinctly different ways, and that final products bear varying relationships to the knowledge and resources supplied by local peoples.[9]

For example, if a community uses a particular oil to soften skin and a company builds on that knowledge to develop a lotion from that oil to soften skin, the claims for the community to compensation will be high. Similarly, if a pharmaceutical company collects a plant because of its traditional use as an anti-diabetic and subsequently isolates a compound to produce a drug for the treatment of diabetes, the community's claims for compensation would be high. But it could be argued that

---

[8] Glaxo Group Research, for example, recently developed a *Policy for the Acquisition of Plant Materials* that addresses as company policy the conservation and development implications of their research, the need to work with reputable collectors, and the negative impact of "unauthorized and/or unrestrained removal of plant materials from their indigenous habitats" (Glaxo, 1992).

[9] Even within-industry variations in collecting practices, research and development can create distinct scenarios. Taking the pharmaceutical industry alone, we find collections conducted randomly, taxonomically, ethnobotanically and based on ecological relationships between species. This might be done in national parks, indigenous reserves, on lands held under communal title, or on private lands. The final product may be closely or distantly related to the original plant compound or traditional use. The collector may be an in-country or outside research institute, or even a for-profit middleman. Each scenario will clearly result in a unique definition of "just compensation".

the claim for compensation here is more tenuous than in the case of the personal care company producing the lotion because the pharmaceutical industry spends millions of dollars and many years on very specialized R&D to develop, test and manufacture the isolated compound.[10] Again, if the company develops an anti-cancer agent from a plant used traditionally as an anti-diabetic, as with the rosy periwinkle, the link with traditional knowledge becomes more tenuous. The relationship between the "product" supplied to companies and the final commercial product is usually built in to negotiations between commercial partners, and will be an issue in negotiations between companies and communities, as well.

Summary

Traditional knowledge plays a significant role in industry R&D programs. Companies cannot be forced to pay exorbitantly for something they feel they can do without, but they can pay fairly for what it is they do use. Because the concept that individuals and communities should benefit from the commercial use of their traditional knowledge is newly and tentatively established, claims to the type of returns communities should receive vary from the overly optimistic (in light of limited commercial demand) and patronizingly small or obscure (due to a lack of conviction some have in these rights and in communities' abilities to negotiate with commercial partners). But traditional knowledge has been and continues to be an element in the commercialization of natural products, it is currently supplied to commercial interests through databases, academic publications or field collections and it should be paid for in some form. This form will to some extent be dictated by the market, but should also be established in light of the fact that traditional knowledge has only recently been considered worthy of recompense and that economic and political power resides unequally among parties; as a result, the market will not reflect the true commercial value of traditional knowledge. Unfortunately, there are few precedents to guide us in this area.

INBio's agreement with Merck galvanized a debate on the components of equitable arrangements for the exchange of biochemical resources. The supply of traditional knowledge for commercial product development, however, produces a number of complex issues not covered in agreements for biochemical samples. The work of companies such as Shaman Pharmaceuticals, The Body Shop, and the institutions currently collecting ethnobotanical data for industry or NCI research programs, such as the New York and Missouri Botanical Gardens and the University of Illinois, can provide us with some indication of the

[10] The current estimate for the research and development costs of a pharmaceutical is $231 million if failures are factored in (Di Masi et al. 1991).

relationships upon which collections are based, how the value for traditional knowledge is currently set, exchanged, and compensated for, the recipients of compensation, and what these compensation "packages" include (advance payments, training, education, health care, agreements for the supply of raw materials and extracts, the nature of royalty provisions should a product be commercialized, etc.).

But traditional knowledge will not be consistently and sufficiently valued through these point-of-collection relatonships alone. Because agreements for the exchange of traditional knowledge require a reconciliation of striking conflicts between commercial, scientific and traditional concepts of knowledge and property, and because they cannot adequately incorporate issues raised by knowledge or materials with no clear ethnic or geographic provenance, they must be designed in the context of international and national laws and policies (as detailed elsewhere in this publication). These laws and policies increasingly address issues of access to, and compensation for, genetic, biochemical and traditional intellectual resources, and provide general principles for the design of equitable relationships. Likewise, the activities of collectors will increasingly be detailed and monitored by professional codes of ethics and institutional policies. Of greatest importance, however, is the ability of individuals, institutions, and communities to negotiate on their own behalf, with complete information on the role of their knowledge in commercial product development, and the choice to involve themselves in this research, or not. If knowledge is supplied for commercial use but the individuals involved do not have sufficient information, they cannot influence the commercial value set for their knowlege, and will depend indefinitely upon "middlemen" to select a balance between traditional, scientific and commercial interests. An understanding of the practical mechanisms by which knowledge is exchanged, and the varying roles it plays in natural product development, is an important first step towards better defining the existing and potential relationships, interests, and values involved in the commercialization of traditional knowledge.

Selected Bibliography [11]

Balick, Michael

1990 Ethnobotany and the Identification of Therapeutic Agents from the Rainforest. In, Bioactive Compounds from Plants (D. J. Chadwick and J. Marsh, eds.). New York, NY: John Wiley and Sons. Pp. 22-39.

Barbier, Edward and Bruce Aylward

1992 What is Biodiversity Worth to a Developing Country? The Pharmaceutical Value of Biodiversity and Species Information. Paper prepared by the London Environmental Economics Center of The International Institute for Environment and Development. IIED.

Bennett, Bradley

1992 Plants and People of the Amazonian Rainforests; The role of ethnobotany in sustainable development. Bioscience. vol. 42, no. 8, September: 599-607.

Biotechnology and Development Monitor

1991 Screeening Plants for New Drugs. no. 9, December: 4-5.

Biotechnology and Development Monitor

1991 Developing Private Biopharmaceutical Capacity in Developing Countries. No. 9, December: 7-8.

Biotics Limited

1991 Forest Focus: A Natural Products-based Action Programme for Tropical Forest Conservation.

Body Shop Plc.

1993 Intellectual Property Rights. Press release, May 26.

Brown, Katrina

1993 Medicinal Plants, Indigenous Medicine and Conservation of Biodiversity in Ghana. CSERGE.

---

[11] Note: At the invitation of the editor, the author has included here a bibliography that goes considerably beyond the citations of the chapter's text. -ed.

Brush, Stephen
1991 Intellectual Property and Traditional Agriculture in the Third World. Paper presented at the Roundtable on Intellectual Property Rights and Indigenous Peoples. 50th Annual Meeting of the Society for Applied Anthropology. March 15.

Business and the Environment
1991 Merck Deal with Costa Rica's INBio Offers Model For future. vol. 2, no. 21, 8 November: 1-3.

Caporale, Lynn
1992 The Merck/INBio Agreement; A Pharmaceutical Company Perspective. Paper presented at the Rainforest Alliance, "Tropical Forest Medical Resources and the Conservation of Biodiversity" symposium, January.

Chapin, Mac
1991 How the Kuna Keep Scientists in Line. Cultural Survival Quarterly. Summer: 17.

Chapman, Audrey
1992 Human Rights Implications of Indigenous Peoples' Intellectual Property Rights. AAAS, Washington, DC.

Cox, Paul Alan
1990 Ethnopharmacology and the Search for New Drugs. In, Bioactive Compounds from Plants (D. J. Chadwick and J. Marsh, eds.). New York, NY: John Wiley and Sons. Pp. 40-55.

CPL Scientific Limited
1990 Possible Funding Mechanisms for a Convention on Biological Diversity. Prepared for the World Wide Fund for Nature, June.

Cultural Survival Quarterly
1991 Intellectual Property Rights -the Politics of Ownership. Summer : 15,3.

Cunningham, A.B.
1992 Ethics, Ethnobiological Research, and Biodiversity. AWWF International Publication. April.

DiMasi, J. and R. Hansen, H. Grabowski, and L. Lasagna
1991 The Cost of Innovation in the Pharmaceutical Industry. Journal of Health Economics 10: 107-142.

Duke, James
1991 Medicinal Plants and the Pharmaceutical Industry. Paper presented at the Second National Symposium on New Crops, October.

Duvick, Donald
1992 Security and Long Term Prospects for Conservation of Plant Genetic Resources. Paper presented to the AAAS symposium, "Managing Genetic Resources" February.

Duvick, Donald
1992 Possible Effects of Intellectual Property Rights on Erosion and Conservation of Plant Genetic Resources in Centers of Crop Diversity. Paper presented at the International Crop Science Congress, July .

Eli Lilly and Company
1992 Tribal Lore Source of Research Leads for Eli Lilly and Company, Shamen Pharmaceuticals, Inc. News of Lilly. October. Indianapolis IN.

Farnesworth, Norman
1990 The Role of Ethnopharmacology in Drug Development. In, Bioactive Compounds from Plants (D. J. Chadwick and J. Marsh, eds.). New York, NY: John Wiley and Sons. Pp. 2-21.

Findeisen, Christina, and Sarah Laird
1991 Natural Products Research and the Potential Role of the Pharmaceutical Industry in Tropical Forest Conservation. A report prepared by the Periwinkle Project of the Rainforest Alliance.

Fowler, Cary, and Eva Lachkovics, Pat Mooney and Hope Shand
1988 The Laws of Life; Another Development and the New Biotechnologies. Development Dialogue 1-2.

Genetic Engineering News
1992 U.S. Refuses to Ratify Rio Treaty on Biodiversity. Vol 12, No. 10, 15 June.

Glaxo Group Research Ltd.
1992 Policy for the Acquisition of Plant Materials. Middlesex, UK.

Gollin, Michael
1991 Using Intellectual Property to Improve Environemtnal Protection. Harvard Journal of Law and Technology 4 (Spring): 193-235.

Gray, Andrew
1991 Between the Spice of Life and the Melting Pot: Biodiversity Connservation and its Impact on Indigenous Peoples. IWGIA.

Harvard Business School Case Study
1992 Agribusiness Case on Merck/INBio Agreement.

King, Steven
1992 Conservation and Tropical Medicinal Plant Research. Paper presented at the Rainforest Alliance "Tropical Forest Medical Resources and the Conservation of Biodiversity" symposium, January.

Kloppenburg, Jr., Jack & Daniel Lee Kleinman
1987 Seed Wars: Common Heritage, Private Property, and Political Strategy. Socialist Review 95 (September/October): 7-41.

Kloppenburg, Jr., Jack.
1992 Conservationists or Corsairs? Seedling. June/July : 12-17.

McNeil, Richard J. & Michael J. McNeil
1989 Ownership of Traditional Information: Moral and Legal Obligations to Compensate for Taking. Northeast Indian Quarterly, Fall: 30-35.

Merck & Co., Inc.
1991 Merck/INBio News Release and "Questions and Answers".

McChesney, James
1992 Biological Diversity, Chemical Diversity and the Search for New Pharmaceuticals. Paper presented at the Rainforest Alliance, "Tropical Forest Medical Resources and the Conservation of Biodiversity" symposium, January.

Miller, James and Stephen Brewer
1992 The Discovery of Medicines and Forest Conservation. Conservation of Plant Genes. Academy Press, Inc.

National Cancer Institute
1992 The Letter of Intent and Material Transfer Agreement.

National Journal
1992 Biodiversity Battle. 8 August: 1827-1830.

Nature
1991 'Hunting License' for Drugs. vol 353, 26 September: 290.

Nature
1992 If Biological Diversity has a Price, Who Sets it and Who Should Benefit?. vol 359, no 6396, 15 October: 565.

New Scientist
1991a The West Pays up for Third World Seeds. 11 May: 18-19.

1991b Prospectors for Tropical Medicines. 19 October: 36-40.

1993 High Hopes Hanging on a 'Useless' Vine. 16 January: 12-13.

NIH, NIMH, NSF and U.S. AID
1992 International Cooperative Biodiversity Groups: Request for Applications. June 12. Washington, D.C.

Pearce, D. and S. Puroshothaman
1993 Protecting Biological Diversity: the Economic Value of Pharmaceutical Plants. CSERGE.

Posey, Darrell
1990 Intellectual Property Rights and Just Compensation for Indigenous Knowledge. Anthropology Today. vol. 6, no. 4, 16 August.

1990 Intellectual Property Rights: What is the Position of Ethnobiology? Journal of Ethnobiology 10,1: 93-98.

Prance, Ghillean
1991 What is Ethnobotany Today? Journal of Ethnopharmacology 32: 209-216.

Reid, Walter V., Sarah A. Laird, Carrie A. Meyer, Rodrigo Gámez, Ana Sittenfeld, Daniel H. Janzen, Michael A. Gollin and Calestous Juma
1993 Biodiversity Prospecting: Using Genetic Resources for Sustainable Development. Washington, D.C.: World Resources Institute (and others).

Royal Botanic Gardens Kew
1992 Memorandum of Understanding; Conditions of acceptance of plant material from external collaborators for collaborative studies in the Biochemistry Section of the Royal Botanic Gardens Kew.

Scientific American
1991 Patenting Life. vol 264, no. 3:40-46.

Schweitzer, J. F., F. Gray Handley, J. Edwards, W. Franklin Harris, M. Grever, S. Schepartz, G. Cragg, K. Snader, and A. Bhat
1991 Summary of the Workshop on Drug Development, Biological Diversity, and Economic Growth. Journal of the National Cancer Institute 83: 1294-1298.

SCRIP World Pharmaceutical News
1992 Redistributing Discovery's Profits - The Schwartz Commentary. No. 1733, 8 July: 15-16.

Sedjo, Roger
1991 Property Rights, Genetic Resources, and Biotechnological Change. Journal of Law and Economics 35, 1: 199-213.

1992 Preserving biodiversity as a resource. Resources for the Future. no. 106, Winter 1992.

Shaman Pharmaceuticals
1992 Supply and Royalty Committments to Countries and/or Institutes Supplying Raw Plant Material to Shaman Pharmaceuticals.

Simpson, R. David
1992 Transactional Arrangements and the Commercialization of Tropical Biodiversity. Resources for the Future Discussion Paper, Washington, D.C.

The Society for Applied Anthropology
1991 Proposal for Ethics Consideration Aspects of Intellectual Property Rights. Drafted by Tom Greaves of Bucknell University.

The Society of Economic Botany
1991 Professional Ethics in Economic Botany: A Preliminary Draft of Guidelines. Drafted by Christine Padoch and Brian Boom of The New York Botanical Garden.

Svoboda, Gordon
1992 The Discovery of the *Catharanthus roseus* Alkaloids and their Role in Cancer Chemotherapy. Paper presented at the Rainforest Alliance symposium, Tropical Forest Medical Resources and the Conservation of Biodiversity. New York, NY. January.

United Nations Development Programme
1991 Ethnobotanical Exchange Between Asia and Amazonia, 9-15 December, Belem, Brazil.

Vromen, Galina
1992 Europe Drug Firms Say Bio-Diversity Pact Harmless. Reuters News Service. London: June 22.

Waitangi Tribunal
1991 Concerning the Treaty of Waitangi Act, 1975. A claim by Hanna Murray (Ngati Kuri) and Dell Withongi (Te Rarawa) and others relating to the Protection, Control, Conservation, Management, treatment, Propagation, Sale, Dispersal, Utilization, and Restriction on the use of and transmission of the knowledge of New Zealand Indigenous Flora and Fauna and the genetic resources contained therein.

The Wall Street Journal
1992 Eli Lilly & Co. Investing in Rain Forest Research. 23 October.

WIPO (World Intellectual Property Organization)
1985 Model Provisions for National Laws on the Protection of Expressions of Folklore Against Illicit Exploitation and Other Prejudicial Actions. Geneva, Switzerland: World Intellectual Property Organization/ United Nations Educational, Scientific and Cultural Organization/ United Nations.

World Resources Institute et al.
1992 Global Biodiversity Strategy: Guidelines for Action to Save, Study, and Use Earth's Biotic Wealth Sustainably and Equitably. Washington, DC: World Resources Institute.IUCN, UNEP.

Chapter
11

Between State and Capital: NGOs as Allies of Indigenous Peoples

Jack Kloppenburg, Jr. and Tirso Gonzales
University of Wisconsin, Madison

NGOs - non-governmental organizations - have become ubiquitous in national and international political processes. Indeed, increasingly the development of governmental policy is done in consultation with these groups, reflecting an awareness of their growing political power. In seeking IPR protections local indigenous groups stand to gain from allying with NGOs, and in many cases the communications capabilities, knowledge, funding and staff labor of NGOs are indispensable to the attainment of the groups' goals. However, there are also drawbacks and costs to these alliances, even when the NGOs are led by leaders who are themselves of indigenous origins. In this chapter and examine the tradeoffs in these alliances that indigenous groups have to weigh. - ed.

11

Between State and Capital: NGOs as Allies of Indigenous Peoples

Jack Kloppenburg, Jr. and Tirso Gonzales[1]
University of Wisconsin, Madison

> 1. The strength of the people is to be who they are.
> 2. The limit of the people is that they cannot, by themselves, stop the forces destroying their possibilities of being.
> 3. The perspective of the people is to reshape their alliances and coalitions to include in their struggle those that can stop or dissolve the forces destroying them.
>
> Gustavo Esteva (1992: 117)

Introduction: The Primacy of the Ethnic Question

The strength of indigenous peoples is to be who they are. It is recognition of this simple truth that lies behind the continuing struggles of indigenous peoples for decolonization and self-determination. Intellectual property rights (IPRs) are a product of the logic and the interests of the states and corporations which have historically been responsible for the cultural, economic, political, and physical violence visited upon indigenous peoples. The question of IPRs has its origins outside indigenous culture and it arises as but one element of the renewed assault against indigenous peoples represented by the promulgation of new economic regimes (e.g., GATT, NAFTA)[2] and new technologies (e.g., genetic engineering). The problem of IPRs must therefore be seen not in isolation, but as part and parcel of what Rodolfo Stavenhagen (1988, 1990) has called the "ethnic question": the

---

[1] Associate Professor and graduate student in the Department of Rural Sociology, University of Wisconsin, Madison, WI 53706, USA, Tel. 608-262-6867, Fax 608- 262-2022, E-mail: kloppenb@ssc.wisc.edu; gonzales@macc.wisc.edu.

[2] Negotiations are presently underway to finalize two global trade liberalization agreements, the Uruguay Round of the General Agreement on Tariffs and Trade (GATT), and the North American Free Trade Agreement (NAFTA). Additionally, a variety of sub-regional agreements, such as the Andean Pact, follow trends similar to those of GATT and NAFTA. Both GATT and NAFTA contain intellectual property rights provisions that strengthen existing regimes of patents and copyrights.

possibilities and prospects for the persistence of social collectivities based on ethnic and cultural affinities in a modern world in which states and corporations seek to homogenize or destroy them.

It may well be, as Gustavo Esteva suggests, that indigenous peoples cannot by themselves successfully oppose the power of the governments and businesses arrayed against them. However, there are other social groups also engaged in parallel struggles. In particular, there are many "non-governmental organizations" (NGOs) which offer opportunities for effective cooperation and mutual support. Should indigenous peoples choose to act in regard to IPRs, there are a variety of NGOs that may be useful allies. In this essay, we give some basic information on NGOs involved in issues related to IPRs, and provide a framework for thinking about the advantages and problems that may be expected in alliances with such organizations.

NGOs and Intellectual Property Rights

There are three main social actors in the world today: the state (governments), capital (corporations, private businesses), and civil society (indigenous peoples, workers, the rest of us). Power is concentrated heavily in governments and corporations. Since civil society encompasses the great mass of the people, the social majority, it is potentially the most powerful. Nevertheless, because the people are largely disorganized, divided, and dispersed, that power is not systematically realized. Still, it is civil society that provides the most latitude for the development of progressive and life-affirming alternatives to capitalist "modernization" and "development."

"NGOs" are non-governmental and non-business organizations. Some NGOs may represent the interests of governments and business, but they are not formal instruments of the state apparatus nor are they engaged directly in profit-making commerce. As such, NGOs often manifest the aspirations and interests of groups of people outside governments or corporations. NGOs are of many types; they may focus on environmental, cultural, educational, religious, ethnic, political, development, religious, human rights, family planning, hunger, legal, or gender issues. Their field of operation may be local, regional, national, or international in scope. They may represent both repressive or liberatory tendencies. At their worst, NGOs are mere reflections of the interests of the powerful. At their best, they are institutional nodes around which oppositional logics are developed and popular resistance to inequality and injustice is mobilized, organized and implemented.

The last decade has seen an enormous growth in the number of NGOs concerned with international development.[3] The increase has been particularly marked in developing nations. There is great diversity in the strength, capacity, talent, interests, and political character of these NGOs. One important distinction is that between "grassroots/local" NGOs and "professional" NGOs. Grassroots/local NGOs are membership-based organizations that are created by people with the objective of defining and realizing their own interests. These NGOs are mostly local and, because they rely on members, they tend to be relatively poor in financial resources and technical expertise. By contrast, professional NGOs are often established by groups of activists who create the organization with the explicit goal of helping people other than their own membership. They are "professional" in the sense that there is a salaried staff with full-time professional commitment. These NGOs frequently operate at the subnational, national and international level, and are relatively rich in financial, material, informational, and technical resources.

In this essay, we will deal principally with professional NGOs, not with grassroots organizations. There are many indigenous and grassroots NGOs working with indigenous peoples, farmers, peasant farmers, and the poor all over the world.[4] But with few exceptions, such NGOs have not been directly concerned with the issue of IPRs. We believe that this is because IPRs have little meaning for peasants and indigenous peoples who are concerned principally with the day to day imperatives of survival or with issues with a much more immediate impact on their lives (say, land titling rather than the intellectual property rights provisions of GATT). NGOs working with such people have properly shared their priorities and have therefore not tended to develop much expertise in issues related to IPRs.

This is not to say that IPRs are unimportant for indigenous communities. But if indigenous peoples do wish to confront the admittedly abstract and longer-term implications of IPRs, they are unlikely to find the guidance they need from local/grassroots NGOs. Instead, they will usually need to contact the professional NGOs at the national and international level which have developed interests and

---

[3] It is estimated that as of 1987 there were 2,640 Third World development-oriented NGOs in the US, the OECD nations, Canada, and Japan (Fowler 1992: 16). In the South itself, there are uncounted NGOs. The Inter-American Foundation has published A Guide to NGO Directories which lists over 11,000 "professional" NGOs in Latin America alone.

[4] A useful listing of NGOs committed to solidarity with indigenous peoples is published by Cultural Survival, see the "Resource Guide to Organizations" in Cultural Survival Quarterly, Fall, 1991, pp. A1-A8. For information on the growth of indigenous organizations see Burger (1990).

expertise in the area of IPRs.[5] This need not be an asymmetric relationship. If indigenous peoples and their indigenous NGOs need national and international NGOs, these professional NGOs need the grassroots as well. Professional NGOs will ultimately have little impact if they do not mobilize people, and to do so they must serve their needs. If professional NGOs are to be something more than an "informal bureaucracy,"[6] parallel to the official bureaucracies, they need to establish better links to the masses of indigenous and non-indigenous peoples from whom the energy for real change must ultimately come.

What are Some Possible Advantages of Working with NGOs?

Indigenous groups and organizations may often lack the experience or particular skills to enable them to pursue their interests effectively in the bureaucratized, politicized, and commodified non-indigenous world. But it is to be hoped that indigenous peoples will not have to struggle alone in their struggle to obtain the rights they are due and to reach the goals to which they aspire. NGOs whose aims are consistent with those of indigenous peoples may prove to be valuable allies. A range of NGOs have demonstrated that they can be useful to indigenous peoples in regard to the question of IPRs. Some of the advantages to indigenous peoples of cooperation with NGOs include:

Provision of Information. The principal advantage of working with NGOs has to do with the information they can provide. Indeed, NGOs may be best understood as organizations designed to collect, process, and transmit information. And it is precisely information about the non-indigenous world that indigenous peoples need if they are to make informed decisions. Yet that information is often very difficult to obtain. This is particularly true of IPRs. Much of the logic and impetus for the extension of property rights law and regulation originates in the corporate boardrooms and trade ministries of the industrialized nations. A wide variety of NGOs have made it their business to seek out such information and to make it widely available.

Premier among these NGOs is Genetic Resources Action International (GRAIN), which for the last decade has been a major clearinghouse for information on the global seed industry, biodiversity, biotechnology, international IPR arrangements, and alternative modes of recognizing and rewarding the rights of farmers and indigenous peoples

---

[5] It is worth emphasizing the very general point that more and better contact and cooperation is needed between local/grassroots NGOs and "professional" NGOs, between national and international NGOs, and, indeed, between all the actors in the NGO sector.

[6] For this phrase, we are indebted to Francisco Berrios, Director de Investigación y Postgrado, Universidad Nacional Agraria, Managua, Nicaragua.

to the genetic materials they produce and reproduce. Other prominent organizations with similar functions include the African Centre for Technology Studies (ACTS), the Consorcio Latinoamericano Sobre Agroecología y Desarrollo (CLADES), India's Gene Campaign, the Rural Advancement Fund International (RAFI), and the South-East Asia Regional Institute for Community Education (SEARICE). Organizations expressly designed to serve the needs of indigenous peoples include Cultural Survival and Native Seeds/SEARCH. These NGOs are adept at gaining access to sources of information on such topics as international agreements (e.g., GATT, NAFTA, UNCED Convention on Biodiversity), property rights law, and the activities of transnational corporations.

In addition, most NGOs try to disseminate information as widely as their resources allow. Monitoring such publications is an effective way for indigenous groups to keep up with current events and issues, and is also a good way to make a preliminary assessment if a particular NGO is one with which it might be productive to cooperate. GRAIN's periodical *Seedling* is the single best source of constantly updated information on IPR issues.

Fund Raising. Working in cooperation with NGOs can also facilitate the efforts of indigenous groups to raise funds for their activities. Virtually all professional NGOs have extensive experience in acquiring financial resources from governments, private donors, and international agencies. Donor agencies are channeling an increasing proportion of their assistance grants through NGOs, and NGOs in the industrialized nations sent $6.4 billion to the Third World in 1989 (Livernash 1992:15). Indigenous groups may have little experience at fund raising. By contrast, most established professional NGOs possess both a track record with donors and a bureaucratic structure to which donors are accustomed. Association with an NGO may permit indigenous peoples to gain access to financial resources from which they might otherwise be excluded.

Technical and Research Assistance. Many professional NGOs have staff with specialized technical or research skills that may be useful for indigenous peoples but are not well developed among them. For example, the Rainforest Alliance has developed a comprehensive model contract for use by indigenous groups in negotiating arrangements with collectors of germplasm (see Laird 1993). Not all indigenous peoples have easy access to the sophisticated legal knowledge needed to draft such a model. Native Seeds/SEARCH has provided biologists who have assisted a variety of Native American groups to identify and recover indigenous crop varieties. And the premier example of a research-oriented NGO is the Kenya-based ACTS, which has produced a wide range of reports prepared under its auspices by university-based academics.

Transfer of Skills. While the skills associated with western-style information collection, fund-raising, and research and analysis may be in relatively short supply among indigenous peoples, they need not remain so. Cooperation between indigenous peoples and NGOs can foster a transfer of such skills and engender an enhanced understanding of the broader context and political economy in which indigenous communities are embedded and to which they must be able to respond effectively.

Networking. As organizations whose life blood is information, most NGOs are connected to networks of similar NGOs. They are also connected to a wide variety of governmental agencies, international agencies, advocacy groups, philanthropic organizations, and even other indigenous peoples. As such, a particular NGO can be a window to other organizations with which indigenous groups might wish to cooperate. More than a window, an NGO might also be a bridge for direct contact between the indigenous group and other organizations that might not otherwise be in touch or have sufficient grounds for extensive cooperation. In Asia, for example, the Indian NGO Gene Campaign has operated as an umbrella organization which has provided a structure within which both indigenous and farm groups can find common ground in opposition to patents on crop varieties as well as to GATT itself. GRAIN, especially, has been instrumental in fostering global networking regarding IPR issues. NGOs, with their technical capacities, can also be useful in publicizing the situation of indigenous peoples and bringing their situation and problems to wider audiences. Many NGOs have sophisticated computer facilities and can extend discussion and awareness through global computer networks such as EcoNet.

What are Some Possible Problems in Working with NGOs?

While indigenous peoples can realize advantages in working with non-indigenous NGOs, there are also potential problems associated with any such relationship. But awareness of some of the pitfalls may help indigenous peoples develop modes of working with NGOs that maximize the benefits of such a relationship and reduce the problems to an acceptable minimum. Some of these potential problems are:

Non-Indigenous Perspective. The source of many misunderstandings and difficulties is the simple fact that the staffs of most NGOs with expertise in IPR issues are almost always composed largely of non-indigenous people. As such, NGOs may have difficulty effectively understanding--or even recognizing--the real nature of indigenous peoples' goals and preferred means of working toward those goals.

Narrow Definition of Interests. Differences in worldview between indigenous peoples and NGO staffs may be compounded by differences in the particular objectives of each. Some NGOs involved in the IPR issue have the welfare of indigenous peoples as their principal concern. Such NGOs--most notably Cultural Survival--came to the question of IPRs through their initial interest in the continuing assault on indigenous rights and livelihood. But most of the NGOs involved in the IPR debate have come to the question of indigenous peoples through a prior concern with the environment, agriculture, or new technologies rather than through prior attention to indigenous peoples. These latter organizations may have more narrowly defined interests or objectives than does the indigenous group with which they are cooperating. For example, there may be a tendency for the NGO to focus on, say, preserving crop germplasm rather than on the preservation of the culture which provides the context and rationale for crop variety preservation. Differences in the priorities and interests of NGOs and indigenous peoples need not preclude cooperation, but any differences must be recognized and clearly addressed if effective cooperation is to be realized.

Financial Dependence. Compounding the problem of interests is the dependence of most NGOs on funding from the North. Dollars do not come without strings attached, though the existence of those strings may be denied by the NGO and the strings may be ideological rather than material. Donor influence on projects can be overt, or it can be very subtle indeed. Donor agencies, whether governmental or non-governmental, tend to give money for purposes they can understand, for objectives they hold, and to organizations with bureaucratic structures that are "efficient" in western terms. Whether purposefully or not, donors tend to create organizations in their own image. Indigenous peoples need to recognize this tendency in the NGOs with which they deal.[7]

Informal Bureaucracy. The staff of professional NGOs is, by definition and behavior, "professional". Professional status almost always implies a salary, office accommodations, communications facilities, travel budgets, and other accoutrements of professional activity. Such resources may well be necessary to accomplish agreed upon tasks and objectives in a bureaucratized world. But such material benefits can also come to be ends in themselves. Given material

---

[7] In a useful review of the funding patterns of Northern NGO donor agencies, Fowler (1992:17) concludes that "A direct implication for southern NGOs in any partnership discussion in the nineties is to ascertain the actual sources of northern NGOs' funds. For without such insight it will be difficult to assess what a potential partner can or cannot negotiate about and the degree of control they may or may not have on decisions."

distinctions and differences in interest between themselves and the people with whom they work, the staff of NGOs can come to view a project or initiative as "theirs." Self-determination ought not to be replaced by any species of paternalism.

Information Centralization. NGOs are particularly good at the collection of information. This does not always mean collection of external information for use by indigenous peoples. In the course of cooperation with indigenous groups, NGOs will likely come into possession of much information about the people, places, and environments in which they operate. Once collected, the movement of information is exceptionally difficult to control. Many national and international NGOs are involved in the systematic collection of databases on human, cultural, and genetic diversity.[8] Governments, corporations, universities, and other organizations have quite surprising ways of using and benefiting from such information. While some of these activities may be innocuous, others may have completely unexpected and negative outcomes for the indigenous peoples from or through whom the information was originally collected (O'Brien and Flora 1992). Considerable care ought to be taken with the custodianship of any information collected by an NGO cooperating with an indigenous group.

A Problematic Model: INBio

Unfortunately, we do not yet have any examples of professional NGOs successfully assisting an indigenous group to establish intellectual property rights to cultural or biological materials. What we do have is an example of the opposite: the exclusion of indigenous peoples from the establishment of IPRs. Costa Rica's National Biodiversity Institute (Instituto Nacional de Biodiversidad - INBio) is worth knowing about for that very reason (Kloppenburg and Rodriguez 1992). It may well be

---

[8] For example, a wide network of centers for the collection of indigenous knowledge and expertise is being developed under the leadership of the Center for International Research and Advisory Networks (CIRAN) and the Center for Indigenous Knowledge in Agricultural Research and Development (CIKARD). The Nature Conservancy's program for Biodiversity Inventories throughout Latin America collects biological rather than cultural information. Both initiatives involve collection of information and recording and centralization of that information in electronic databases. While these organizations envision progressive applications of the information they collect, the people and nations from whom the data was collected no longer have control over the disposition of that information. And information benefits those with the capacity to use it. And need we point out that capacity lies disproportionately in the industrialized nations?

that, for indigenous peoples, the struggle over IPRs will be as much to *prevent* appropriation of those rights by others as to establish them for the indigenous groups themselves.

Despite its name, INBio is *not* a government institution, it is an NGO. INBio was founded in October 1989 as a private, non-governmental, non-profit organization. Its purpose is two-fold: 1) to inventory the biological resources extant in Costa Rica and, 2) to protect that biodiversity by making it available for productive purposes and--by establishing its utility--thereby generating the financial resources to protect the natural resources. A central tactic in this strategy is raising money through the contractual supply of organisms to private companies searching for new sources of drugs, industrial materials, and agricultural inputs. The first initiative of this type is an arrangement with the North American pharmaceutical transnational Merck & Company, Inc. The Merck deal raises US$ 1 million for INBio's activities and so has received praise from many quarters as an innovative method for generating funding for conservation efforts. But this unprecedented sale of genetic resources has also drawn criticism from environmental organizations and other NGOs within Costa Rica which oppose granting the right to the disposition of Costa Rican biological resources to a private organization.

But what many in the debate have failed to realize is that the biological resources in question are not necessarily most equitably conceived of as Costa Rican. Although INBio's collection activities take it to the Talamanca Indian Reserve, Costa Rica's indigenous peoples were not consulted at any point in the process, nor are they considered to have any rights in the materials being taken from their land. There are no provisions to reward the people of Talamanca Reserve should valuable drugs be developed from the genetic resources extracted from their reserve. It is true that in one sense, the INBio/Merck contract represents an important advance. It sets a precedent for compensation for the appropriation of genetic resources by companies. On the other hand, it establishes a model of information extraction that focuses on national rather than local or ethnic sovereignty over biodiversity and it ignores the rights of indigenous peoples.

The INBio model has been extolled by both the US National Academy of Science and The Royal Society of Britain as an ideal model. Already, similar institutions are being planned for Mexico and Indonesia. And a bill has been proposed in the US congress to provide systematic and global financial support for the creation of other NGOs in the image of INBio. Indigenous peoples must be aware of this proliferation of extractive institutions and be prepared to confront them.

Conclusion

Indigenous peoples and their organizations are now faced with the accelerating appropriation of their biological and cultural resources by an increasingly acquisitive set of corporate and political entities. Developing a familiarity with intellectual property issues may well be a prerequisite to effectively responding to this challenge. A variety of professional NGOs with established expertise in the area of IPRs are available to assist indigenous peoples and their organizations to negotiate this new conceptual and legal terrain. We hope that this essay has provided information that can be a vehicle for the establishment of productive alliances between indigenous groups and NGOs involved in the IPR debate.

Bibliography

Burger, Julian
1990 The Gaia Atlas of First Peoples: A Future for the Indigenous World. New York, NY: Anchor Books.

Cernea, Michael M
1988 Nongovernmental Organizations and Local Development. World Bank Discussion Paper 40, Washington, DC: The World Bank.

Esteva, Gustavo
1992 The Limits, Strengths and Perspectives of Indigenous and Alternative Practices. In, Proceedings of the International conference Living With the Earth: Cross-Cultural Perspectives on Sustainable Development: Indigenous and Alternative Practices. Quebec: Intercultural Institute of Montreal. Pp. 115-129

Fowler, Alan
1992 Building Partnerships Between Northern and Southern NGOs: Issues for the Nineties. Development (Journal of the Society for International Development) 1: 16-23.

Kloppenburg, Jack, Jr. and Silvia Rodriguez
1992 Conservationists or Corsairs? Seedling 9:2 & 3 (June/July): 12-17.

Laird, Sarah
1993 Contracts for Biodiversity Prospecting. In, Walter Reid et al., Biodiversity Prospecting. Washington, DC: The World Resources Institute. Pp. 99-130.

Livernash, Robert
1992 The Growing Influence of NGOs in the Developing World. Environment 34:5 (June): 12-20, 41-43.

O'Brien, William E. and Cornelia Butler Flora
1992 Selling Appropriate Development vs. Selling out Rural Communities: Empowerment and Control in Indigenous Knowledge Discourse. Agriculture and Human Values 2:9 (Spring): 95-102.

Stavenhagen, Rodolfo
1988 Derecho Indígena y Derechos Humanos en América Latina. México, DF: Instituto Interamericano de Derechos Humanos.

1990 The Ethnic Question: Conflicts, Development, and Human Rights. Tokyo: United Nations University Press.

Suggested Contacts

Center for International Research and Advisory Networks (CIRAN)
P.O. Box 90734
2509 LS The Hague
The Netherlands
Tel. 31-70-351-0574, Fax 31-70-351-0513
Publication: Indigenous Knowledge and Development Monitor

Center for Indigenous Knowledge in Agricultural Research and Development (CIKARD)
318 Curtiss Hall
Iowa State University
Ames, IA 50011, USA
Tel. 515-294-0938, Fax 515-294-1708

African Centre for Technology Studies (ACTS)
Attn: Calestous Juma
P.O. Box 45917
Nairobi, Kenya
Tel. 254-2-744-047, Fax 254-2-743-995

Consorcio Latinoamericano Sobre Agroecología y Desarrollo (CLADES)
Attn: Camilla Montecinos
CET, Casilla 97, Correo 9
Santiago, Chile
Tel. 56-2-234-1141, Fax 56-2-233-8918
Publication: Agroecología y Desarrollo

Cultural Survival
Attn: Ted MacDonald
215 1st Street
Cambridge, MA 02142, USA
Tel. 617-621-3818, Fax 617-621-3814
Publication: Cultural Survival Quarterly

EcoNet
Institute for Global Communications
18 De Boom Street
San Francisco, CA 94107, USA
Tel. 415-442-0220, Fax 415-546-1794

Gene Campaign
Attn: Suman Suhai
F-31, Green Park (Main)
New Delhi-110 016, India

Genetic Resources Action International (GRAIN)
Attn: Henk Hobbelink, René Vellvé
Jonqueres 16, 6° D
08003 Barcelona, Spain
Tel. 34-3-310-5909, Fax 34-3-310-5952
Publication: Seedling

Instituto Nacional de Biodiversidad (INBio)
Attn: Ana Sitenfeld
Apartado Postal 22-3100
Santo Domingo, Heredia, Costa Rica
Tel. 505-36-4269, Fax 506-36-2816

Native Seeds/SEARCH
Attn: Gary Nabhan
2509 North Campbell Street #325
Tucson, AZ 85719, USA
Tel. 602-327-9123

Publication: The Seedhead News

Rainforest Alliance
270 Lafayette Street, Suite 512
New York, NY 10012, USA
Tel. 212-941-1900, Fax 212-941-4986

Rural Advancement Fund International (RAFI)
Attn: Pat Mooney
130 Slater Street, Suite 750
Ottawa, Ontario K1P 6E2, Canada
Tel. 613-567-6880, Fax 613-594-8705

South-East Asia Regional Institute for Community Education (SEARICE)
Attn: Rene Salazar
P.O. Box EA-31, Ermita
Manila, Philippines
Tel. 63-2-96-9071, Fax 63-2-521-1319

Chapter
12

A Legal Paradigm for Protecting Traditional Knowledge

David J. Stephenson, Jr.
Center for Cultural Dynamics, and
Bucholtz, Bull and Ewing, P.C.
Denver

Intellectual property rights law of the capitalist West presents a hostile setting for indigenous intellectual property rights. It protects individual creations rather than those created by tradition, defines knowledge as a commodity, and eventually conveys all intellectual property into the public arena where any use is a fair use, and where, in time, no compensation to the originator is required. Western intellectual property law fuels a global entrepreneurial search for ideas to exploit, while raising forbidding obstacles to anyone who would seek to maintain control over traditional knowledge. The barrier posed by Western-style intellectual property law is not, however, without its fissures. David Stephenson here analyzes recent legal accommodations to the unusual features of computer software, finding some intriguing possibilities for legal defense of traditional cultural knowledge. - ed.

12

A Legal Paradigm for Protecting Traditional Knowledge

David J. Stephenson, Jr.
Center for Cultural Dynamics, and
Bucholtz, Bull and Ewing, P.C.
Denver

In my view, any indigenous society has the right to just compensation for the use and development of its collective, intellectual products by nonindigenous persons.[1] Indigenous peoples have had difficulty

---

[1] The articulation and acceptance of this premise by social scientists and other nonindigenous persons is of relatively recent vintage. Despite fits and starts since the inception of applied anthropology early in this century, anthropologists did not make concerted efforts to join hands with advocates for indigenous peoples' rights until the early 1970's (Maybury-Lewis 1985; Paine 1985; Turner 1979; Wright 1988:385). The notion that indigenous peoples have intellectual property rights that can be advocated for is at the cutting edge of applied anthropology. In a 1992 survey on anthropology and law, Merry (1992:368-69) discusses numerous scholars concerned with indigenous human rights and sovereignty almost exclusively in terms of treaty rights or land tenure rights and nowhere explicitly discusses or cites research concerned with rights to intellectual property. However, Messer (1993: 236), a year later, recognizes this emerging concern in a survey on anthropology and human rights. Whether there are such things as universal human rights, including intellectual property rights, that can or should be advocated for on behalf of any given social group is still a lively debate among anthropologists (Berg 1991; Brush 1993; Coombe 1993a, 1993b; Downing & Kushner 1988; Levitt 1987; Renteln 1990).

Whatever the outcome of such ivory tower debate, however, indigenous societies are confronting real assaults on their territory and inundation by the worst characteristics of "frontier capitalism", including poverty, massive unemployment, and diseases--including AIDS and alcohol and drug addiction--at least in part due to the exploitation of their intellectual heritage without just compensation. The property of indigenous peoples--in the form of specialized knowledge, music, material products, and great works of art--has been used, enjoyed, or developed by nonindigenous persons without any significant compensation to the indigenous societies since prehistoric times (Kloppenburg 1991; Kloppenburg 1988). Control and conscious ownership by indigenous peoples of their traditional knowledge might serve to enhance their solidarity and pride under such assault, and financial returns from that ownership might assist them in their struggles. If the intellectual traditions of indigenous societies are literally valued monetarily for what they are worth to the world, these rich traditions will stand a better chance of thriving, and we will all be richer in the long run.

Fortunately, many articulate, applied social scientists have recently recognized this human rights crisis and have begun vigorously advocating, in partnership with or in

finding a legally viable means for protecting this right, however. Nevertheless, the law is constantly evolving and it is rapidly adapting to the booming telecommunications and software industry in order to protect the ownership rights of computer software creators. Surprisingly, computer software appears to share certain key characteristics with the traditional knowledge systems of indigenous peoples. In this chapter I propose a paradigm, or model, for providing legal protection for the intellectual property rights of indigenous peoples based on the developing legal protections of computer software.

The Paradigm-- A Licensing Agreement

A typical computer software licensing agreement offers a potentially fruitful model for indigenous peoples to adopt as a means for legally protecting their right to just compensation for the acquisition and use of their intellectual products. Traditional knowledge within an indigenous society is usually a collective, evolving product. Many persons contribute to it over time, and it is modified and enhanced as it is used over time and passed on from generation to generation. The question arises, then, how can relatively amorphous, community knowledge that changes over time be legally protected so that the indigenous society will receive fair compensation whenever such knowledge is used by non-members of the indigenous society?[2]

The licensing agreements that computer software companies have developed to license their proprietary software may offer a solution to this problem. The computer software that is licensed to many businesses is usually modified daily by both computer company programmers and in-house programmers for the business users of the software in order to adapt the software to the varying and changing needs of the businesses to which it is licensed.

Computer software licensing agreements are written to protect such communal, evolving products in two primary ways. First, such licenses are typically non-transferable, non-exclusive, and perpetual. That is, many businesses may obtain the right to use the same software, and each user has the right to use the software perpetually, but none of the user companies have the right to transfer the software to another person or company; that right remains exclusively with the computer software company that "owns" the software. Second, many computer

---

collaboration with indigenous peoples, for justly compensating indigenous peoples for the tapping of indigenous knowledge by nonindigenous persons (Anders 1989; Boom 1990; Cunningham 1991; Kloppenburg 1991; Kloppenburg and Kleinman 1987; Posey 1991, 1990). It is in this historical context and for these reasons that the paradigm, or model, in this paper is proposed for protecting the intellectual property rights of indigenous peoples.

[2] See Brush 1993: 663-4.

software license agreements define the protected software *very* comprehensively, by language such as the following:

> The term Licensed Software refers to all the proprietary software products marketed by [the computer software company], including, but not limited to, application, programming language, and interface software, software modifications, regardless of form, as well as associated logic diagrams, flow charts, specifications, and procedure manuals.

Therefore, the computer software company retains ownership rights in all modifications of the software, regardless of form. This protects the company's ownership rights to the software used by its customers even though it is modified daily by both the owning company's programmers and user, licensee in-house programmers, and even though the "form" of the software licensed to the customer on the first day of a customer's use is different from the form of the software used by the same customer many years later.

Other features of a standard computer software licensing agreement may include provisions for an annual licensing fee, which give the user the right to updated versions of the software for a fee, and provisions for consulting fees, which establish an ongoing business relationship between the computer software company and its customers, thus providing the owner company with an ongoing source of income from such licensee users.

These provisions of a standard computer software licensing agreement have special utility to an indigenous society seeking to protect its traditional knowledge. Once a corpus of indigenous knowledge is identified, it can then be licensed for the nonexclusive, perpetual use of other societies. Even if the other societies add to, enhance, or in any manner modify the basic corpus of knowledge, title to the knowledge, even as modified, will remain with the indigenous society.

Similarly, if the corpus of knowledge licensed to other societies is improved upon by the indigenous society itself, it not only retains title to the original corpus, but it may be able to share its more highly-evolved corpus of knowledge for a special, additional fee, or members of the indigenous society could share this enhanced knowledge with other societies for consulting fees.

There are some practical prerequisites for the implementation of such licensing arrangements by indigenous peoples. The indigenous societies would have to either establish communally owned corporations or otherwise pragmatically define the communities of peoples who can legitimately claim legal title to, or ownership interests in, the evolving communal knowledge that the indigenous peoples want to protect from unauthorized use (Brush 1993: 663-4). The licenses would have to be written so that they comply with an agreed-upon set, or agreed-upon sets, of controlling laws (e.g., the U.S. Code and applicable federal regulations, applicable laws of a recognized sovereign indigenous group, such as a Native American nation, or a specified set of international laws that could be enforced by a mutually recognized international law enforcement body).

Suggested Implementation Steps in an Ethnographic Context

It can be better seen how this paradigm might be applied if it is examined in two different ethnographic contexts, the Kuna of Panama, and the Alaska Natives.

The Kuna of Panama. In 1988, the Kuna Indians of Panama promulgated a set of rules entitled "Research Program: Scientific Monitoring and Cooperation" with the words "Information for Researchers" written clearly on the cover (Chapin 1991; Kloppenburg 1991). These rules require payments from nonindigenous scientists wanting to engage in research or collection on their land. Moreover:

> [R]ecognizing that real control of genetic information lies ultimately in knowing more about what it is and especially about how it might be used (and what it might be worth) in an industrial society, the Kuna require that an indigenous assistant accompany the scientist and that they have access to any reports resulting from the research or collection (Kloppenburg 1991:17).

Specifically, any information about plant breeds and associated farming techniques learned by outside scientists from the Kuna are properly intellectual property of the Kuna and the Kuna should be justly compensated for the use and development of this information (Kloppenburg 1991:17-18). This 1988 research program implemented by the Kuna provides them with the potential for tracking the use of indigenous knowledge by nonindigenous scientists and for negotiating licensing agreements with scientists who use the information. This 1988 Kuna research program established a research organization, PEMASKY (Project for the Study of the Management of Wildlife Areas of Kuna Yala), which could be used to implement, monitor, and, with the assistance of legal counsel, enforce such licensing agreements. Importantly, in such a context, PEMASKY would exercise control over cultural *information*, not just plant races or other physically tangible objects (compare to Brush 1993).

A Caveat--The Alaska Natives Case. Athough this paradigm may appear promising at first blush, its rosy appearance must be viewed skeptically. It presumes that indigenous societies can either formally incorporate or define comparable communities so that they can legally protect their collective intellectual property.[3] The experience of some Alaska Natives with the Alaska Native Claims Settlement Act (ANCSA) serves as a warning that incorporating indigenous societies in order to preserve indigenous property rights can exacerbate the disintegration of the societies (Anders 1989).

ANCSA mandated that everyone in Alaska who was at least one quarter Alaska Native blood (Indian, Eskimo, or Aleut) born before December 18, 1971, be enrolled as a shareholder in specially-formed regional and complementary village corporations and that distributions of land and money go to these corporations instead of tribal entities.

A critical analysis of ANCSA by Anders (1989) found that Alaska Natives, on the whole, have received "minuscule benefits from ANCSA" (1989:297). ANCSA has instead primarily benefited white professionals--lawyers, accountants, and business consultants--and a small number of privileged natives due to the complexity of its administration (1989:297). Most native leaders have lost control over these native corporations that were at least ostensibly established for the benefit of the natives (297). Anders concludes that ANCSA has left the majority of Alaska Natives as shareholders in estranged corporations that they do not even understand, let alone control (1989:289).

Therefore, if the paradigm proposed in this paper is adopted, careful attention will have to be paid to the indigenous corporations or other comparable groups that are formed or identified to implement the paradigm. Legal constraints should be imposed to assure that indigenous leaders remain in the control of the benefits derived from such licensing agreements.

Conclusion: The Paradigm in the International Context

The paradigm proposed in this paper is neither a panacea nor an exclusive solution but merely one of a wide variety of tools that indigenous societies could draw on to protect their intellectual property and thereby improve their viability within the international political economy. To date, however, although many international governmental and nongovernmental organizations (NGOs) and several United Nations agencies have explored means for protecting indigenous intellectual property rights, none have developed a framework that is at once practical, widely-accepted, and enforceable (Posey 1991; Wilkerson

[3] Identifying discrete cultural communities for the purpose of protecting intellectual property can be a practical and political challenge. For example, the United States government enacted the Indian Arts and Crafts Act in 1990 in a effort to prevent arts and crafts that were not genuinely Native American from being labeled and sold as Native American products. However, as of June of 1993, this legislation *had never been enforced* due to practical and political problems encountered attempting to identify who true Native American artists and craftspeople are (Knight 1993).

1993). In a comprehensive survey of such efforts by Posey (1991), he reviews shortcomings in the multitude of efforts that have been broached by numerous agencies and organizations, including the United Nations World Intellectual Property Organization (WIPO), the Union for the Protection of New Varieties of Plants (UPOV), and the International Union for the Conservation of Nature (IUCN). Specifically, he observes that even though 123 United Nations member states have reached broad agreements on industrial property and trademark that these agreements have never been applied to indigenous knowledge or handicrafts (1991:31). He argues that it would be both feasible and desirable for consumers, NGOs, and professional organizations to take advantage, on behalf of indigenous peoples, of industrial property conventions by insisting that products originating from indigenous peoples carry "appellations of origin" which could be used by the marketers only upon guarantees that the products were produced in an ecologically sustainable manner, that fair prices have been paid to the indigenous people, and that a fair percentage of the profits will be returned to the indigenous societies (1991:32).

The licensing agreement paradigm proposed in this paper offers a means for implementing such appellations of origin. Whether such agreements ultimately are enforceable, and whether they are enforceable in a manner that benefits indigenous peoples, will likely be determined only after efforts by interested parties to the agreements to enforce them, either through the means prescribed in the agreements or through some other judicial forum and law enforcement venue. Enforcing such agreements at the national level, however, may be the most effective short-run method for protecting indigenous intellectual property rights until pertinent international conventions are more widely accepted and vehicles for enforcing international laws more firmly established (1991:32).

References Cited

Anders, Gary C.
1989 Social and Economic Consequences of Federal Indian Policy: A Case Study of the Alaska Natives. Economic Development and Cultural Change 37: 285-303.

Berg, Jeff
1991 Moral Rights: A Legal, Historical and Anthropological Reappraisal. Intellectual Property Journal 6: 341-376.

Boom, B. M.
1990 Giving Native People a Share of the Profits. Garden 14,6: 28-31.

Brush, Steven B.
1993 Indigenous Knowledge of Biological Resources and Intellectual Property Rights: The Role of Anthropology. American Anthropologist 95,3: 653-686.

Chapin, Mac
1991 How the Kuna Keep Scientists in Line. Cultural Survival Quarterly 15,3: 17.

Coombe, Rosemary J.
1993a Cultural Appropriations: Intellectual Property, Colonialism, and Contemporary Politics. Forthcoming from Routledge, Chapman and Hall.

1993b Cultural and Intellectual Properties: Occupying the Colonial Imagination. Political and Legal Anthropology Review 16: 8-15.

Cunningham, A. B.
1991 Indigenous Knowledge and Biodiversity. Cultural Survival Quarterly 15,3: 4-8.

Downing, Theodore E. and G. Gushner, eds.
1988 Human Rights and Anthropology. Cambridge, MA: Cultural Survival, Inc.

Kloppenburg, Jack, Jr.
1988 First the Seed: The Political Economy of Plant Biotechnology. Cambridge, MA: Cultural Survival, Inc.

1991 No Hunting: Biodiversity, Indigenous Rights, and Scientific Poaching. Cultural Survival Quarterly 15,3: 14-18.

Kloppenburg, Jack, Jr. and Daniel Lee Kleinman
1987 Seed Wars: Common Heritage, Private Property and Political Strategy. Socialist Review 17: 7-41

Knight, Al
1993 The Government Has No Business Deciding the Purity of Indian Art. Rocky Mountain News, March 23, 1993, p. 1D.

Levitt, Leon
1987 On Property, Intellectual Property, the Culture of Property, and Software Pirating. Anthropology of Work Review 8,1:7-9.

Maybury-Lewis, David
1985 A special sort of pleading - anthropology at the service of ethnic groups. In, Advocacy and Anthropology (R. Paine, ed.). Newfoundland: Inst. Soc. Economic Research. Pp. 130-148.

Merry, Sally E.
1992 Anthropology, Law and Transnational Processes. In, Annual Review of Anthropology 1991. (B. J. Siegel, ed.). Palo Alto, CA: Annual Reviews, Inc. Pp. 357-379.

Messer, Ellen
1993 Anthropology and Human Rights. In, Annual Review of Anthropology 1993 (B. J. Siegel, ed.). Palo Alto, CA: Annual Reviews, Inc. Pp. 221-249.

Paine, R., ed.
1985 Advocacy and Anthropology. Newfoundland: Inst. Soc. Economic Research.

Posey, Darrell A.
1990 Intellectual Property Rights and Just Compensation for Indigenous Knowledge. Anthropology Today 6,4: 13-16.

1991 Effecting International Change. Cultural Survival Quarterly. 15,3: 29-35.

Renteln, Alice D.
1990 International Human Rights: Universalism versus Relativism. Newbury Park, CA: Sage.

Turner, Terrance
1979 Anthropology and the Politics of Indigenous Peoples' Struggles. Cambridge Anthropologist 5,1: 1-43.

Wilkerson, S. Jeffrey K.
1993 Intellectual Property: The Need for a Shared International Perspective. National Geographic Research and Exploration 9,1: 3-11.

Wright, R. M.
1988 Anthropological Presuppositions of Indigenous Advocacy. In, Annual Review of Anthropology 1988 (B. J. Siegel, ed.). Palo Alto, CA: Annual Reviews Inc. Pp. 355-390.

Chapter
13

Human Rights and Cultural Heritage: Developments in the United Nations Working Group on Indigenous Populations

Dean B. Suagee
Hobbs, Straus, Dean & Wilder
Washington, D.C.

The UN Working Group on Indigenous Populations is the principal venue in which such societies can interact with the community of nation-states, in exercise of their own sovereignty and contribution to the human community in general. Consequently, the deliberations of the UN Working Group on Indigenous Populations are now central to the actions of indigenous societies on the international stage. Created in 1982, the Working Group has produced a number of documents which are shaping the directions which national and international law will likely take as the international community gradually recognizes the presence of indigenous peoples and their distinctive and urgent needs. In this chapter Dean Suagee presents the current agenda of the Working Group, identifies key documents it has recently produced, and details the important and ongoing controversy regarding whether IPR has to been seen as a competing priority that should be subordinated to more pressing indigenous needs, such as land and sovereignty, or whether these objectives can be pursued in concert. Suagee develops a justification for the latter. - ed.

13

Human Rights and Cultural Heritage: Developments in the United Nations Working Group on Indigenous Populations[1]

Dean B. Suagee
Hobbs, Straus, Dean & Wilder
Washington, D.C.

Introduction

International human rights law should be a key component of any realistic strategy to use international law to protect the rights of indigenous peoples to their intellectual property. Although the existing international law for the protection of human rights does not adequately protect the rights of indigenous peoples, a new body of law on the rights of indigenous peoples has begun to emerge. Over the last decade, the United Nations has become the primary forum in which indigenous peoples have sought to gain international recognition and protection of their collective human rights. The focal point of these efforts has been the U.N. Working Group on Indigenous Populations, which has fashioned a draft universal declaration on the rights of indigenous peoples.[2] The Working Group also serves as a forum for representatives of indigenous peoples and national governments to present reports on developments in the field of the human rights of indigenous peoples.

This paper presents an introduction to the Working Group's draft declaration of the rights of indigenous peoples, with an emphasis on those rights that most directly relate to the protection of cultural knowledge. This paper also presents an overview of recent developments relating to indigenous intellectual and cultural property that have come before the Working Group, including a study commissioned by the

---

1 Portions of this chapter have been adapted from Suagee, 1992.

2 *Discrimination Against Indigenous Peoples: Report of the Working Group on Indigenous Populations on its eleventh session*, United Nations, Economic and Social Council, Commission on Human Rights, Sub-Commission on Prevention of Discrimination and Protection of Minorities, E/CN.4/Sub.2/1993/29, (hereinafter "*Working Group 1993 Report*"), Annex I, page 50-60 (Aug. 23, 1993).

Working Group[3] and an international conference that was convened under the auspices of the Working Group. The conference issued a declaration[4] calling for the development of a new legal regime under international law for the protection of the intellectual and cultural property rights of indigenous peoples. The study includes a similar recommendation, but the study also concludes that the most effective way to protect the cultural heritage of indigenous peoples is to secure recognition and protection of the the right of indigenous peoples to the collective possession and use of their traditional territories, including the ability to control access by outsiders. In the conclusion of this paper, I suggest that efforts to secure rights to autonomous self-government within traditional territories need not conflict with efforts to establish a legal regime under international law for the protection of indigenous intellectual and cultural property, and I offer some suggestions for the general approach that might be taken in designing such a regime.

The United Nations Working Group on Indigenous Populations

The founding of the United Nations at the end of the Second World War marked the beginning of a new era in international law, during which most of what is now considered "international human rights law" emerged.[5] In 1948, the United Nations General Assembly adopted the Universal Declaration of Human Rights[6] and the Convention

---

3 Erica-Irene Daes, Special Rapporteur of the Sub-Commission on Prevention of Discrimination and Protection of Minorities and Chairperson of the Working Group on Indigenous Peoples, United Nations, Economic and Social Council, Commission on Human Rights, Sub-Commission on Prevention of Discrimination and Protection of Minorities, *Study on the protection of the cultural and intellectual property of indigenous peoples*, E/CN.4/Sub.2/1993/28 (1993) (hereinafter *"Chairperson's Study"*).

4 United Nations, Economic and Social Council, Commission on Human Rights, Sub-Commission on Prevention of Discrimination and Protection of Minorities, First International Conference on the Cultural and Intellectual Property Rights of Indigenous Peoples, held at Whakatane, Aotearoa, New Zealand, June 12-18, 1993, *The Mataatua Declaration on Cultural and Intellectual Property Rights of Indigenous Peoples*, E/CN.4/Sub.2/AC.4/1993/CRP.5 (hereinafter *"Mataatua Declaration"*), included as an annex to the Chairperson's Study. See note 3.

5 See Bilder 1984. The United Nations Charter includes "promoting and encouraging respect for human rights and fundamental freedoms for all" in its statement of purposes and principles. U.N. CHARTER art. I, ¶ 3. The U.N. Charter was signed at San Francisco on June 26, 1945 and entered into force on October 24, 1945. *Ibid.*

6 G.A. Res. 217, U.N. GAOR, 3rd Sess., U.N. Doc. A/810 (1948).

on the Prevention and Punishment of the Crime of Genocide.[7] In 1966 the General Assembly adopted and opened for signature by states the two principal multilateral treaties for the protection of human rights, the International Covenant on Civil and Political Rights[8] and the International Covenant on Economic, Social and Cultural Rights.[9] The Covenants proclaim the rights of individuals against states,[10] and they constitute important limitations on a state's sovereignty over matters within its domestic jurisdiction.

During this same period, the rights of all peoples to self-determination gained currency.[11] In 1960 the General Assembly adopted the Declaration on the Granting of Independence to Colonial Countries and Peoples,[12] and in 1966 the right of peoples to self-determination also was enshrined in the first article of both of the International Human Rights Covenants.[13] The right of self-determination differs from other human rights in that it is a collective rather than an individual right. In exercising its right of self-determination, a people determines for itself its political status from a range of options, including status as a sovereign

---

7 Convention on the Prevention and Punishment of the Crime of Genocide, G.A. Res. 260, U.N. GAOR, 3rd Sess., 179th plen. mtg., pt. 1 page 174, U.N. Doc. A/810 (1948). For further discussion on the Genocide Convention, see generally Robinson, 1960.

8 International Covenant on Civil and Political Rights, G.A. Res. 2200, U.N. GAOR, 21st Sess., Supp. No. 16, page 52, U.N. Doc. A/6316 (1966).

9 International Covenant on Economic, Social and Cultural Rights, G.A. Res. 220, U.N. GAOR, 21st Sess., Supp. No. 16, at 49, U.N. Doc. A/6316 (1966). These two International Covenants, together with the Universal Declaration and the Optional Protocol to the International Covenant on Civil and Political Rights sometimes are referred to collectively as the International Bill of Human Rights. See Burke 1989, page xi. The United Nations and other international organizations have adopted a number of other human rights instruments as well. *See generally* Bilder 1984.

10 See Hannum 1989, pg. 17, noting that even Article 27 of the Covenant on Civil and Political Rights, where "the protection of groups is clearly the primary concern," has been applied to protect individual members of groups and not groups themselves).

11 See Hannum 1989, pg. 7-9 (discussing the evolution of the concept of self-determination from a "principle" to a "right").

12 G.A. Res. 1514, U.N. GAOR, 15th Sess., Supp. No. 16, page 66-67, U.N. Doc. A/4684 (1960).

13 Both the Covenant on Civil and Political Rights, and the Covenant on Economic, Social and Cultural Rights, begin with an identical Article 1, the first section of which proclaims: "All peoples have the right of self-determination. By virtue of that right they freely determine their political status and freely pursue their economic, social and cultural development." International Covenant on Economic, Social and Cultural Rights, see footnote 9, page 49; International Covenant on Civil and Political Rights (see footnote 8) page 53.

independent state, free association with a state, various forms of autonomy within a state, and integration into a state.[14]

In the 1970s, an international movement emerged seeking to use international law to protect the rights of indigenous peoples.[15] Indigenous peoples soon discovered, however, that international human rights law lacked specific provisions to address many of their concerns. Indigenous peoples are primarily concerned with their collective rights as distinct peoples,[16] while international human rights law is mainly concerned with the rights of individuals against states.[17] Their demands for self-determination, the principal human right that is collective in nature, have met with negative reactions from states, in large part because self-determination implies the right to choose independent statehood.[18] Although the Declaration and the Covenants say that "all" peoples have the right of self-determination, in practice the right has been limited to former colonies which had been ruled by overseas powers.[19] Even within former colonies, the right of self-determination

---

14 Hurst Hannum 1988.

15 *Ibid.* page 658-60; see also Williams 1990.

16 See Clinton 1990.

17 Although indigenous peoples mainly are concerned with collective rights, there are instances in which indigenous individuals have been successful in using international human rights law to protect their interests, and in doing so have advanced the rights of other indigenous individuals. One example is Sandra Lovelace, a Maliseet Indian woman who filed a complaint with the U.N. Human Rights Committee challenging a Canadian law which prohibited her from residing on her Band's reserve because of her marriage to a non-Indian. The Human Rights Committee ruled that the Canadian law violated her right under Article 27 of the Covenant on Civil and Political Rights "in community with the other members of [her] group, to enjoy [her] own culture." *Views of the Human Rights Committee Under Article 5(4) of the Optional Protocol to the International Covenant on Civil and Political Rights Concerning Communication No. 24/1977 Sandra Lovelace*, 36 U.N. GAOR Supp. No. 40, pages 166, 177, U.N. Doc. A/36/40 (1981), *reprinted in* Human Rights Committee, Selected Decisions Under The Optional Protocol, pages 86-87, U.N. Doc. CCPR/C/OP/1, U.N. Sales No. E.84.XIV.2 (1985). This decision contributed to the enactment of amendments to Canada's Indian Act, R.S.C., ch. 32, § 7(2)(3) (1st Supp. 1985) (Can.), which allows Indian women (and their children) to be registered as Indians. The amendments also allow bands to assume control of their own membership. *Ibid.* § 10(1).

Another example of a complaint before the U.N. Human Rights Committee based on Article 27 of the Covenant on Civil and Political Rights is *Ominayak and the Lubicon Lake Band v. Canada, Report of the Human Rights Committee*, U.N. GAOR, 45th Sess., Annex IX, Supp. No. 40, pages 1-30, U.N. Doc. A/45/40 (1990). The case is discussed and analyzed in McGoldrick 1991.

18 See Hannum 1988, page 672, and Morris 1992, pages 77-79.

19 See Hannum 1989, page 9, and Anaya 1990, pages 214-215. *see also* John Humphrey, who argues that there is little support in the legislative history of the two International Covenants for the view that the General Assembly intended to limit the

has not benefitted indigenous peoples. In the Americans and Australia, most indigenous peoples live within the boundaries of states that achieved independence long before the founding of the United Nations. Elsewhere, borders previously drawn by colonial powers remained in effect and became the borders of newly independent states with little regard for territories of indigenous peoples living within or astride those borders.[20]

In the 1980s, after a decade-long study by a Special Rapporteur, the United Nations established the Working Group on Indigenous Populations[21], and this Working Group has become the focus of the efforts of indigenous peoples to gain international legal recognition of their human rights. By establishing the Working Group, the United Nations in effect acknowledged that the existing international law of human rights was not adequate to protect the human rights of indigenous peoples. The Working Group is comprised of five experts who serve in their individual capacities rather than as representatives of states, and its annual meetings are open to representatives of indigenous peoples and nongovernmental organizations, as well as representatives of states.[22] The Working Group is charged with a two-part mandate: (a) to review developments pertaining to the human rights of indigenous peoples; and (b) to develop standards to protect their rights.[23]

In carrying out the first part of its mandate, the Working Group has become a forum for indigenous peoples to present information about specific instances where the actions of national governments and transnational corporations have come into conflict with the rights and interests of indigenous peoples. Representatives of national governments have used the Working Group as a forum in which to report on developments in domestic law that provide some measure of autonomy for indigenous peoples or otherwise provide legal recognition for their distinctiveness. Participants in Working Group sessions also have devoted attention to the recent revision of the International Labour Organisation Convention on tribal and indigenous peoples.[24] By serving

---

meaning of the word "peoples" to include only colonial peoples (Humphrey 1984: 193-96).

20 Hannum 1989, page 9.

21 The formation of the Working Group on Indigenous Populations was proposed by the Sub-Commission on Prevention of Discrimination and Protection of Minorities in its resolution 2(XXXIV) of September 8, 1981, was endorsed by the Commission on Human Rights in its resolution 1982/19 of March 10, 1982, and was authorized by the Economic and Social Council in its resolution 1982/34 of May 7, 1982.

22 Stomski 1991, page 579.

23 *Working Group 1993 Report, (see foot*note 2) page 4.

24 *Ibid.* page 582. The first multilateral treaty to specifically address the issue of indigenous peoples was the Convention Concerning the Protection and Integration of

as a forum for the discussion of these issues, the Working Group has performed a critical service for indigenous peoples and for the community of nations.

The Draft Declaration on the Rights of Indigenous Peoples

In recent years, emphasizing the second part of its mandate, the Working Group has been fashioning a Declaration on the rights of indigenous peoples for adoption by the United Nations General Assembly. Such General Assembly declarations, however, do not necessarily have the force of international law,[25] but rather they more commonly are adopted as a step in the development of positive international law. When the principles expressed in a General Assembly declaration are written into a multilateral treaty, they become binding on states that become parties to that treaty.[26] The Declaration on the rights of indigenous peoples, when adopted, should carry significant weight in international law because it will interpret existing norms of positive and customary international law which are enshrined in the two International Covenants and other international human rights instruments. Regardless of the legal force of the Declaration, the extent to which states honor the principles of the Declaration will be a function of the moral force behind the Declaration and the effectiveness with which indigenous peoples and their advocates bring that moral force to bear on the conduct of states.

The principles expressed in the draft Declaration reflect the aspirations of indigenous peoples as tempered by the demands of states. They include the full enjoyment of all human rights under existing human rights instruments, the preservation of cultural identities, the use

---

Indigenous and Other Tribal and Semi-Tribal Populations in Independent Countries (I.L.O. Convention No. 107), June 26, 1957, 328 U.N.T.S. 247. See Hurst, 1990, pages 76-78. Indigenous peoples objected to the assimilationist approach of ILO Convention No. 107, and, in response to these objections, a new ILO Convention No. 169 was adopted in 1989 which rejects assimilation as a norm and generally supports the right of indigenous peoples to live and develop as distinct communities. Convention Concerning Indigenous and Tribal Peoples in Independent Countries (I.L.O. Convention No, 169), Official Bulletin, volume 72, Series A, No. 2 (1989), pages 59-70. *See generally* Anaya 1991, noting that almost all of the states that have been active in the U.N. Working Group also took visible roles on the committee that drafted Convention 169); Barsh 1990, (analyzing the new ILO Convention No. 169); and Swepston 1990 (discussing the new ILO Convention No. 169).

25 See Schachter 1991, pages 84-105, and also Kerwin 1983 (arguing that the political character of the General Assembly should prevent resolutions from being treated as authoritative). Some General Assembly declarations are, by their own terms, authoritative in international law. *See, e.g., Declaration on Principles of International Law, supra* note 51, G.A.Res. 2625, U.N. GAOR, 25th Sess., Annex, Agenda Item 85, U.N. Doc. A/Res/2625 (XXV) (1970).

26 Schacter 1991, pages 84-105.

of lands and waters on which the indigenous cultures depend, and autonomy and self-government within their traditional territories. A detailed discussion of the full scope of the draft Declaration is beyond the scope of this paper. The draft Declaration annexed to the Working Group's report on its eleventh session, which was held in 1993, consists of 45 articles and a number of preambular statements.[27] More than a third of the articles deal with the rights of indigenous in their own distinctive cultures. These articles include specific provisions addressing such matters as language, religion, education, the manifestations of culture, and repatriation of items of cultural patrimony and human remains.[28] Two of these articles explicitly acknowledge the rights of indigenous peoples in their cultural and intellectual property. These two articles, numbers 12 and 29, state:

> "Indigenous peoples have the right to practise and revitalize their cultural traditions and customs. This includes the right to maintain, protect and develop the past, present and future manifestations of their cultures, such as archaeological and historical sites, artifacts, designs, ceremonies, technologies and visual and performing arts and literature, as well as the right to the restitution of cultural, intellectual, religious and spiritual property taken without their free and informed consent or in violation of their laws, traditions and customs."[29]

> "Indigenous peoples are entitled to the recognition of the full ownership, control and protection of their cultural and intellectual property. They have the right to special measures to control, develop and protect their sciences, technologies and cultural manifestations, including human and other genetic resources, seeds, medicines, knowledge of the properties of fauna and flora, oral traditions, literatures, designs and visual and performing arts."[30]

Article 12 lays a foundation for the repatriation of items of cultural, intellectual and religious property that have been taken from indigenous peoples without their consent or in violation of their laws. While Article 29 also applies to the repatriation context, this Article looks as well toward preventing the future alienation of indigenous cultural and intellectual property. But what does it mean to have such a "right to special measures"? In the context of the Declaration, the term

27 *Working Group 1993 Report*, footnote 2, Annex I, pages 50-60.

28 *Ibid.* pages 50-60 (e.g., articles 3, 4, 7, 12-17, 21, 24-26, 28-31, 38).

29 *Ibid*, pages 53-54.

30 *Ibid.* page.57.

"special measures" generally refers to measures to be taken by states to protect the rights of indigenous peoples, recognizing that, for a variety of reasons, general measures to protect the rights of other citizens are often not adequate to protect the rights of indigenous peoples. In the context of intellectual property rights, however, special measures at the national level are not likely to be sufficient. The legal regimes for protecting rights in intellectual property are based on multilateral treaties, as discussed in the following section of this paper. State parties implement these treaties through national legislation, but for intellectual property law at the national level to be effective in protecting the rights of indigenous peoples in their cultural and intellectual property, the "special measures" must be fashioned to fit into the international law framework. This may require the adoption of amendments to the governing multilateral treaties. In the last few years, the Working Group has devoted a substantial amount of attention to this subject, and, in doing so, has begun the process of developing the "special measures" to which indigenous peoples are entitled.

Toward Special Measures for Indigenous Cultural and Intellectual Property

The idea of using intellectual property law to protect the rights of indigenous peoples in their cultural property has been discussed at several recent sessions of the Working Group. This paper takes note of three documents that have been considered by the Working Group: (1) a report issued under the auspices of the Secretary-General of the United Nations entitled *Intellectual property of indigenous peoples: concise report of the Secretary-General* (herein "*Concise Report*");[31] (2) a study on cultural property of indigenous peoples that the Working Group assigned to the Chairperson-Rapporteur of the Working Group, and which was released under her name as a draft at the Working Group's 1993 session;[32] and (3) the Mattatua Declaration, which was adopted at the first international international conference on the cultural and intellectual property rights of indigenous peoples.[33]

The Secretary-General's Concise Report, which was issued in July 1992, just prior to the commencement of the Working Group's tenth session, was prepared in response to a request by the Sub-Commission on the Prevention of Discrimination and the Protection of Minorities.

---

31 *Discrimination Against Indigenous Peoples: Intellectual property of indigenous peoples: concise report of the Secretary-General*, U.N. ESCOR Comm. on Human Rights, 9th Sess., U.N. Doc. E/CN/.4/Sub.2/1992/30 (1992), [hereinafter "*Concise Report*"].

32 *Chairperson's Study* (see footnote 3).

33 *Mataatua Declaration* (see footnote 4).

The Sub-Commission asked the Secretary-General to prepare a report on "the extent to which indigenous peoples can utilize existing international standards and mechanisms for the protection of their intellectual property."[34] The Concise Report includes a brief introduction to two of the multilateral treaties for protecting rights in intellectual property and discusses some of the ways in which the field of intellectual property rights may be relevant to the concerns of indigenous peoples. The two main branches of intellectual property are: *copyrights*, which include literary, musical, artistic, photographic and audiovisual works; and *industrial property*, which includes inventions, trademarks and industrial designs. The principal multilateral treaty for the protection of copyrights is the Berne Convention for the Protection of Literary and Artistic Works, which was first adopted in 1888 and has been amended many times since then. For industrial property, the principal multilateral treaty is the Paris Convention for the Protection of Industrial Property, first adopted in 1883. While these two treaties establish much of the international law of intellectual property, states that are parties to these treaties generally carry out their obligations under these treaties through the enactment and enforcement of national legislation.

The Concise Report suggests that the intellectual property of indigenous peoples can be divided into three categories: (a) folklore and crafts, including "oral literature, music, dance, artistic motifs and designs, crafts"; (b) biodiversity, including "plant varieties which have been developed through experiment and cultivation for use as food, medicine or materials for house, boat or other kinds of construction or use"; and (c) indigenous knowledge "held, evolved and passed on by indigenous peoples about their environment, plants and animals, and the interaction of the two."[35] With respect to folklore, the Concise Report concludes that copyright has proven an ineffective means of protection, in large part because copyright protects a work through the lifetime of the author and for a short period afterwards and works of folklore are collective, without precise authorship or moment of creation.[36] The Concise Report notes that in 1982 the World Intellectual Property Organization adopted model provisions for the protection of folklore through national legislation, but it draws no conclusion as to whether these model provisions have served to protect the rights of indigenous peoples in their folklore. The Concise Report does conclude that the existing international agreements have been ineffective in protecting the traditional knowledge of indigenous peoples.[37] Noting that this is a complex field which is largely unresearched, the Concise Report

---

34 *Concise Report* , page 1 (see footnote 31).

35 *Concise Report*, page 2-3 (see footnote 31).

36 *Ibid.* p.age 4.

37 *Ibid.* page 6.

suggests that consideration be given to the development of amendments to the multilateral treaties to specifically address the concerns of indigenous peoples.[38]

The *Chairperson's Study*[39] discusses a number of international instruments for protecting rights in intellectual property, including the Berne Convention and the Paris Convention and several others.[40] The *Study* does recommend that a group of experts be convened to develop possible future revisions to both the Berne and Paris Conventions to address the concerns of indigenous peoples,[41] but this recommendation is not presented as an item for immediate attention. Rather, with respect to cultural and intellectual property that is still in the possession of indigenous peoples, the *Study* concludes that the most effective protection is for indigenous peoples to be able to control their own territories.[42] With respect to items of cultural property that have been alienated from indigenous peoples, the Study concludes that existing mechanisms under national and international law are inadequate and that the United Nations should establish a new mechanism for the return of cultural property across international borders.[43] Whatever new mechanisms are fashioned must provide for the recognition of collective ownership of cultural and intellectual property.[44]

In a more fundamental sense, the *Chairperson's Study* challenges the premise that intellectual property rights law offers an appropriate legal framework for protecting indigenous cultural knowledge and suggests that using the concept of intellectual property transforms knowledge into a commodity that can be bought and sold. The *Study* concludes that the mechanisms such as copyright and patent law are "not only inadequate for the protection of indigenous peoples' heritage but *inherently unsuitable*" because these mechanisms provide protection for a limited period of time and because the basic philosophy behind these mechanisms conflicts with the philosophy of most indigenous peoples toward their cultural knowledge.[45] The *Study* calls for protection of a

---

38 *Ibid.* page 8.

39 See footnote 3. While the *Study* identifies the Chairperson-Rapporteur as the author, it was prepared under a contract with the Mikmaq Grand Council.

40 The *Study* also discusses a variety of legal regimes under national laws for the protection of places that have historic, cultural or religious significance and for the repatriation of sacred objects and artifacts and human remains. A discussion of these legal regimes is beyond the scope of this paper. For a brief description of U.S. laws to protect culturally important places, see Suagee and Funk 1993.

41 *Chairperson's Study,* page 67. See foonote 3.

42 *Ibid.* page 66.

43 *Ibid.* page 65.

44 *Ibid.* page 64.

45 *Ibid.* pages 13-14 (emphasis added).

broader conception of the collective "heritage" of each indigenous people, which it describes as:

> ...everything that belongs to the distinct identity of a people and which is theirs to share, if they wish, with other peoples. It includes all of those things which international law regards as the creative production of human thought and craftsmanship, such as songs, stories, scientific knowledge and artworks. It also includes inheritances from the past and from nature, such as human remains, the natural features of the landscape, and naturally-occurring species of plants and animals with which a people has long been connected.[46]

The *Study* says that most indigenous peoples do not regard their heritage in terms of *property* but rather in terms of individual and community *responsibility*, and that heritage is more appropriately seen as a bundle of relationships rather than a bundle of economic rights.[47] Under this conception, heritage is something that can be shared but which should never be alienated from the culture that produced it. The *Study* also suggests that it is inappropriate to subdivide heritage into separate legal categories with different levels of protection but that, rather, heritage "should be managed and protected as a single, interrelated whole."[48]

The Mataatua Declaration provides some evidence that many indigenous peoples believe that it is acceptable to subdivide heritage into different categories for purposes of fashioning mechanisms for legal protection. Many of the statements in the Mataatua Declaration reinforce many of the points made in the *Chairperson's Study*, but there seems to be little reluctance to use the concepts of intellectual and cultural property to fashion a new legal regime to protect the rights of indigenous peoples in their cultural knowledge. In particular, the Mataatua Declaration calls for the development of a new legal regime, specifying that the new regime should incorporate: collective ownership, retroactive coverage, protection against "debasement of culturally significant items," cooperative framework, and multi-generational coverage.[49]

The Mataatua Declaration also calls for a second international conference to be convened on the cultural and intellectual property rights of indigenous peoples, and that the conference should be hosted by the Coordinating Body for the Indigenous Peoples Organisations of the

46 *Ibid.* page 11.

47 *Ibid.* page 12.

48 *Ibid.* page 13.

49 Mataatua Declaration, page 5 (see footnote 4).

Amazon Basin. Clearly, there is a substantial amount of interest on the part of indigenous peoples in using the concepts of intellectual property law to protect some aspects of their heritage. Accordingly, the Working Group has decided to take further steps in this area, including convening a workshop with relevant academic and indigenous experts, expanding and updating the Chairperson's Study, and placing the subject of the development of new legal instruments on its agenda for its twelfth session in 1994.[50]

Conclusion

The emerging international law of the human rights of indigenous peoples may prove to be a more effective legal mechanism for protecting indigenous cultural knowledge than the international law of intellectual property rights. Indigenous peoples that have recognized rights to autonomous self-government under national law are better situated to protect their cultural knowledge and the environments on which that knowledge depends than are indigenous peoples who lack such recognized rights. By adopting a declaration on the human rights of indigenous peoples which includes among those rights the collective right of autonomous self-government within a recognized territory, the United Nations General Assembly and the community of nations can take a major step to empower indigenous peoples to protect their rights in their cultural knowledge.

Efforts to fashion a new regime for the protection of the intellectual and cultural property of indigenous peoples, however, need not detract from the campaign for international recognition that the human rights of indigenous peoples include rights of autonomous self-government. Rather, both campaigns can support each other. The Chairperson-Rapporteur addressed this point in the eleventh session of the Working Group, saying that:

> ...the protection of cultural and intellectual property of indigenous peoples [is] closely related to the realization of their most fundamental rights, such as their territorial rights, the right to self-determination, the right to preserve their traditions, knowledge and values, as well as to maintain their social organization and manage their environment and [is] thus essential for maintaining, developing and restoring indigenous societies.[51]

---

50 *1993 Working Group Report,* page 48 (see footnote 2).

51 *Ibid.* page 35.

It is generally true that for indigenous peoples cultural heritage is a complex whole in which the various parts are so interrelated that it makes little sense to think about any one part in isolation. But to make national and international law work to protect the rights of indigenous peoples in their heritage, we must be able to focus on the parts as well as on the whole. Principles and mechanisms drawn from the law of intellectual property could be useful in fashioning a new legal regime to protect some parts of the whole. The new regime need not be either copyright or industrial property, as such, but rather should be more in the nature of "neighboring rights," rights which bear a resemblance to intellectual property but which reflect the distinct nature of the interests that are to be protected.[52] The process of developing the new regime must begin with indigenous peoples defining the interests that they want to have protected, and there must be genuine interaction among the academic and the indigenous experts and the others involved in the lawmaking process. The new regime must include recognition of the legitimacy and importance of the laws and customs of indigenous peoples, but the new regime must also work at the international level, and so it must be international law. The mechanisms used by the new regime may bear a resemblance to intellectual property law, and they most likely will also include mechanisms to protect culturally important places, including sacred sites, as well as cultural knowledge. In any event, whatever form the new regime takes, it must be clear that the interests to be protected are not just property interests but, rather, are human rights.

---

[52] *See generally* Stewart 1983: 174-201. In March, 1993, a group of lawyers, literary critics, computer scientists, publishers, environmentalists and scholars of cultural heretage held a conference in Bellagio, Italy: Bellagio Conference on Cultural Agency/Cultural Authority: Politics and Poeticsof Intellectual Property in the Post-Colonial Era. The Participants at the conference issued a document entitled the "Bellagio Declaration" which calls for the consideration of neighbouring rights in fashioning legal regimes to protect works of folklore, works of cultural heritdage and the biological and ecological know-how of traditional peoples. Copies of the Bellagio Declaration may be obtained from Professor Peter Jaszi, Washington College of Law, The American University, 4400 Massachusetts Ave., N.W., Washington, D.C. 20016.

Bibliography

Anaya, S. James

1990 The Rights of Indigenous Peoples and International Law in Historical and Contemporary Perspective. Harvard Indian Law Symposium, 1989.

1991 Indigenous Rights Norms in Contemporary International Law. Arizona Journal of International Law 8.

Barsh, Russel L.

1990 An Advocate's Guide to the Convention on Indigenous and Tribal Peoples, Oklahoma City University Law Review 15:209-253.

Bilder, Richard B.

1984 An Overview of International Human Rights Law, in Guide To International Human Rights Practice (Hurst Hannum ed.) Philadephia: University of Pennsylvania Press. Pp. 3-19.

Burke, Kathryn J.

1989 Introduction , New Directions In Human Rights (Ellen L. Lutz et al. eds.) Philadephia: University of Pennsylvania Press. Pp. xi-xiv.

Clinton, Robert N.

1990 The Rights of Indigenous Peoples as Collective Group Rights. Arizona Law Review 32: 739-747.

Hannum, Hurst

1988 New Developments in Indigenous Rights. Virginia Journal of International Law 28: 649-678.

1989 The Limits of Sovereignty and Majority Rule: Minorities, Indigenous Peoples, and the Right to Autonomy, in New Directions In Human Rights (Lutz et al., eds.). Philadelphia: University of Pennsylvania Press. Pp. 3-24.

1990 Autonomy, Sovereignty and Self-Determination: the Accommodation of Conflicting Rights. Philadephia: University of Pennsylvania Press.

Humphrey, John P.

1984 Political and Related Rights, *in* Human Rights In International Law, Vol. 1 (Theodor Meron ed.) Pp. 171-203.

Kerwin, Gregory J.
1983 The Role of United Nations General Assembly Resolutions in Determining Principles of International Law in United States Courts. Duke Law Journal 1983: 876-899.

McGoldrick, Dominic
1991 Canadian Indians, Cultural Rights and the Human Rights Committee. International and Comparative Law Quarterly 40: 658-669.

Morris, Glenn T.
1992 International Law and Politics: Toward a Right to Self-Determination for Indigenous Peoples. In, The State Of Native America: Genocide, Colonization, And Resistance (M. Annette Jaimes, ed.). Boston: South End Press. Pp. 55-86.

Robinson, Nehemiah
1960 The Genocide Convention. New York: Institute of Jewish Affairs.

Schachter, Oscar
1991 International Law In Theory And Practice. Norwell, MA: Kluwer Academic Publisher.

Stewart, Stephen M.
1983 International Copyright and Neighbouring Rights . London: Butterworth & Co.

Stomski, Laura
1991 The Development of Minimum Standards for the Protection and Promotion of Rights for Indigenous Peoples. American Indian Law Review 16: 575-596.

Suagee, Dean B.
1992 Self-Determination for Indigenous Peoples at the Dawn of the Solar Age Michigan Journal of Law Reform 25: 671-749.

Suagee, Dean B. and Karen J. Funk
1993 Cultural Resources Conservation in Indian Country. Natural Resources and Environment 7,4: 30-33,61-63.

Swepston, Lee
1990 A New Step in the International Law on Indigenous and Tribal Peoples: ILO Convention No. 169 of 1989. Oklahoma City University Law Review 15: 677-714.

Williams, Jr., Robert A.
1990 Encounters on the Frontiers of International Human Rights Law: Redefining the Terms of Indigenous People's Survival in the World. Duke Law Journal 1990: 660-704.

Chapter
14

Human Rights Implications of Indigenous Peoples' Intellectual Property Rights

Audrey R. Chapman,
American Association for the Advancement of Science

What are the prospects of linking the intellectual property rights of indigenous peoples to the slowly growing corpus of internationally recognized human rights? Historically the main thrust of those rights has been to endow individuals with rights, while the essential needs of indigenous peoples *as peoples* rest in group rights, especially in two hotly debated rights categories, economic and cultural rights. Across the past two decades pressure on national states has grown to publicly commit themselves to a broad set of rights in these categories. Nation-states, however, have trenchantly resisted these pressures, regarding them as threats to the states' authority over the citizens and lands within their respective boundaries. Thus, internationally honored agreements have been slow to come. Audrey Chapman reviews the complex texture of human rights agreements currently in force, and suggests four strategies where progress toward the protection of indigenous intellectual property rights might be gained. - ed.

14

Human Rights Implications of Indigenous Peoples' Intellectual Property Rights

Audrey R. Chapman
American Association for the Advancement of Science

Is it possible to utilize international human rights standards to protect the intellectual property rights of indigenous peoples? If feasible, this strategy could have several advantages. Human rights are fundamental moral and legal norms which protect people from political, economic, and social abuse. International human rights instruments enumerate internationally recognized economic, social and cultural rights as well as civil and political rights. States which ratify these instruments become states parties to them and are legally bound to respect and implement their provisions. The United Nations has established a series of oversight bodies to monitor the performance of states parties to specific instruments. Non-governmental organizations and/or individuals have recourse to bring cases of human rights violations to some of these bodies. A human rights approach would also link advocates of indigenous peoples' intellectual property rights to the international human rights movement.

Limitations of Human Rights Approaches

The Universal Declaration of Human Rights adopted by the United Nations General Assembly in 1948 and subsequent human rights instruments based on the Universal Declaration have a comprehensive understanding of international human rights.[1] (Center for the Study of Human Rights 1992). The Universal Declaration recognizes two broad categories of rights. The first 21 articles of the Declaration enumerate civil and political rights similar to those found in the Bill of Rights in the U.S. Constitution. Articles 22 through 27, however, go beyond these civil and political rights to list rights to economic, social, and cultural benefits, such as social security, an adequate standard of living, and education. Article 27 is particularly relevant to the issue of intellectual property rights in that it recognizes that:

---

[1] The text of the Universal Declaration of Human Rights can be found in many collections, among them Center for the Study of Human Rights, Twenty-Four Human Rights Documents (New York: Columbia University, 1992), pp. 6-9.

(1) Everyone has the right to participate in the cultural life of the community, to enjoy the arts, and to share in scientific advancement and its benefits.

(2) Everyone has the right to the protection of the moral and material interests resulting from any scientific, literary, or artistic production of which he is the author.

Nevertheless there are major problems associated with utilizing human rights standards to protect the intellectual property rights of indigenous peoples.The prevailing paradigm of human rights is highly individualist. Concepts of economic rights, collective rights, and cultural rights are not well developed and their validity is being challenged.

(1) Individualistic bias of prevailing paradigms of human rights. Late twentieth century understandings of human rights still reflect the eighteenth century liberal individualism which gave rise to notions of natural rights. The radical individualism underlying human rights theory ignores the social character of personhood and human life. While acknowledging that western individualistic models do not fit many other cultures and societies, western human rights theorists, who dominate legal and philosophical interpretations of human rights, continue to claim that human rights rest solely on the inherent dignity of the individual person: "Human rights as they have been understood, rest on a view of the individual person as separate from and endowed with inalienable rights held primarily in relation to society, and especially the state" (Donnelly 1989: 145).

Intellectual property rights of indigenous peoples, however, are a collective right held corporately by virtue of membership in the group. Like other collective rights, they pertain to protection of the non-reducible collective interests and to promotion of the common good.

Human rights theorists have been reluctant to recognize such collective or solidarity rights as authentic human rights. Typically these critics assert that because solidarity derives from a relationship among persons or groups and confers benefits on the basis of membership in a particular community, "Any rights that might arise from solidarity would not be human rights" (Donnelly 1989:144). Some philosophers and legal scholars of human rights are willing to acknowledge the existence of a category of collective rights, but they refuse to categorize such rights as human rights. Moreover, they often denigrate collective rights by linking them to a traditional world view incompatible with modernization.[2]

There are other reasons why human rights analysts have been reluctant to acknowledge a category of collectively based human rights. Many link collective rights with the position of "cultural relativists" who argue that the group orientation of non-western societies renders individually based human rights inappropriate or less important. To maintain the universal status of human rights as proceeding from and protecting the dignity of the individual, western human rights specialists deny the validity of all collective rights claims.[3] Anticipating that the claims of the individual may conflict with the interests of a community or group in which she/he is a member, human rights specialists scrupulously confer priority to protecting the rights of the individual in such situations (Donnelly 1989: 143-146). Some analysts also are suspicious that collective rights tend to become exclusivist rights, overriding the rights of members and implying denial of valid rights claims of others outside of the group (Howard 1992:97-98). They speak about the alleged provincialism of collective rights in contrast to the cosmopolitanism of individual rights (McDonald 1992:145). Relatedly, liberal human rights analysts maintain (without clear rationale) that group rights, unlike individual rights, appear to be nonjusticiable (cannot be adjudicated) because they are inherently political (McDonald 1992: 141).

(2) Economic and cultural rights are both challenged and not as well developed as civil and political rights. Although the Universal Declaration and the major human rights covenants are premised on the interdependence and indivisibility of all human rights, many western human rights specialists argue for the precedence of civil and political rights, some to the point of declaiming the authenticity of economic, social, or cultural rights as rights. This position reflects their assumption that rights, first and foremost, constitute negative constraints on the operations of governments so as to protect individuals. Arguing that economic rights require positive action on the part of governments whereas human rights imply restraint, many conservatives and libertarians have sought to undermine the status of economic, social and cultural rights. (Other analysts more correctly point out that virtually all rights, whether civil and political or economic, social, and cultural, actually require both positive action and restraint.)

---

2 See for example Galienkamp 1991.

3 Jack Donnelly, for example, is reluctant to recognize third generation human rights because they emanate from the notion of solidarity, which is a relationship among persons or groups, and according to Donnelly human rights "derive from the inherent dignity of the human person." See his discussion in Donnelly, *op.cit*., p.144.

Despite ratification by over 100 countries, the International Covenant on Economic, Social and Cultural Rights has encountered far more difficulties in acceptance and implementation than the parallel International Covenant on Civil and Political Rights. In contrast with the Human Rights Committee charged with oversight of the Civil and Political Covenant, the Committee on Economic, Social and Cultural Rights has little domestic or international jurisprudence serving to clarify the Covenant's norms. With the exception of labor-related rights, the range of rights recognized in the Covenant was considerably in advance of most national constitutional and legislative enactments. In the absence of clear standards, states' reports on implementation of economic, social and cultural rights have been very inadequate, and states' representatives have manifested a distinct reluctance to engage in a meaningful exchange of views with the Committee on these issues (Alston 1992: 489-491). Moreover, the right to property, the paramount economic right in a capitalist society, is not specifically recognized in the covenant.

Cultural rights provisions as developed in the United Nations system do not provide applicable standards for questions of the ownership and control of the cultural property of indigenous peoples. Like other rights enumerated in the International Covenant on Economic, Social, and Cultural Rights, Article 15, which recognized the right of everyone "to benefit from the protection of the moral material interests resulting from any scientific, literary or artistic production of which he is an author" is an individual entitlement, as is the related right of everyone "to take part in cultural life" (Center for the Study of Human Rights 1992: 14). Cultural property is defined by the principal relevant international instrument, the UNESCO Convention on the Means of Prohibiting and Preventing the Illicit Import, Export, and Transfer of Ownership of Cultural Property, adopted in 1970, as "property which, on religious or secular grounds, is specifically designated by each State as being of importance for archeology, prehistory, history, literature, art or science" (UNESCO 1986). The UNESCO Convention places importance on the antiquity of cultural property, not its contemporary cultural relevance or economic worth. It also fails to cover such indigenous cultural property as oral history or acquired knowledge. Moreover, the impetus behind this document is fairly narrow - regulating the illicit acquisition of, and trafficking in, cultural property. In connection with the protection of folklore, UNESCO and the World Intellectual Property Organization drafted Model Provisions for National Laws on the Protection of Expressions of Folklore against Illicit Exploitation and Other Prejudicial Actions in 1985. The provisions do recognize that expressions of folklore deserve to be protected in a manner consistent with other productions of intellectual creativity (UNESCO/WIPO 1985).

On broader issues the World Intellectual Property Organization (WIPO), the UN agency which protects patents, has told the UN Human

Rights Centre that it does not recognize the standing of indigenous peoples. In a dismissive letter, the Director General of WIPO wrote to the Centre that intellectual property is distinguished by the type of intellectual creation and not by the groups responsible for its creation. This position reflects WIPO's insistence on individual authorship as a prerequisite for patent protection.[4]

To seek to resolve these dilemmas, some human rights specialists have offered a model of generations of rights. They distinguish between the "first generation" of human rights based on the idea of liberty and providing protection against state violations of the person and the "second generation" of economic, social, and cultural rights grounded in equality and guaranteeing positive access to essential social and economic goods, services, and opportunities. "First generation" rights include such traditional civil and political rights as freedoms of speech, movement, assembly, rights to a fair trial and free elections, and protection against the state from arbitrary arrest and cruel and unusual punishment. In contrast, "second generation" rights encompass welfare entitlements like rights to health, to work in safe conditions, to receive a fair wage, to have a basic education. This schema also has a "third generation" of rights based on solidarity and requiring new forms of international cooperation. These "third generation" rights would incorporate the rights of groups or collectivities.[5] Examples of "third generation" rights are the rights to self-determination and rights to development. The language of generations is, however, ambiguous and unsatisfactory because it implies that second and third generation rights are inferior to and require the prior implementation of earlier generations of rights. Moreover, even those human rights advocates who argue for the authenticity and equal status of economic, social, and cultural rights are reluctant to recognize the existence of a category of collective or solidarity rights.

Alternative Strategies under Human Rights Regimes for Gaining Recognition of Indigenous People's Intellectual Property Rights

Confronted with these ideological biases, I believe that there are four possible strategies for using human rights approaches to promote recognition of indigenous people's intellectual property rights:

(1) Articles in human rights instruments recognizing the right of peoples to self-determination can be applied to indigenous intellec-

---

[4] "WIPO does not recognize indigenous peoples," For the Record, Human Rights Internet, 1991, p.19.

[5] See the discussion in Donnelly, *ibid.*, pp. 143-144 on the rationale.

tual property rights: Both the International Covenant on Civil and Political Rights and the International Covenant on Economic, Social and Cultural Rights recognize the right of people to self-determination. By virtue of this right, people may determine not only their political status, but also pursue economic, social and cultural development. A second paragraph of this right declares that people may freely dispose of their natural wealth and resources. A final paragraph states that "In no case may a people be deprived of its own means of subsistence." The text of the first two paragraphs of Article 1, enumerating the right to self-determination, as it appears in the International Covenant on Civil and Political Rights is that:

(1) All peoples have the right to self-determination. By virtue of that right they freely determine their political status and freely pursue their economic, social and cultural development.

(2) All peoples may, for their own ends, freely dispose of their natural wealth and resources without prejudice to any obligation arising out of international economic cooperation, based upon the principles of mutual benefit, and international law. In no case may a people be deprived of its own means of subsistence.[6]

To date, states have been reluctant to grant subnational minorities the rights of peoples. Most international conventions, for example, refer to indigenous societies as indigenous "people." One option would be to prepare a case to take to the United Nations Human Rights Committee, the body which monitors states parties compliance with this covenant, arguing that the failure to recognize indigenous people's intellectual property rights constitutes deprivation of their means of subsistence. The objective would be to elicit an interpretation of this article that would give indigenous peoples standing and explicitly cover and provide recognition to indigenous intellectual property rights.

While both major international covenants enumerate the right of all peoples to self-determination, it would be more feasible to gain standing under the International Covenant on Civil and Political Rights than the International Covenant on Economic, Social and Cultural Rights. The Optional Protocol related to the Civil and Political Covenant recognizes the competence of this Committee to receive and consider communications with individuals or groups of individuals who claim to be victims of violations by states parties. Individuals currently lack such standing under most other international human rights instruments. Also, the U.S. is a state party to this covenant but not its

---

[6] Center for the Study of Human Rights, 1992, p.11.

counterpart International Covenant on Economic, Social and Cultural Rights.

(2) Collective rights can be interpreted as the rights of individuals acting as members of social groups: Some human rights specialists who refuse to recognize the validity of collective or group rights are willing to speak of "third generation" human rights if such rights are interpreted merely as the rights of individuals acting as members of social groups.[7] Apparently even classic liberals do not object in principle to such a formulation of individuals pooling their rights as long as the transfer is subject to an important procedural condition: each member must give free and informed consent to the association (McDonald 1992: 349-351). The obvious disadvantage of such an approach is that it would relegate indigenous peoples to the status of a voluntary association, corporation, or partnership and would deny rights to the group as such. Yet it might provide standing under international human rights instruments and possibly domestic human rights legislation to address some intellectual property rights issues.

(3) The ILO Convention Concerning Indigenous Tribal Peoples in Independent Countries provides potential recourse: In 1989 the International Labour Organization adopted Convention 169, entitled a Convention Concerning Indigenous and Tribal Peoples in Independent Countries. While not strictly a human rights treaty, ILO conventions are among the most effective international instruments. Convention 169 is a revision of a previous convention (107) which was drafted on the paternalistic assumption that indigenous people would eventually assimilate. In contrast, convention 169 assumes that indigenous people want to remain distinct and separate but not sovereign entities.

While Convention 169 does not directly address intellectual property rights, it has several provisions that might bear on these issues. Under the Convention, governments have the responsibility for promoting the full realization of the social, economic and cultural rights of indigenous and tribal peoples with respect to their social and cultural identity, their customs and traditions and their institutions (article 2, 1). Other provisions specify that governments respect the special importance of peoples' relationships with the land for their cultures and spiritual values (article 13, 1). The Convention also states that the right of the peoples concerned to the natural resources pertaining to their land shall be specially safeguarded (article 15).[8]

---

7 One such case, albeit with some reluctance, is Donnelly, *ibid.*, p. 147-148.

8 The text of Convention 169 is reprinted in Center for the Study of Human Rights, *ibid.*, pp.97-105.

In principle, ILO mechanisms allow complaints from grassroots organizations if they are submitted through an NGO which has status with the ILO. Every year a committee of legal experts monitors the performance of governments and makes recommendations to the annual conference which rebukes the worst offenders. Nevertheless, even though the Convention 169 came into force in 1991, very few countries have ratified it, and its provisions do not apply to nonsignatories.

(4) Groups can challenge the fundamental assumptions that preclude recognition of indigenous people's intellectual property rights as a human right: The predominant paradigm of liberal individualistic interpretations of human rights is not writ in stone. While many western human rights analysts reject the existence of collective human rights, Third World human rights specialists and grass roots organizations frequently advocate recognition of broad categories of collective or group rights. In 1986 the General Assembly adopted a Declaration on the Right to Development which appears to recognize a category of collective rights. The text acknowledges the massive and flagrant violation of the human rights of the peoples, as well as individuals. It states that the human right to development implies the full realization of the right of peoples to self-determination, including the exercise of their inalienable right to full sovereignty over all their natural wealth and resources (article 1). Nevertheless, like other human rights instruments, it identifies the human person and not communities as the central subject of development and the active participant and beneficiary of the right to development.[9]

A recent UN expert Seminar on Appropriate Indicators to Measure Achievements in the Progressive Realization of Economic, Social and Cultural Rights, for which this author served as rapporteur, broke new ground on this subject. It underscores the need to recognize group rights as well as individual rights as one component of a holistic approach.[10]

The Sub-Commission on Prevention of Discrimination and Protection of Minorities, which serves as the general research arm of the United Nations Commission on Human Rights, also issued a working paper on "Discrimination Against Indigenous Peoples" in 1991. The purpose of this working paper is to propose a tentative framework which might guide further elaboration and study. It considers two aspects: (1) return and restitution of cultural property of indigenous peoples; and (2)

---

[9] The text of the Declaration on the Right to Development can be found in Resolutions and Decisions of the 41st Session of the General Assembly (United Nations, 1986).

[10] Par. 12, "Conclusions and Recommendations," UN Seminar on Appropriate Indicators to Measure Achievements in the Progressive Realization of Economic, Social and Cultural Rights, January 1993, Document 9884Q.

protection and preservation of existing cultural property of indigenous peoples, including their human or skeletal remains, folklore, crafts and skills. The author of the working paper recommends that the Sub-Commission on Prevention of Discrimination and Protection of Minorities consider authorizing further study of the question of ownership and control of the cultural property of indigenous peoples.[11]

Yet another initiative underway is work on a universal declaration on indigenous rights by the Working Group on Indigenous Populations, one of the few UN bodies on which indigenous peoples have some representation. The draft universal declaration of indigenous rights, first issued in 1991, provides comprehensive affirmation of collective rights in any UN document. Several paragraphs refer to rights to maintain and develop cultural characteristics and property. The right to special measures for protection as intellectual property of cultural manifestations, seeds, genetic resources, medicine, or knowledge of the useful properties of fauna and flora.[12] The revised text completed in 1993 has the following provisions (Article 29):

> Indigenous peoples are entitled to the recognition of the full ownership, control and protection of their cultural and intellectual property.
>
> They have the right to special measures to control, develop and protect their sciences, technologies and cultural mechanisms, including human and other genetic resources, seeds, medicines, knowledge of the properties of fauna and flora, oral traditions, literatures, designs and visual and performing arts.[13]

The comprehensive protections for indigenous peoples outlined in the text, however, make many governments reluctant to approve the declaration. Particularly the use of the term "peoples" in international law implies the right to full self-determination, including political independence. Because 1993 is the International Year of the World's Indigenous People there may be a possibility for building momentum for its adoption. Even if it is voted by the General Assembly, as a declaration it

---

[11] Discrimination Against Indigenous Peoples: Working paper on the question of the ownership and control of the cultural property of indigenous peoples prepared by Ms. Erica-Irense Daes, Sub-Commission on Prevention of Discrimination and Protection of Minorities, Commission on Human Rights, United Nations Economic and Social Council, 43rd session, 3 July 1991.

[12] Draft document on the Rights of Indigenous Peoples, Report of the Working Group on Indigenous Populations on its tenth session, UN Commission on Human Rights. E/CN4/Sub.2/1992/93, Annex I. pp. 44-52 (August 20).

[13] Draft Declaration as Agreed Upon by the Members of the Working Group on Indigenous Peoples at its Eleventh Session, E/CN.4/Sub.2/1993/29, p.57.

would have the status of a statement of principles which is not binding or justiciable.

The text of the Vienna Declaration and Programme of Action, issued in June 1993 at the close of the World Conference on Human Rights, has a section on indigenous people. Again, disappointing the large number of representatives from indigenous communities, the diplomats scrupulously avoided conferring the full right to self-determination implied in the term peoples. Included in the World Conference text are recommendations to renew the mandate of the Working Group on Indigenous Populations, for the United Nations system to provide advisory services and technical assistance which would be of direct benefit to indigenous people, and for the General Assembly to proclaim an International Decade of the World's Indigenous People, to begin from January, 1994, that would include action-oriented programs, to be decided in partnership with indigenous people. The World Conference also urged States "to ensure the full and free participation if indigenous people in all aspects of society, in particular in matters of concern to them."[14]

Bibliography

Alston, Philip

1992 The Committee on Economic, Social and Cultural Rights. In, The United Nations and Human Rights: A Critical Appraisal (Philip Alston, ed.). Oxford: Clarendon Press.

Center for the Study of Human Rights

1992 Twenty-Four Human Rights Documents. New York: Columbia University Press.

Daes, Erica-Irense

1991 Discrimination Against Indigenous Peoples: Working paper on the question of the ownership and control of the cultural property of indigenous peoples. Sub-Commission on Prevention of Discrimination and Protection of Minorities, Commission on Human Rights, United Nations Economic and Social Council, 43rd Session.

Donnelly, Jack

1989 Universal Human Rights in Theory and Practice. New York: Cornell University Press.

---

[14] These citations are from the text of the Vienna Declaration and Programme of Action made available by the United Nations at the close of the World Conference. This version does not have an official number. The section on indigenous people is on pp. 21-22.

Galienkamp, Marlies
1991 Collective Rights: Much Ado About Nothing? A Review Essay. Netherlands Quarterly of Human Rights. 3: 291-307.

Howard, Rhoda E.
1992 Dignity, Community, and Human Rights. In, Human Rights in Cross-Cultural Perspectives: A Quest for Consensus (Adullahi Ahmed An-Na'im, ed.). Philadelphia: University of Pennsylvania Press. Pp. 81-102.

Human Rights Internet
1991 WIPO Does Not Recognize Indigenous Peoples. For the Record. 19.

McDonald, Michael
1992 Should Communities Have Rights? Reflections on Liberal Individualism. In, Human Rights in Cross-Cultural Perspectives: A Quest for Consensus (Adullahi Ahmed An-Na'im, ed.). Philadelphia: University of Pennsylvania Press. Pp. 133-161.

UNESCO
1986 Standard-Setting Instruments, IV.A.4.

UNESCO/WIPO
1985 Model Provisions for National Laws on the Protection of Expression of Folklore Against Illicit Exploitation and Other Prejudicial Actions.

United Nations
1986 Resolutions and Decisions of the 41st Session of the General Assembly.

1993a Conclusions and Recommendations. UN Seminar on Appropriate Indicators to Measure Achievements in the Progressive Realization of Economic, Social and Cultural Rights, Par. 15. Document 9884Q.

1993b Draft Document on the Rights of Indigenous Peoples, Report of the Working Group on Indigenous Populations on its Tenth Session. UN Commission on Human Rights. E/CN4/Sub.2/1992/93, Annex I. pp. 44-52.

1993c Draft Declaration as Agreed Upon by the Members of the Working Group on Indigenous Peoples at its Eleventh Session, E/CN.4/Sub. 2/1993/29.

1993d Vienna Declaration and Programme of Action. Made available by the United Nations at the close of the World Conference.

Chapter
15

International Agreements and Intellectual Property Right Protection for Indigenous Peoples

Darrell A. Posey
Institute for Social and Cultural Anthropology
St. Antony's College, Oxford University
and
Museu Paraense Emilio Goeldi/CNPq
Belem, Brazil

In this chapter, Darell Posey explores the high degree of flux in which the concept of IPR for indigenous peoples is currently found within international law and practice. At the same time, he identifies nine areas of international agreements where elements of IPR relevant to indigenous peoples occur, and out of which a more solid base of assumptions and definitions about these rights could emerge. He argues, however, that the lead must be taken by indigenous peoples themselves, and that the definition and boundaries of the concept should not be defined prematurely lest new applications, indigenous input, and sources of strength be precluded. - ed.

15

International Agreements and Intellectual Property Right Protection for Indigenous Peoples

Darrell A. Posey
Institute for Social and Cultural Anthropology
St. Antony's College, Oxford University
and
Museu Paraense Emilio Goeldi/CNPq
Belem, Brazil

Introduction

Intellectual Property Rights (IPR) is a rubric under which a great variety of concerns have accumulated. As interest has grown, IPR has become increasingly difficult to define. For indigenous peoples, IPR is an alien construct that roughly refers to "culture". Since sacred sites are reflections, if not foci, of "culture", then "intellectual" property may have physical and spiritual manifestations.

IPR developed as a Western concept that was essentially established to protect individual, technological and industrial inventions. Until recently, it has been considered an unlikely tool to protect the collective, trans-historical and obliquely defined qualities of indigenous cultures. Many think, as do I on some occasions, that IPR is not an appropriate mechanism to strengthen and empower traditional and indigenous peoples. Yet, I continue to pursue the nebulous and incorrigibly difficult precepts upon which IPR is based for one principal reason: it is a subject that challenges every category of thinker and thereby stimulates dialogue.

The Last Frontier

Valuing biodiversity through biotechnology development and establishing the ground rules for "the sharing of benefits" from biogenetic resource acquisition and manipulation were the underlying motives for The Earth Summit.[1] The global gathering recognized that genetic resources, and the knowledge of traditional and indigenous peoples about those resources, are the bonanzas of the future--they are the newest "last frontier" that will justify explorations and drive future economies.

---

1 The Earth Summit is the more popular name for the United Nations Conference on Environment and Development that was held in Rio de Janeiro in June, 1992.

Will indigenous peoples be a part of that future? Undoubtedly, since their knowledge has irrefutably been shown to reveal sources for valuable new medicines, fertilizers, foods, oils, essences, repellents and insecticides, building materials, dyes, colorings, etc. The lands and territories they have defended, occupied, and ecologically molded over the millennia are the sources of this new wealth (Posey 1990a). The question is: will they benefit from these developments, or will they become yet again the victims of an expanding frontier?

I question if any of us will benefit in the long run. The Earth Summit was more of a political game to re-divide the world's resources between new global players than a gathering to address the issues of poverty and environmental degradation. Environmentally rich countries want to be given as much power as technologically rich countries. One has to admit that "bio-culturally rich" vs "industrially rich" is at least more pleasant to the ear than "developed" vs "un- or under-developed countries", "northern" vs "southern" , or "first" vs "third world". No matter the dichotomy in vogue, the consumer society will eat its way to the collapse of the global environment and/or economy (which ever comes first).

There may be no stopping it! Best strategy: try to support, protect, strengthen, and empower those indigenous and traditional societies which are still relatively free from the destructive system. IPR alone will certainly not do that, but it will probably buy some time--and may even help. Minimally, demanding that knowledge of non-literate, indigenous and traditional peoples should be held on a par with industrial knowledge of the "civilized" world, will provoke major change (Posey 1990b). GATT and TRIPS[2] would certainly become more interesting than the boring "free market" discourse of today. WIPO[3] might even function in a more dynamic manner with a shaman, not an IPR lawyer, as its head.

So, my question is, does anyone have a better mechanism than IPR to provoke a new, more socially just and ecologically sound paradigm of "wealth", to strengthen positions of local communities, or to recognize the intellectual contribution of indigenous peoples to human patrimony? Alternative strategies are welcome and needed. But the deadly serious race is to conserve the biological and cultural diversity of the Planet is on: IPR seems to be one of the most interesting intellectual, legal, economic and political tools available to us at the present.

---

[2] GATT (General Agreement on Tariff and Trade) and TRIPS (Trade Related Intellectual Property) offices are located in Geneva and are the principal trade negotiation institutions of the United Nations.

[3] WIPO (World Intellectual Property Rights Organization) is based in Geneva and is responsible for implementation of international conventions on intellectual property rights (see Yamin and Posey 1993).

Creating IPR

To protect indigenous knowledge, the existing legal concepts that circumscribe intellectual property rights can be accepted as they now exist, or the term can be purposefully molded, expanded, and re-designed. The former is said by most IPR lawyers to be impossible, given the industrial property connotations, individual property bias, and inequality of access to legal structures faced by local communities. The latter, therefore, seems to be the better option--albeit it a very challenging and difficult one.

I have identified a number of areas that overlap sufficiently to provide the synthetic and ideological basis for a newly designed IPR (that will surely also have to be renamed). These are: (1) labor law; (2) human rights laws and agreements; (3) economic and social agreements; (4) intellectual property and plant variety protection; (5) farmers' rights; (6) environmental conventions and law; (7) religious freedom acts; (8) customary law and traditional practice; (9) cultural property/cultural heritage. This paper will follow the same topical sequence. A final section will discuss the practical aspects of implementing an IPR agreement.

1. IPR and the ILO

The International Labor Organization (ILO) was the first U.N. organization to deal with indigenous issues. A Committee of Experts on Native Labor was established in 1926 to develop international standards for the protection of native workers. The ILO developed a special Convention (107) known as the Convention Concerning the Protection and Integration of Indigenous and Other Tribal and Semi-Tribal Populations in Independent Countries (June 5, 1957). The Convention was revised in June, 1989, as Convention 169, Convention Concerning Indigenous Peoples in Independent Countries, and much of the "integrationist language" of the original was removed.

Its seventh preambular paragraph refers to "the distinctive contributions of indigenous and tribal peoples to...ecological harmony of humankind". Article 7 guarantees the right of indigenous peoples to decide their own development priorities and to control their own economic, social and cultural development.

Article 13(1) states that governments "shall respect the special importance of the cultures and spiritual values of the peoples concerned of their relationship with the lands or territories, or both as applicable, which they occupy or otherwise use, and in particular the collective aspects of this relationship". The recognition of *collective aspects* is a critical aspect of the Convention and is important in intellectual property rights issues, since collectivity is fundamental to transmission, use and protection of traditional knowledge.

ILO 169 has not been sufficiently utilized with implementation of IPR in mind. The Convention is not even mentioned in the Secretary-General's Concise Report on IPR and indigenous peoples. Nonetheless, it is has widely agreed upon terminology that should be exploited in defining the new IPR concept.

2. Intellectual Property and Human Rights

The 1948 Universal Declaration of Human Rights (UDHR) and subsequent International Covenant on Economic, Social and Cultural Rights (ICESCR, 1966) guarantee: fundamental freedoms of personal integrity and action; political rights; social and economic rights; and cultural rights. The principal problem with the "human rights approach" to cultural protection, is that action (or inaction) is directed toward Nation-States and does not easily "provide a basis for claims against multinational companies or individuals who profit from traditional knowledge".[4] Nonetheless, Article 1 (ICESCR, art. 1) establishes the right of self-determination, including the right to dispose of natural wealth and resources. This also implies the right to protect and conserve resources, including intellectual property.

Article 7 (UDHR) allows for equal protection under the law, thereby implying that IPR protection should be available to indigenous peoples as well. Article 17 provides for the right to own collective property and not to be arbitrarily deprived of that property. And Article 23 (UDHR) guarantees the right to just and favorable remuneration for work, which can be interpreted as work related to traditional knowledge.

Finally, Article 27 (UDHR) provides for the right to culture and recognition of interest in scientific production, including the right to the protection of the moral and material interests resulting from any scientific, literary or artistic production.

This language is echoed in the Draft Declaration on the Rights of Indigenous Peoples, which in paragraph 18 states: "Indigenous peoples have the right to the protection and, where appropriate, the rehabilitation of the total environment and productive capacity of their lands and territories, and the right to adequate assistance including international cooperation to this end". It is clear that IPR should to be seen as a basic human right and that human rights organizations should take up the cause as a major part of their activities.

---

[4] For a detailed discussion and citations of relevant documents, see Dinah Shelton, "Legal Approaches to Obtaining Compensation for the Access to and Use of Traditional Knowledge of Indigenous Peoples." Draft Report to the World Wide Fund for Nature -- International, Gland, Switzerland, 1993.

3. ECOSOC and Working Group on Indigenous Populations

In 1972, the United Nations Economic and Social Council (ECOSOC) authorized the Commission on Human Rights to form a special Sub-Commission "to conduct a broad study of the problem of discrimination against indigenous peoples" (Kahn & Talal 1987: 121). After lengthy delay, a voluminous report found that present international instruments are NOT "wholly adequate for the recognition and promotion of the specific rights of indigenous populations as such within the overall societies of the countries in which they now live" (UN Document No. E/CN.4/Sub.2/1986/7/ Add.4).

ECOSOC created in 1982 a Working Group on Indigenous Populations. Since that time, the Working Group has worked to prepare a Declaration on Rights of Indigenous Peoples and has become the most open international forum for indigenous representatives and advocates of indigenous rights.

Resolution 1990/27 of the Sub-Commission recommended that any UNCED convention "Provide explicitly for the role of indigenous peoples as resource users and managers, and for the protection of indigenous peoples' right to control of their own traditional knowledge of ecosystems". Resolution 1991/31 called for a study on the applicability of collective rights regarding property, including intellectual property.

In 1991, the Sub-Commission on Prevention of Discrimination and Protection of Minorities requested that the Secretary-General prepare a concise report on the extent to which indigenous peoples can utilize existing international standards and mechanisms for the protection of their intellectual property, drawing attention to any gaps or obstacles and to possible measures for addressing them. WIPO was also specifically requested to help in "formulating recommendations for the effective protection of the intellectual property of indigenous peoples" (UN Doc. E/C.4/Sub.2/1992/30). Unfortunately, the report, prepared by Erica Irene-Daes, Special Rapporteur of the Working Group, is weak and adds little to advancing an understanding of IPR issues.

In May, 1992, the United Nations held in Santiago, Chile, a Technical Conference on Indigenous Peoples and the Environment. The Conference established some basic principles that include: "recognition, protection and respect for indigenous knowledge and practices that are essential contributions to the sustainable management of the environment". It was also recommended that the United Nations system take effective measures to protect property rights of indigenous peoples, including intellectual property, cultural property, genetic resources, biotechnology and biodiversity (UN Doc. E/CN.4/Sub.2/1992/31).

In these declarations and recommendations, as in the Draft Declaration, there has been a clear call from the Human Rights

Commission for protection of and just compensation for the intellectual property rights of indigenous and tribal peoples. Since this forum can activate other U.N. agencies, it may provoke important results on the international level.

4. IPR, Folklore, and Plant Variety Protection

The United Nations Educational, Scientific and Cultural Organization (UNESCO) should be a logical forum for IPR discussion, but, although UNESCO has heard "petitions" of complaints by native peoples related to the fields of education, science, culture and information, indigenous questions are still only marginal to its agenda. The World Intellectual Property Organization (WIPO) in Geneva has 123 Member States that have already reached broad agreements on "industrial property" and "copyright".[5] Folklore, however, represents traditions that transcend the life span of individuals and, therefore, are collective property and not protectable.

In 1984, WIPO, together with UNESCO developed "Model Provisions for National Laws on the Protection of Expressions of Folklore Against Illicit Exploitation and Other Prejudicial Actions (WIPO 1985).[6] Both individual and collective folklore traditions are recognized. The words "expressions" and "productions" are used instead of "work" to emphasize that the provisions are sui generis and that copyright laws have not proven effective in the protection of folk traditions. Under the Model Provisions, folklore need not be "reduced to material form" (i.e., written down) to be protected.[7]

---

5 "Industrial property" deals chiefly with inventions, trademarks, industrial designs, and appellations of origin. "Copyright" deals chiefly in literary, musical, artistic, photographic and cinematographic works. The application of "industrial property" agreements has never been applied to indigenous knowledge or handicrafts. "Copyright" laws have proven ineffective because they depend upon the identification of "individuals" who produced the "work" to be copyrighted.

6 The Model Provisions were stimulated by "the multiple abuses", "distortions" and "mutilation" of folklore traditions being provoked by the "spectacular development of technology" in audiovisual productions, phonograms, broadcasting, cable television, etc. The Model Provisions specifically refer to the problem that "no share of the returns from ... exploitation is conceded to the communities who have developed and maintained it [folklore]".

7 The Model Provisions avoid dealing with the concept of "ownership", since the "owners" of folkloric traditions in some countries is legally the State. Emphasis is given to authorization of use by the "competent authority" or "community concerned". Compensation for "authorized use" would, therefore, be negotiated during the authorization process. The "competent authorities" are specifically granted the legal right to "fix and collect a fee" (WIPO 1989b:8). Unauthorized use or willful distortion of folklore that is "prejudicial to the cultural interests of the

Although the Model Provisions have never been adopted, there is renewed interest in the basic issues, especially in the recognition of collective and individual "expressions" and "productions" that remove folk expressions from the necessity of having the "personality" of a creator/artist as required by copyright law. Establishment of the principle that unwritten or oral expressions can be protected and that fees for such expressions should be paid, with criminal penalties for those who disrespect the necessity of authorization, are critical elements. The most important contribution is the application of "neighboring rights" to protect native performers, allowing folkloric expressions to be considered the same as the "performance of a work" and, therefore, protected under international copyright agreements as set out in the 1961 Rome Convention for the Protection of Performers.

For indigenous peoples, it is critical that plant (and animal) genetic resources also be seen as a unique part of their cultural heritage. This approximation is not unusual, in as much as plant genetic resource protection falls under WIPO's jurisdiction within the United Nations. The Union for the Protection of New Varieties of Plants (UPOV) is an independent, intergovernmental organization linked to WIPO in that its secretariat is located in the same building as WIPO and its Secretary-General is also the Director General of WIPO. UPOV established a Convention in 1961 (amended in 1972 and 1978) for the protection of breeders of new plant varieties. Under the international convention, natural or legal persons resident in Member States can acquire protection for plant varieties that they have developed that are "clearly distinguishable", "sufficiently homogeneous", and "stable in essential characteristics" (WIPO 1989: 41).

The Convention calls for compensation of the breeder for use of the protected variety. No cases have appeared before UPOV in which native peoples are considered the "breeders" of distinctive varieties, although ethnobiologists, geneticists, and botanists can now clearly show that the origins of hundreds of domesticated varieties lie with indigenous selection for, and improvement of, genetic traits. Even "wild" varieties may show extensive selection for millennia with resultant genetic improvements, although these varieties were never brought into a "domesticated" status (Posey & Overal 1988).

The critical factor here is to link folklore and plant genetic resources with intellectual property. It is this complicated legal linkage that allows for expansion of the concept of IPR to include traditional knowledge not only about species use, but also species management. Thus, ecosystems that are "molded" or modified by human presence are a product of indigenous intellectual property, and, consequently, are products themselves--or offer products--that are protectable.

---

community concerned" would be considered a punishable offense. Fines, seizure, and imprisonment are foreseen as enforcement measures.

Furthermore, "wild", "semi-domesticated" (or "semi-wild"), as well as domesticated plant and animal species, are products of human activity and should also be protectable.

5. FAO Farmers Rights

The UN Food and Agriculture Organization (FAO) has tackled in a series of conferences the question of "farmers' rights" and "breeders' rights". A major goal was to find ways that developing countries and "Third World farmers" could get a share in the huge seed market. Basic food crops, like rice, maize, and wheat, were originally acquired from native peoples and genetic material from "wild stock" is still essential to breed into existing varieties the resistance necessary to sustain economic production (Mooney 1983; Kloppenburg 1988; Juma 1989; Kloppenburg & Kleinman 1987). Third World countries are in enviable positions, since they "possess the greatest genetic wealth of edible plants at a time when plant genes are in greatest demand in the flourishing biotechnology industry" (Hurtado 1989:96; see also Scoones et al. 1992; Hamburger et al. 1991; Balick 1990; Reid et al. 1993). Yet developing countries continue to be reluctant and timid to press their demands of IPR for their genetic resources (Farrington 1989).

In 1987, FAO established a fund for plant genetic resources. The idea was to establish with contributions linked to the volume of total seed sales a fund to finance projects for sustainable use of plant genetic resources in the Third World. Unfortunately, contributions were voluntary and the fund wholly inadequate. Major seed producers, like the USA, have opposed mandatory contributions to the fund. The USA has, in fact, even refused to participate in FAO discussions on the matter. Instead, it has pushed for patent rights for all laboratory improved varieties. Opponents to the US position warn that, if the US gets its way, "the only forms of human innovation that will not be patentable will be those of informal innovators in the Third World (Hurtado 1989: 96).

6. IPR and the Environment: Life After U.N.C.E.D.

The links between biological and cultural diversity are inherent in the Biodiversity Convention that was signed by 126 Heads of State during "The Earth Summit" in June of 1993.

a. The Rio Declaration. The Rio Declaration clearly establishes the relevance of indigenous peoples and the central importance of their protection in order to attain sustainable development. Given the squeamishness of Nation-States regarding indigenous peoples' rights in the past, the tone of the Rio Declaration might even be interpreted to be progressive and welcome. Principle 22 states:

> Indigenous people and their communities, and other local communities, have a vital role in environmental management and development because of their knowledge and traditional practices. States should recognize and duly support their identity, culture and interests and enable their effective participation in the achievement of sustainable development.

b. The Biodiversity Convention. Article 1 of the Convention states:

> The objectives of this Convention ... are the conservation of biological diversity, the sustainable use of its components and the fair and equitable sharing of the benefits arising out of the utilization of genetic resources, including by appropriate access to genetic resources and appropriate transfer of relevant technologies, taking into account all rights over those resources and to technologies, and by appropriate funding.

The underlying logic behind these objectives is that biodiversity can only be conserved if it is sustainably utilized, particularly by the biotechnology industries, and the economic benefits of such utilization flow back to conservation activities, particularly in developing countries. States retain sovereign rights to their biological and cultural resources, and are responsible for ensuring that the benefits flowing from the utilization of biological resources reach their citizens.

Indigenous peoples, who have largely been marginalized by such processes in the past (if not totally eliminated), are understandably skeptical that this time things will be better. However, for the first time, at least indigenous and local communities embodying traditional lifestyles are expressly mentioned in the Convention. and their central contributions to biodiversity conservation recognized. Signatories to the Convention have pledged to:

> ... respect, preserve and maintain knowledge, innovations, and practices of indigenous and local communities embodying traditional lifestyles relevant for the conservation and sustainable use of biological diversity and promote their wider application with the approval and involvement of the holders of such knowledge, innovations and practices and encourage the equitable sharing of the benefits arising from the utilization of such knowledge, innovations and practices [Article 8 (j)].

Yet, again, indigenous groups doubt that existing international and national laws will adequately recognize and protect their knowledge, innovations and practices. They are even more skeptical that "trickle-down benefits" will occur, since historically they have rarely benefited from the goodwill of Nation-States.

c. Agenda 21. Chapter 26 of "Agenda 21" deals specifically with indigenous peoples, traditional knowledge and sustainable development. This list of "priorities for action" is more than adequate to direct major global resources into the use, application--and protection--of indigenous peoples, their cultures, and physical and intellectual resources.

The language of the Rio Declaration, Biodiversity Convention and Agenda 21 is vague and will be molded by future political and economic actions. Given that indigenous and traditional peoples are recognized as having special rights and benefits, and that economic livelihood is linked to development and conservation of natural resources, it is definitely worthwhile that energies and efforts be directed toward pushing the relevant sections in the direction of indigenous rights, including the recognition and protection of, as well as compensation for, intellectual property. GATT, FAO, and WIPO will all have to accommodate to this reality in future negotiations due to the large number of signatories expected on the Biodiversity Convention.

7. Religious Freedom and IPR

In a seminar on IPR at the United Nations Human Rights Convention in Vienna, June, 1993, Ray Apoaka of the North American Indian Congress suggested that IPR is essentially a question of religious freedom for indigenous peoples. "Much of what they want to commercialize is sacred to us. We see intellectual property as part of our culture--it cannot be separated into categories as [Western] lawyers would want." Pauline Tangipoa, a Maori leader, agrees: "Indigenous peoples do not limit their religions to buildings, but rather see the sacred in all life".

The Human Genome Project is an example of the dangers indigenous peoples see in the unbridled research and commercialization of genetic resources. In a brochure distributed by the World Council of Indigenous Peoples, a frantic alarm is raised over the genetic "research" that is taking place on indigenous peoples in the name of global health (WCIP 1993). They are concerned that such research will not only not be used to benefit them, but even be utilized to destroy or weaken them. Minimally, they are concerned that someone else is going to commercially benefit (and in a big way) from their genetic material--and they have not even as much as been consulted on the matter. Certainly no sharing of profits is mentioned, even in the fine print.

The Human Genome Project clearly infringes not only upon the human rights of indigenous groups, but upon their religious freedom. For many of the groups "chosen" to provide samples of their hair, skin, blood, and other body materials for laboratory examination, the taking of such material is against their religious beliefs.

8. Indigenous Perspectives and Non-Western Models of IPR

As previously stated, intellectual property rights is a foreign concept to indigenous peoples. Until very recently, the subject was not on the agenda of indigenous groups. Within the past 2 years, however, that has changed. For example, in the Charter of the Indigenous-Tribal Peoples of the Tropical Forests (Article 44) IPR concerns are explicitly stated:

> Since we highly value our traditional knowledge and believe that our biotechnologies can make an important contribution to humanity, including "developed" countries, we demand guaranteed rights to our intellectual property, and control over the development and manipulation of this knowledge[8]

In the current Draft of the Declaration on the Rights of Indigenous Peoples, such concerns are also clearly stated in paragraph 19 (see E/CN.4/Sub.2/1992/28):

> Indigenous peoples have the right to special measures for protection, as intellectual property , of their traditional cultural manifestations, such as literature, designs, visual and performing arts, medicines and knowledge of the useful properties of fauna and flora.

During informal hearings held during the III Prep-Com for the United Nations Conference on Environment and Development (UNCED),[9] indigenous representatives discussed their concerns and skepticism regarding the use of intellectual property rights regimes to protect their cultural heritage. Several problems were specifically pointed

---

[8] Charter of the Indigenous-Tribal Peoples of the Tropical Forests: Statement of the International Alliance of the Indigenous-Tribal peoples of the Tropical Forest, Penang, Malaysia, 15 February, 1992.

[9] Declaration on Intellectual Property Rights and Indigenous Peoples, from a symposium organized by D. Posey for the Global Coalition for Biological and Cultural Diversity, July, 1992, Geneva at the III Preparatory Committee Meeting, United Nations Conference on Environment and Diversity.

out: (1) the categories between cultural, intellectual, and physical property are not as distinct and mutually exclusive for indigenous peoples as in the Western legal system. "Sacred sites", for example, are frequently types of ecological reserves that are the result of human knowledge in management and conservation, as well as cultural centers that have both physical and spiritual significance; (2) knowledge is generally communally held, and, although some specialized knowledge may be held by certain ritual or society specialists (such as shamans), this does not give that specialist the right to privatize communal heritage; (3) even if legal IPR regimes were to be implemented, most indigenous communities would not have the financial means to implement, enforce, or litigate. It was clear that under *some circumstances* commercialization of knowledge and plant genetic resources might be desirable, but the prime desire for indigenous peoples was an IPR regime that gave them the right to say no to privatization and commercialization.

One of the areas of IPR research that is most lacking is that of non-western IPR regimes. Up to now, the debate has centered around United Nations and Western concepts of intellectual and genetic property. There are, of course, ancient systems of property utilized by Muslim, Hindu, Chinese, and many other civilizations. But what about the property regimes of indigenous peoples themselves? Cunningham (1992) mentions a few African examples, and numerous other examples are to be found scattered about in many places. A synthesis and analysis of non-Western systems would be very helpful in finding creative solutions to IPR protection.

9. Cultural Property

In recent years, indigenous peoples have been increasingly successful in reclaiming the tangible aspects of their cultures, or "cultural property", from museums and institutions (Messenger 1989). Although the term has no clearly defined meaning (O'Keefe 1993), it has come to refer to everything from objects of art to archaeological artifacts, traditional music and dance, and sacred sites. Crewdson (1984) has argued that there is ample justification for establishing a "distinct legal code" for cultural property. Likewise, Rodata (1988) holds that cultural property already constitutes a "new category of goods" and needs its own set of new rules.

"Cultural heritage" has appeared as a related "legal instrument" to link knowledge and information to the cultural artifact. The concept assumes that the property to be protected is not just of historical significance, but is of central interest to living and future generations (O'Keefe et al, 1984). Cultural heritage also includes protection for human remains in as much as the ancestors are vitally important to modern society. To date, successful use of "cultural heritage" as a legal tool has been limited to Australia; however, it has recently provoked great interest in international debates.

Although indigenous peoples are interested in following the successes of both cultural heritage and cultural property battles, they have not abandoned the intellectual property rights option. During the 1993 United Nations Year for the World's Indigenous Peoples, IPR was on the agenda of nearly every major encounter. One of the most significant was the "First International Conference on the Cultural & Intellectual Property Rights of Indigenous Peoples" convened by the nine Mataatua Tribes in Whakatane, Aotearoa New Zealand. The resulting "Mataatua Declaration on Cultural and Intellectual Property Rights of Indigenous Peoples" reflects the concerns of the 150 delegates from 14 countries who were present.[10] The Declaration states that cultural and intellectual property are central to the right of determination and that, although the knowledge of indigenous peoples is of benefit to all humanity, the first beneficiaries of indigenous knowledge must be the direct indigenous descendants of such knowledge. In the Preamble, the Declaration recognizes that "Indigenous Peoples are capable of managing their traditional knowledge themselves, but are willing to offer it to all humanity provided their fundamental rights to define and control this knowledge are protected by the international community".

It is in this spirit that fruitful discussion will proceed, and then, only if indigenous peoples themselves take the lead. It would appear from the Mataatua Declaration that indigenous peoples have indeed found that the concepts of intellectual and cultural property are of use to them in the strengthening and protection of their societies.

Other Relevant Activities

The World Commission on Environment and Development pointed out in 1987 that "tribal and indigenous peoples' lifestyles can offer "modern society many lessons in the management of resources in complex forest, mountain and dryland ecosystems" (WCED 1987: 12). Increasingly scientists are documenting the complex nature of indigenous scientific and ecological knowledge in order to emphasize the profound importance of such information in the development of alternative models of sustainable natural resource use, management, and conservation. The International Union for the Conservation of Nature (IUCN) has begun a Task Force on Indigenous peoples in order to articulate more coherent and effective policies in the conservation of nature through the involvement of indigenous peoples and the use of traditional knowledge in effective conservation activities (IUCN 1993). Likewise major environmental

---

10 This Declaration can be obtained from the Conference Secretariat, P.O. Box 76, Whakatane, Aotearoa, New Zealand (Fax 64-7-307-0762).

groups, such as WWF have taken on intellectual property rights issues as a key mechanism for the more just and equitable partnerships necessary to conserve biological and cultural diversity (Cunningham 1993). World Resources Institute and the Rainforest Alliance have carried out pioneering efforts to integrate IPR concerns into public policy as well as into the practical language of legal contract (Reid et al. 1993).

In 1988, the International Society for Ethnobiology in its first world congress in Belem, Brazil, established a set of principles for research and work with indigenous and local communities. The Declaration of Belem was the first to call attention to the "inextricable link" between the conservation of biological diversity with the preservation of cultural diversity. It was the first international declaration to call specifically for the protection of and compensation for IPR, that is treated as "an inalienable right". Principle 4 of the Declaration states that "Procedures be developed to compensate native peoples for the utilization of their knowledge and their biological resources.

During the Second International Congress of Ethnobiology in Kunming, China, ISE founded The Global Coalition for Biological and Cultural Diversity in order to implement the Declaration of Belem. The Global Coalition, through extensive consultation with indigenous peoples and IPR specialists, has developed A Covenant on Intellectual, Cultural, and Scientific Property to establish guidelines for responsible businesses, institutions, and scientists. The Principles of this Covenant can be found in Appendix 1.

Codes of ethics & professional behavior similar to the Declaration of Belem have been developed by the International Society of Chemical Ecology (1989), Society of Economic Botany (1991), NIH/NCI (1991), Global Biodiversity Strategy (WRI/IUCN/UNEP), and AMOMPS (Asian Symposium for Medicinal Plants, Spices, and other Natural Products, 1992) and American Society of Pharmacognosy (1992) (for details, see Cunningham, 1993).

The most celebrated compensation-for-biodiversity agreement to date is between INBio (Instituto Nacional de Biodiversidad) of Costa Rica and Merck Pharmaceuticals. In the Agreement, Merck paid $1 million "up front" for collecting and screening privileges. If any new products are developed, Merck retains the patent rights, but must share profits (to date the royalty figure is undisclosed, but is thought to be 3%) with INBio, who, in turn, will invest the funds in conservation activities (Joyce 1991; WRI 1992; Stone 1992). Indigenous peoples and local communities do not figure in this agreement and there is no guarantee that they will even be consulted on conservation priorities and projects.

The U.S. National Institute of Health's (NIH) National Cancer Institute (NCI) has also developed a set of general principles to govern its vast collecting across the globe. [see also Cragg et al., Chapter 6, this volume - *ed.*] Compensation for traditional knowledge and biogenetic resources is central, with "compensation" being interpreted as including "training, institution building and information transfer" (Schweitzer et al. 1991). Similar arrangements have been set up with the New York Botanical Garden and Kew Royal Botanical Gardens, with beneficiaries being the state governments.

"Guidelines for Equitable Partnerships in New Natural Products Development" have also been developed by the World Wide Fund for Nature, together with UNESCO, and the Kew Gardens "People and Plants" Initiative (Cunningham 1993). The "Code of Practice" considers the wide range of subjects related to equitable relationships between institutions and corporations with local communities and indigenous peoples. While recognizing that governments hold sovereignty over biogenetic resources, the Code calls upon governments to "accept the responsibility for establishing or implementing national policies for the conservation and use of biological diversity" (Section 1.1), while collectors are urged to "respect local social values, traditional, and customary law" (Section 5.4). While encouraging "ethno-directed" screening and collection, the Code leaves the IPR issue up to national governments who "should be free to decide whether or not to adopt IPR protection for new natural products" (Section 8.3). There is very little in the Code to console, encourage, or even orient local communities as to how to deal with IPR issues.

The obvious problem of these arrangements is that local communities in general, and indigenous peoples in particular, are benefited only if the government or non-government organization so desires. This very basic point has brought all agreements existing to date under much-deserved criticism, since indigenous and traditional peoples are no longer interested in "intermediaries" or "patrons".

Indigenous peoples and developing countries have taken steps on their own to deal with misappropriation and misuse or unauthorized use of traditional knowledge. In 1979, the Organization of African Unity urged that herbal medicine research be carried out in secrecy to prevent multinational companies from developing new drugs and selling them back to developing countries at high prices (Hanlon 1979). The Kuna Indians of Panama developed a 26-page manual in 1988 to regulate scientific research in their area (Chapin 1991). The Kayapo Indians of Brazil are currently negotiating an IPR code and contract with the Body Shop to regulate commercial activities in their region, especially regarding the development of new products based on traditional knowledge and local biogenetic resources.

Conclusion

Intellectual Property Rights has become a very central issue to debates in many major fields of international politics and law, including human rights, labor law, environment and development, trade, religious freedom and cultural property/cultural heritage. Problems central to the implementation of existing IPR tools (copyright, patent, trade secret, appellation of origin, trademark, etc.) include the collective nature of traditional knowledge and necessity to identify the initiator or inventor of certain knowledge and/or genetic resources. ILO 169 has established an international precedent for the recognition of "collective" rights, as has the United Nations Commission of Human Rights and the Convention on Biodiversity. "Neighboring rights", as first described in the WIPO Model Provisions on Folklore, but subsequently recognized in a wide range of law relating to expressions of artists, serves as a major advance in the protection of traditional knowledge. Indigenous/traditional knowledge as "science", however, has only been marginally conceived, but will hopefully be developed as a result of the Declaration of Rights of Indigenous Peoples and other developments called for by the Secretary General of the United Nations. Religious freedom guarantees have, to date, not been adequately utilized to defend IPR, while the provisions of the Convention on Biodiversity (together with Agenda 21) are only now being analyzed in order to develop effective strategies to empower local communities and indigenous peoples. Two major steps now need to be taken: (1) IPR debates need to be translated into practical tools for indigenous, traditional peoples and local communities so they can begin to experiment with on-the-ground methods of dealing with the problem of IPR as *they* define it; and (2) non-Western models of intellectual/cultural property need to be analyzed to the end of redefining IPR as an entirely new concept. Both of these steps must be led by indigenous peoples themselves. The role of scientist, scholar, and lawyer should be to provide information and ideas, not to undertake the redefining of IPR. That should occur as the result of practice and experimentation by local communities. One thing is for certain: we are dealing with a concept that is not defined, and indeed, *should not* be defined for a while to come.

Bibliography

Kahn, S. and H. Talal

1987 Indigenous Peoples: A Global Quest for Justice. London: Zed Books.

Balick, M.

1990 Ethnobotany and the Identification of Therapeutic Agents From the Rainforest. In, Bioactive Compounds from Plants (Chadwick, D. & J. Marsh, eds). Ciba Foundation Symposium no. 154. Chichester: J. Wiley & Sons. Pp. 22-39

Chapin, M,
1991 How the Kuna keep the Scientists in Line. Cultural Survival Quarterly 15(3): 17.

Crewdson, R.
1984 Cultural Property--A Fourth Estate. Law Society Gazette 18: 126.

Cunningham, A.
1992 Ethics, Ethnobiological Research, and Biodiversity, Gland, Switzerland: WWF-International.

Farrington, J.
1989 Agricultural Biotechnology: Prospects for the Third World. London: Overseas Development Institute.

Hamburger, M., Marston, A., and K. Hostettemann.
1991 Search for New Drugs of Plant Origin. Advances in Drug Research 20: 167-215

Hanlon, J.
1979 When the Scientist Meets the Medicine Man. Nature 279: 284-285.

Hurtado, M.
1989 Seeds of Discontent. South, September 15: 95-96.
IUCN

1993 Indigenous Peoples and Strategies for Sustainability: Inter-Commission Task Force on Indigenous Peoples. IUCN, Gland, Switzerland.

Joyce, C.
1991 Prospectors for Tropical Medicines. New Scientist, 19 October, 32-36.

Juma, C.
1989. The Gene Hunters: Biotechnology and the Scramble for Seeds. Princeton University Press, Princeton, New Jersey

Kloppenberg, J. Jr.
1988 Seeds and Sovereignty. Duke University Press, London

Kloppenburg, J. Jr. & D. Kleinman
1987 Seed Wars: Common Heritage, Private Property, and Political Strategy. Socialist Review 95 (September/October): 7 - 41.

Messenger, P.
1989 The Ethics of Collecting Cultural Property: Whose Culture? Whose Property? Albuquerque: University of New Mexico Press.

Mooney, P.
1983 The Law of the Seed. Development Dialogue 1-2: 1-172. London: Zed Books, Ltd.

O'Keefe, P.
1993 Intellectual Property, Cultural Property, Cultural Heritage: Do These Further Indigenous Interests? A paper presented at the First International Conference on the Cultural and Intellectual Property Rights of Indigenous Peoples, Whakatane, Aotearoa New Zealand, June, 1993.

O'Keefe, P., L. Prott, and L. Law
1984 Law and the Cultural Heritage. London: Butterworths.

Posey, D.
1990a Intellectual Property Rights: What is the Position of Ethnobiology? Journal of Ethnobiology 10,1: 93-98.

1990b Intellectual Property Rights and Just Compensation for Indigenous Knowledge. Anthropology Today 6,4: 13-16.

Posey, D. & W. Overal
1988 Ethnobiology: Implications and Applications. Proceedings of the First International Congress of Ethnobiology. Museu Paraense Emilio Goeldi. ldi/CNPq. Belem (Brazil).

Reid, W., et al.
1993 Biodiversity Prospecting: Using Genetic Resources for Sustainable Development. Washington, D.C.: World Resources Institute (and others).

Rodata, S.
1988 Explanatory Memorandum in Council of Europe. The Art Trade: Report of the Committee on Culture and Education, Strasbourg (Document 5834).

Schweitzer, J., F. Handley, J. Edwards, W. Harris, M. Grever, S. Schepartz, G. Cragg, K. Snader, and A. Bhat.
1991 Summary of the Workshop on Drug Development, Biological Diversity and Economic Growth. Journal of the National Cancer Institute. Pp. 1294-1298.

Scoones, I. , M. Melnyk, & J. Pretty.
1992 The Hidden Harvest: Wild Foods and Agricultural Systems--A Literature Review and Annotated Bibliography, IIED/WWF, London.

Shelton, D.
1993 Legal Approaches to Obtaining Compensation for the Access to and Use of Traditional Knowledge of Indigenous Peoples, Draft Report to the World Wide Fund for Nature--International, Gland, Switzerland.

Stone, R.
1992 The Biodiversity Treaty: Pandora's Box or Fair Deal? Science 256: 1624.

WCED (World Commission on Environment and Development)
1987 Our Common Future. World Commission on Environment and Development,Oxford University Press.

WCIP (World Council of Indigenous Peoples)
1993 "Presumed Dead...but Still Useful as a Human By-Product" Ottawa, Canada: World Council of Indigenous Peoples,

WIPO (World Intellectual Property Organization)
1985 Model Provisions for National Laws on the Protection of Expressions of Folklore Against Illicit Exploitation and Other Prejudicial Actions. Geneva, Switzerland: World Intellectual Property Organization/ United Nations Educational, Scientific and Cultural Organization/ United Nations.

WIPO (World Intellectual Property Organization)
1989 General Introductory Course on Copyright and Neighboring Rights: Protection of Expressions of Folklore. Geneva, Switzerland: WIPO/ UN.

WRI (World Resources Institute)
1992 Global Biodiversity Strategy: Guidelines for Action to Save, Study and Use Earth's Biotic Wealth Sustainably and Equitably. Washington, D.C.: WRI, IUCN, UNEP.

Yamin, F. & D. Posey
1993 Intellectual Property Rights, Indigenous Peoples and Biotechnology. Review of European Community and International Environmental Law 2, 3: 141-148.

Appendix 1

A Covenant on Intellectual, Cultural, and Scientific Property: A Basic Code of Ethics and Conduct for equitable partnerships between responsible corporations, scientists or institutions, and indigenous groups.

Prologue

Indigenous peoples are unanimous in identifying their primary concern as being self-determination, which subsumes such basic rights as recognition of and respect for their cultures, societies, and languages, as well as ownership over their own lands and territories, and control over the resources that are associated with those lands and territories. Intellectual property rights (a term that at present is inadequate to describe the broad category of concerns indigenous peoples have for their cultural, sacred, and communal property) is seen as a mere starting point to defining a more useful category of traditional values, knowledge, and resources that have often been used and misused without authorization, recognition of origin, or just compensation. This COVENANT should not be viewed as a finished *product* defining equitable partnerships, but rather a tool for redefining intellectual property rights through a *process* of consultation, debate, discussion, and creative thinking from the many peoples and groups concerned about establishing a new basis for sustainable development that is socially just and ecologically sound. The end result will undoubtedly be a concept that is no longer known as intellectual property rights.

The COVENANT should in no way be construed as being a call for commoditization/commercialization of culture, biogenetic resources, or knowledge; nor is it a justification for bringing indigenous peoples unwillingly into commercial relationships with other societies. The COVENANT recognizes that trade relationships have been generally harmful to local communities in the past. It is exactly for this reason, together with the fact that an increasing number of indigenous and traditional communities are opting for or are being forced into dangerous trade relationships, that a COVENANT is necessary. This is an attempt to provide a basic code of ethics and conduct that will hopefully form the basis for equitable partnerships that lead to economic independence for local communities, while providing for the conservation of natural resources.

The COVENANT is proposed as a mechanism to build upon IPR concepts utilizing already established "neighboring rights" in the areas of: (1) Labor law; (2) Human Rights laws and agreements; (3) Economic and Social agreements; (4) Intellectual Property and Plant Variety Protection; (5) Farmers' Rights; (6) Environmental conventions and law; (7) Religious freedom acts; (8) customary law and traditional practice; (9) Cultural property and heritage.

Practically, the COVENANT is proposed as a model that can be tried in many parts of the world by many partners. There will undoubtedly be failures, but hopefully there will be many successes. The accumulation of these experiences will produce a new category that will replace IPR with a more powerful and decisive concept that, ideally, will catalyze the replacement of markets for temporary gain with trade based upon long term commitments that result in mutual advantages--turning businesses from being vanguards of destruction into equitable partners with local communities in the conservation of biological and cultural diversity.

Preamble

A COVENANT is a special agreement that carries with it all the responsibilities of friendship and long lasting relationships that celebrate the essence of sharing and satisfaction of mutual relationship. This COVENANT on Intellectual Property Rights has nothing to do with short term commercial exploitation, but everything to do with long term partnership expressed through responsible trade and exchange for mutual benefit.

Implementation of the COVENANT will be a long-term process that will require nurturing, patience, and tolerance. The process can only work successfully if both parties come to understand and appreciate the other, and if both see the relationship as a means to improving not just their own lots, but the whole of our Earth.

SPIRIT OF THE COVENANT

--THIS COVENANT IS CELEBRATED IN ORDER TO:

> SUPPORT INDIGENOUS AND TRADITIONAL PEOPLES IN THEIR FIGHT AGAINST GENOCIDE AND FOR THEIR LAND, TERRITORY, AND CONTROL OVER THEIR OWN RESOURCES, WHILE STRENGTHENING THE CULTURE AND LOCAL COMMUNITY THROUGH RECOGNITION AND SUPPORT OF THE GROUPS' OWN GOALS, VALUES, AND OBJECTIVES, BY HELPING TO FIND NEW WAYS OF RESPONSIBLY UTILIZING, WHILE CONSERVING, THE BIOLOGICAL/ECOLOGICAL/ CULTURAL RICHNESS OF THE REGION, THROUGH EQUITABLE AND RESPONSIBLE TRADE, SOURCING, RESEARCH, AND DEVELOPMENT, THEREBY ESTABLISHING A LONG TERM RELATIONSHIP BUILT THROUGH JOINT DECISION-MAKING BASED UPON THE PRINCIPLES OF EQUALITY OF RELATIONSHIPS AND PROTECTION OF

TRADITIONAL VALUES, KNOWLEDGE AND CULTURE; IF THESE BASIC ELEMENTS ARE NOT RESPECTED, THEN THE COVENANT IS ENDANGERED, AND ALONG WITH IT, THE SPIRIT OF TRUST AND PARTNERSHIP BETWEEN RESPONSIBLE BUSINESSES/SCIENTISTS/ INSTITUTIONS AND LOCAL COMMUNITIES THAT IS ESSENTIAL FOR THE FUTURE WELL-BEING OF THE PLANET --

WHAT IS BEING PROTECTED:

Although the essence of this Covenant is about the development of equitable and responsible trade, any Intellectual Property Rights agreement must inevitably deal with protection. The first concern of indigenous peoples is their right NOT to sell, commoditize, or have expropriated from them certain domains of knowledge and certain sacred places, plants, animals, and objects. All other elements of the Covenant are preconditioned by this basic right, which is considered a fundamental element of self-determination.

Thus, the first category for protection is:

1. Sacred property (images, sounds, knowledge, material culture, or anything that is deemed sacred and, thereby, not commoditizable).

The following categories are recognized as providing the basis for protection and just compensation, if, and only if authorized by the community, society and cultural group.

2. Knowledge of current use, previous use, potential use of plant and animal species, as well as soils and minerals, known to the cultural group;

3. Knowledge of preparation, processing, storage of useful species;

4. Knowledge of formulations involving more than one ingredient;

5. Knowledge of individual species (planting methods, caring for, selection criteria, etc.);

6. Knowledge of ecosystem conservation (that protect or preserve the resource that may be found to have commercial value, although not specifically used for that purpose or other practical purposes by the local community or the culture);

7. Biogenetic resources that originate (or originated) on indigenous lands & territories;

8. Cultural property (images, sounds, crafts, arts, performances);

9. Classificatory systems of knowledge.

All of these are protected as part of the larger need to protect land, territory, resources and to stimulate self-determination for indigenous/traditional peoples.

BASIC PRINCIPLES TO BE EXERCISED BY ALL PARTNERS:

I. Equity of Partners, including profit-sharing, joint planning and goal setting, informed consent, and full disclosure in all aspects of the project, including results.

II. Working to insure that compensation is equitably shared within and between groups, and that compensation is in a form that strengthens the community and ethnic group;

III. Non-exclusivity of relationships, meaning that both parties are free to enter into agreements with other parties; priority for exchange will obviously be between Partners;

IV. Confidentiality of information and resources, meaning that information imparted by the indigenous group to the Partner cannot be passed on to others without consent of the Giver;

V. Continual dialog and mutual review, supported by independent monitoring and, if necessary, mediation by a third party (as agreed by Partners); mandatory review is required if there is a change of status of either Party or in the law;

VI. Diversification of the economic base through diversification of collecting, ingredients, and products based upon traditional knowledge, cultural practice and local resources, as well as diversification of markets;

VII. Cooperation with local (indigenous and non-indigenous) educational, health, research, and non-governmental institutions;

VIII. Insuring ecological and cultural sensitivity in all phases of any project, including collecting, screening, sourcing, production, and manufacture;

IX. Encouragement of community autonomy and control over all aspects of the projects as early as possible.

ADDITIONAL PRINCIPLES TO BE OBSERVED BY THE COMPANY, SCIENTIST, OR INSTITUTION:

X. Responsibility to be informed about local, regional, and national laws, customs, and cultures;

XI. Judicial recognition and registration of this agreement, followed by appropriate legal protection to enable the indigenous group to protect its knowledge and biogenetic resources.

ADDITIONAL PRINCIPLES TO BE OBSERVED BY THE INDIGENOUS GROUP:

XII. Establishment of a consensus on representation, group participation, ethnic boundaries and "legal personality(ies) of Partner(s)";

XIII. Commitment to work toward assuming legal, economic and financial independence.

ADDITIONAL PRINCIPLES FOR INDEPENDENT MONITORS:

IXV. Must have no conflict of interests and be able to act as arbitrators or mediators for all parties;

XV. Must have the professional qualifications and relevant experiences to represent all parties equitably;

XVI. Must practice full information disclosure and provide a public statement of working procedures and principles;

XVII. Must serve as the guardian of the COVENANT, providing audits when requested by either party, but at least once annually, on actual practice in all areas of the agreement.

SPECIFIC RESPONSIBILITIES OF THE PARTNERSHIP

A. TO THE CULTURE:

A.1. Respect for Sacred Places, knowledge, and things;

A.2. Respect for specialized and secret knowledge;

A.3. Respect for privacy;

A.4. Respect for secrecy (obligation not to reveal things divulged in secret or under special circumstances, such as during rituals);

A.5. Respect for the integrity of the larger cultural/ethnic group (it would be against the spirit of the Covenant if any action were to weaken the cohesion and harmony of the whole culture);

A.6. Consultation and joint development of publications, documentaries, advertisements and other materials that represents the indigenous culture;

A.7. Respect for cultural patrimony by insuring that all publications, video and audio documentation, as well as other materials that may be developed by the institutions involved (or their sub-contractees) and based on indigenous culture be provided to the indigenous peoples (recognizing that in many instances, this may mean setting up local archives &/or museums, but in all cases involves agreements on who and how the materials are held).

B. TO THE COMMUNITY (RESPECT FOR THE COMMUNITY AND ITS RELATIONSHIP WITH THE NATION, TRIBE, BAND, CULTURAL OR ETHNIC GROUP)

B.1. Responsibly define the "legal personality" of the indigenous Partner (who signs any legal agreement, how is the Partner defined vis a vis the community/sub-group/larger ethnic entity; is that definition acceptable to all parties);

B.2. Respect for consensus decision-making process that generally characterizes indigenous societies;

B.3. Respect for internal social structure and cultural values;

B.4. Full disclosure to and promotion of community discussion about all possible positive AND negative effects, caring especially not to create false or unrealistic hopes and expectations;

B.5. Joint setting of collection and production schedules and goals;

B.6. Joint planning for quality control, delivery, accounting, pricing structures, and accountability;

B.7. Development of education and training programs with the community in order to make all aspects of the project independent of non-indigenous elements as soon as feasible.

C. TO THE SOCIETY (IMPLICATIONS OF SOCIAL AND POLITICAL CHANGES)

C.1. Promotion of in-depth discussions on implications of cultural, social, and economic change;

C.2. Development of a mechanism for income sharing and distribution;

C.3. Development of a community plan for improvement of communal life;

C.4. Development of a plan for income allocation to strengthen the larger ethnic group.

D. TO THE ENVIRONMENT (IMPLICATIONS OF ECOLOGICAL CHANGES)

D.1. Description of traditional methods of natural resource use and conservation;

D.2. Preparation of environmental and social impact studies (pre-, duration, and post-project);

D.3. Monitoring of environmental and social changes;

D.4. Development with the community of group plans for environmental conservation, and, where appropriate, enrichment of ecosystems and restoration/renovation of damaged areas;

D.5. Development of ecologically and socially responsible plans for expansion of production, including agricultural intensification, if necessary, desirable, and culturally appropriate.

E. TO THE REGION (LOCAL AND REGIONAL DEVELOPMENT)

E.1. Commitment to value added development (including local processing, production, packaging) on location and/or in the region, given that joint decision-making prevails on how, where, and with whom such projects should proceed;

E.2. Commitment to strengthening local and regional research institutions in screening, analyzing, and sourcing, as well as marketing, ingredients and products;

E.3. Support of local and regional educational (official and non-governmental) activities in support of conservation of biological and cultural diversity;

E.4. Working toward long term harmony and stability of social and economic relations between and within indigenous groups and non-indigenous people;

E.5. Development of local and regional networks, cooperatives, and institutions to aid in sourcing, production, and market diversification.

About the Authors

Stephen B. Brush

Stephen Brush is professor in the Applied Behavioral Sciences Department at the University of California, Davis. He hold a Ph.D. in Anthropology from the University of Wisconsin (1973). He served on the faculty of the College of William and Mary, 1973-1984 and as staff associate and then director of the Anthropology Program at the National Science Foundation, 1980-1983. At the University of California, Davis, Brush as been academic administrator for international agricultural development, 1984-1988. His research concerns agricultural ecology and genetic resource conservation. Brush has done field work in Peru in 1972 and also 1977-1986, Turkey (1990-present), Mexico (1988) and California (1986 to present). He has been consultant to the World Bank, United Nations Development Programme, UNESCO, and the Office of Technology Assessment. Contacts: Dept. of Applied Behavioral Science, Univ. of California, Davis; Davis, CA 95616 USA. Telephone: 916-752-4368. Fax: 916-752-5660. Internet: sbbrush@ ucdavis.edu

Audrey R. Chapman

Audrey R. Chapman, director of the Science and Human Rights Program of the American Association for the Advancement of Science, holds a Ph.D. degree in public law and government from Columbia University and graduate degrees in theology and ethics from New York Theological Seminary. She has been a member of the faculty of Barnard College, University of Ghana, and University of Nairobi. She has also directed peace, justice, and human rights programs for the international agency of the United Church of Christ. She is the author or coauthor of six books and numerous monographs and articles on human rights, ethnic conflict, and development issues. Her current professional focus is conceptual and measurement issues relating to economic, social, and cultural rights. In the past two years she has served as the rapporteur for the first United Nations expert seminar on this subject, coorganizer of the first international conference exploring linkages between environmental protection and human rights, and research director of a project exploring a human rights approach to health care reform. Contacts: Science and Human Rights Program, American Association for the Advancement of Science, 1333 H Street, N.W., Washington, D.C. 20005, USA. Telephone: 202-326-6795. Fax: 202-289-4950. Internet: AChapman@ AAAS. ORG.

Gordon M. Cragg, Michael R. Boyd, Michael Grever and Saul A. Schepartz

Dr. Gordon Cragg obtained his Ph.D. from Oxford University and after periods of service on the faculties of various universities, he joined the NCI in 1984. He is Chief of the Natural Products Branch of the NCI and coordinates the acquisition of natural products for the drug discovery program from over 25 countries worldwide. Dr. Michael Boyd is Chief of the Laboratory of Drug Discovery Research and Development Program of the DTP and leads the NCI research team responsible for the discovery and early development of novel anticancer and anti-AIDS drugs from natural sources. He obtained his M.D. and Ph.D. degrees from Vanderbilt University in Tennessee, and has served the NCI since 1977 in a number of senior positions, including that of Associate Director of the DTP from 1984 to 1990. Dr. Michael Grever is Associate Director of the Developmental Therapeutics Program (DTP) which is responsible for all aspects of the drug discovery and development at the National Cancer Institute. He obtained his M.D. from the University of Pittsburgh and led the Investigational Chemotherapy Program and Oncology Unit at the Ohio State University prior to joining the NCI in 1989. Dr. Saul Schepartz obtained his Ph.D. from the University of Wisconsin and joined the NCI in 1958. Among the senior positions he has held are Associate Director of the Drug Research and Development Program and Deputy Director of the Division of Cancer Treatment. He is currently Deputy Associate Director of the DTP. The authors have all played prominent roles in the establishment of the NCI policies for collaboration with, and compensation of, source countries participating in the NCI collection programs. Contacts: Developmental Therapeutics Program, Division of Cancer Treatment, National Cancer Institute, 9000 Rockville Pike, Bethesda, Maryland 20892, USA. Telephone: 301-496-8720. Fax: 301-402-0831.

Tom Greaves

Tom Greaves presently serves as professor of anthropology at Bucknell University. As a former president of the Society for Applied Anthropology and first chair of its Policy and Issues Committee, he has furthered the Society's continuing involvement in IPR and other indigenous issues. He has served as editor-in-chief of the American Anthropologist, president of the Society for the Anthropology of Work, and program chair for the annual meeting of the American Anthrpological Association. Currently his professional focus is on the political struggles of indigenous societies in the Western Hemisphere, with particular emphasis on those taking place in the United States and Canada. Previous field- and applied work and professional writing has dealt with agriculturalists and field hands in Peru, nutrition in Colombia, tin miners and tropical forest colonists in Bolivia, and others. Tom Greaves obtained his Ph.D. in anthropology from Cornell University. Contacts: Department of Sociology

(Tom Greaves, continued)

and Anthropology, Bucknell University, Lewisburg, PA 17837, USA. Telephone: 717-524-3406. Fax: 717-524-3760. Internet: Greaves@ Bucknell. edu

Steven R. King

Steven R. King is currently Vice President for Ethnobotany and Conservation for Shaman Pharmaceuticals, Inc. He has conducted ethnobotanical research with native people in the Peruvian Amazon, where he worked for 11 months in 1978 and 1982. Previously he was the Chief Botanist for the Latin American Science Program at the Nature Conservancy, where he focused on integrating ethnobotanical and taxonomic information into the international plant conservation activities of the Latin American Conservation data centers. Prior to joining the Nature Conservancy, Dr. King worked with the National Research Council's Committee on Managing Global Genetic Resources, where he focused on the management of forest genetic resources. He has worked extensively with Andean crops and was a scientific panel member of the National Academy of Sciences book, "Lost Crops of the Incas." He served as the principal ethnobotanical consultant and future section team leader for the Smithsonian Institution's 1992 "Seeds of Change" exhibit. Steven earned his Ph.D. in Biology from City University of New York as part of the Institute of Economic Botany at the New York Botanical Garden. Contacts: Shaman Pharmaceuticals, Inc., 213 East Grand Avenue, South San Francisco, CA 94080, USA. Telephone: 415-952-7070. Fax: 415-873-8367.

Jack Kloppenburg, Jr. and Tirso Gonzales

Jack Kloppenburg is interested in the social ramifications of knowledge production. His current research focuses on the emergent social impacts of biotechnology, and on the distinction between "scientific" and "local" knowledges. He is also analyzing the global political economy of access to and control over genetic resources, the processes of genetic erosion and species extinction, and the prospects for "sustainable agriculture" in the U.S. and the less developed nations. He is the author of First the Seed: The Political Economy of Plant Biotechnology, 1492-2000 (Cambridge University Press, 1988) and is editor of Seeds and Sovereignty: Use and Control of Plant Genetic Resources (Duke University Press, 1988). Tirso Gonzales is a Peruvian Ph.D. candidate in the Department of Sociology, University of Wisconsin, Madison. His dissertation deals with the "Political Ecology of Peasant Communities, Native Crop Genetic Resources and NGOs in Contemporary Mexico and Peru." He is an active member of the "NGO and Democratization Seminar" as well as of the "Development Group" at the UW-Madison. He has been a research assistant in the project on "Comparative Political Studies of the Contemporary

(Jack Kloppenburg, Jr. and Tirso Gonzales, continued)

State in the Andes" at the Instituto de Estudios Peruanos in Lima, Peru, and has worked in rural development-related activities at Centro 'Bartolome de las Casas' in Cusco, Peru. Contacts: Department of Rural Sociology, University of Wisconsin, Madison, WI 53706, USA. Telephones: 608-262-6867 and 608-262-1562. Internet: Kloppenburg@macc.wisc.edu; Gonzales@macc.wisc.edu

Sarah Laird

Sarah Laird is currently a research fellow at the Rainforest Alliance, and is conducting independent research for NGOs and companies into the ethical sourcing and marketing issues surrounding the commercialization of genetic, biochemical and non-timber forest products from the tropics. As a former director of the Rainforest Alliance's Periwinkle Project, her work included research into the ethical, legal, marketing and sourcing issues surrounding the utilization of plants in traditional, herbal and pharmaceutical medicine. The fruits of this research were incorporated into collaborations with field researchers and community projects attempting to integrate the sustainable use of medicinal species into local conservation and development efforts, including those promulgated through the Edelstein Fellowship for Medicinal Plant Research in Brazil, which she developed in 1990. She recently contributed to the World Resources Institute, Institute of Biodiversity, Rainforest Alliance and African Center for Technology Studies publication, *Biodiversity Prospecting*, of which she was also a co-editor. Sarah Laird obtained her MSc in forestry from the University of Oxford. Contacts: c/o Rainforest Alliance, 65 Bleeker St., New York, NY 10012, USA. Telephone: 212-677-1900. Fax: 212-677-2187.

Janet McGowan and Iroka Udeinya

Janet McGowan presently serves as general counsel to Cultural Survival, Inc. an NGO working to secure human rights and economic and social justice for indigenous peoples and ethnic minorities. She negotiates contracts and licenses for Cultural Survival's trading arm which markets rain forest commodities, prosecutes CS's trademarks, and advises on non-profit tax law. She has served as the manager of Cultural Survival's Indigenous Intellectual Property Project, worked on the development of the Biodiversity Conservation Network's Ethical Guidelines, and has lectured and written on intellectual property law as it affects indigenous peoples. Previously she was an attorney at the Conservation Law Foundation, an environmental law NGO, and a judicial law clerk on the District of Columbia Court of Appeals. She is a graduate of Harvard Law School and Antioch College. Contacts: Cultural Survival, Inc., 215 First St., Cambridge, MA 02142, USA. Telephone: 617-621-3818. Fax: 617-621-3814.

(Janet McGowan and Iroka Udeinya, continued)

Iroka Udeinya presently serves as research associate professor in the College of Medicine at Howard University. His research has focused on traditional medicines and tropical diseases, particularly malaria. Currently he is studying the medicinal properties of the Neem tree. He is keenly interested in the issue of compensating traditional healers and local people for their knowledge of traditional medicines. A Nigerian citizen, he has performed most of his field collecting in that country. He has published many articles on his research. Previously, he was a senior lecturer at the Pharmacology and Therapeutics Department in the College of Medicine at the University of Nigeria. He received his Ph.D. in Toxicology and Pharmacology from West Virginia University and a B.A. from Brandeis University. He did post-doctoral research at the National Institutes of Health. Contacts: Department of Pharmacology, College of Medicine, Howard University Hospital, 2041 Georgia Ave. NW, Washington, D.C. 20060 USA. Telephone: 202-806-6311. Fax: 202-806-7934.

Katy Moran

Katy Moran is the Executive Director of the Healing Forest Conservancy. As an ethnobiologist, her thesis research, "Traditional Elephant Management in Sri Lanka and its Implications for Conservation and Development," was sponsored by the Smithsonian Institution. She organized two symposia for the Smithsonian, "Culture: The Missing Element in Conservation and Development" in 1987 and "Can Nuts Save the Rainforest? The Promise of Ethnobiology and Non-timber Forest Products" in 1992. She also worked as legislative assistant and press secretary for Members of Congress in the US House of Representatives where she specialized in global environment and human rights issues. Moran received a Masters in applied anthropology from American University. Contacts: The Healing Forest Conservancy, 3521 S Street, NW, Washington, D.C. 20007, USA. Telephone and Fax: 202-333-3438.

Sandra Lee Pinel and Michael J. Evans

Sandra Lee Pinel, AICP, is an executive program analyst and regional planner currently employed by the State of New Mexico. For the previous 12 years she worked as a program developer and policy analyst for several Indian pueblos in New Mexico, national Indian rights organizations and for the New Mexico Office of Indian Affairs. IPR is one aspect of her interest in defining how anthropological research methods can be used by governmental planners and policy makers to enhance community and cultural identity and economic options. She is a member of the SfAA Ethics Committee and serves on the American Planning Association Task Force for Women and Minorities, Small Town and Rural Planning Division, and is a contributing author to "An Agenda for America's Communities." Pinel obtained her M.S. in Urban and Regional Planning from the University of Wisconsin, Madison, and her B.A. in

(Sandra Lee Pinel and Michael J. Evans, continued)

Anthropology from Brandeis University where she received a Sachar award for research on traditional medicine in Peru. Contacts: State of New Mexico Department of Finance and Administration, Local Government Division, Santa Fe, NM 87503, USA. Telephone: 505-827-4950.

Michael J. Evans is an Assistant Research Scientist in the Bureau of Applied Research in Anthropology (BARA) at the University of Arizona. Specializing in cultural resource issues, Evans has worked extensively in Native American social impact assessment, cultural resource management, and Native American consultation primarily in the southwestern and western United States. He has also worked in cultural resource management and cultural production in Micronesia. Evans received the Ph.D. in Anthropology from the University of Florida in 1988. Contacts: Bureau of Applied Research in Anthropology, University of Arizona, Tucson, AZ, 85721, USA. Telephone: 602-621-6282. Fax: 602-621-9608.

Darrell Addison Posey

Darrell Addison Posey is currently Visiting Scholar at The Institute for Social and Cultural Anthropology and Senior Member of St. Anthrony's College, Oxford University, England. He is Titled Researcher of the Brazilian National Council for Science and Technology (CNPq) and Head of the Program of Ethnobiology of the Goeldi Museum, Belem, Brazil. He is one of the founders and Past President of the International Society for Ethnobiology and currently serves as Executive Director of The Global Coalition for Biological and Cultural Diversity and received a UN "Global 500" award in 1993.. He has coordinated the International Working Group on IPR since its founding in 1989 and is presently working to develop a Covenant on intellectual and cultural property for indigenous peoples. He received his Ph.D. in anthropology from the University of Georgia. Contacts: The Institute for Social and Cultural Anthropology, St. Anthony's College, Oxford University, 61 Banbury Road, Oxford 0X2 6PE, England. Telephone and Fax: 44-865-327-358.

Dave Ruppert

Dave Ruppert presently holds the position of Regional Cultural Anthropologist for the National Park Service in Denver, Colorado. As as federal employee for the past 15 years he has sought to apply anthropological research methods and perspectives to the management of natural resources. Before joining the National Park Service in 1991, he served in similar positions with the Bureau of Land Management and the Office of Federal Inspector. He has taught at the University of Alaska and presently serves as adjunct assistant professor of anthropology at Regis University and at the University of Colorado at Denver.

(Dave Ruppert, continued)

His applied work has primarily focussed on natural resource use and management of the environment by indigenous societies in the western United States and Alaska. Related applied work and publications deal with the application of anthropological research methods in the field of computer-human interface design as it relates to geographic informations systems. Dave Ruppert obtained his Ph.D. in anthropology from the University of Arizona. Contacts: National Park Service, Rocky Mountain Regional Office, Division of Cultural Resources, 12795 Alameda Parkway, Denver, Colorado 80225, USA. Telephone: 303-969-2879.

Daniela Soleri, David Cleveland, Donald Eriacho, Fred Bowannie, Jr., and Andrew Laahty

Daniela Soleri is Co-Director of the Center for People, Food and Environment is Tuscon, Arizona, and consultant on crop genetic resources issues. She served as consultant on the Zuni Sustainable Agriculture and Zuni Folk Varieties Projects, especially in project organization, crop genetic resources, and intellectual property rights. She has an M.S. in international agricultural education and is a Ph.D. candidate in the College of Agriculture, University of Arizona, researching the agronomic and genetic implications of farmer management of crop genetic resources. Her main interests are biological and cultural diversity in agriculture, farmer selection and maintenance of folk crop varieties, small-scale household food systems, and community development.

David A. Cleveland is Co-Director of the Center for People, Food and Environment in Tucson, Arizona. He served as Director of the Zuni Sustainable Agriculture Project from May, 1992, to October, 1993. He is now a consultant to this project. He is director of the Zuni Folk Varieties Project. He has a Ph.D. in anthropology and an M.S. in genetics from the University of Arizona. He did research on agriculture and demography with Kusasi farmers in northeast Ghana, research on crop genetic resources with Hopi farmers, worked with farmers on an irrigation project in northern Pakistan, and has experience with farmers in Egypt and Mexico. He has managed international development projects in the College of Agriculture and taught in the Department of Anthropology at the University of Arizona. His main interests are cultural and biological diversity, stability, and productivity in small-scale sustainable farming.

Donald Eriacho is a Zuni farmer and rancher and past President of the Pescado Irrigation Unit of the Zuni Irrigation Association. He started as Assistant Director on the Zuni Sustainable Agriculture Project in November, 1992, and became the Director in November, 1993. He is in charge of the peach orchard

(Daniela Soleri, David Cleveland, Donald Eriacho, Fred Bowannie, Jr., and Andrew Laahty, continued)

interviews, and the folk variety interviews for the Zuni Folk Varieties Project for which he is Assistant Director.

Fred Bowannie, Jr., is a Zuni farmer and rancher and President of the Nutria Irrigation Unit of the Zuni Irrigation Association from April, 1992, to November, 1993, at which time he became Vice President. He is currently being hired as an Assistant Director on the Zuni Sustainable Agriculture Project. With Andrew Laahty he supervises the Nutria Pilot Project portion of ZSAP, including interviews of fellow farmers and field mapping using the GPS for input to a GIS data base.

Andrew Laahty is a Zuni farmer and rancher and Vice President of the Nutria Irrigation Unit of the Zuni Irrigation Association from April, 1992, to November, 1993, at which time he became President. He is currently being hired as an Assistant Director on the Zuni Sustainable Agriculture Project.

Contacts: Soleri and Cleveland: Center for People, Food and Environment, 344 South Third Avenue, Tucson, Arizona 85701, USA; Telephone and Fax: 602-624-5379. Eriacho, Bowannie and Laahty: Zuni Folk Varieties Project, P.O. Box 630, Zuni, NM 87327, USA; Telephone: 505-782-5851, Fax: 505-782-2726.

David J. Stephenson, Jr.

Dave Stephenson practices law in Denver, Colorado. He has had extensive experience litigating computer software trade secret cases. He has both a law degree (J.D., U. of Denver) and a Ph.D. in Anthropology (U. of Colorado, 1982). He majored in Anthropology as an undergraduate at Dartmouth College. Besides authoring his paper in this volume, he has previously drawn on his combined background in law and anthropology in published articles concerning international human rights law and through participation in several culture change projects that have significantly influenced comprehensive legislation in areas such as school finance, health and safety, and consumer protection. He is currently working with a group of judges, lawyers, anthropologists, and other social sicentists that is studying the cultural dynamics of professionalism within the American legal system with a view toward implementing systemic change. He participates actively as an applied anthropologist on the Board of the Center for Cultural Dynamics (based in Denver, Colorado) and with affiliated organizations that are concerned with cultural dynamics and socioeconomic development locally, nationally, and internationally. Contacts: Bucholtz, Bull & Ewing, P.C., 1666 So. University Blvd., Suite A, Denver, CO 80210-2890, USA. Telephone: 303-778-8822. Fax: 303-778-0070. Internet: jgp@ csn.org

Dean B. Suagee

Dean Suagee is an attorney who is of counsel to the Washington, D.C., law firm of Hobbs, Straus, Dean and Wilder. The firm specializes in representing American Indian and Alaska Native tribal governments and tribal organizations, and Mr. Suagee specializes in environmental law and cultural preservation. He received his J.D. from the University of North Carolina and holds a Master of Laws (LL.M.) in international legal studies from the American University. He is the author of several law review articles, including "Self-Determination for Indigenous Peoples at the Dawn of the Solar Age," 25 U Mich. J.L. Ref. 671 (1992). He recently helped in the founding and currently serves on the board of a national intertribal organization, Keepers of the Treasures: Cultural Council of American Indians, Alaska Natives and Native Hawaiians, which is dedicated to supporting tribal efforts to maintain and revitalize tribal cultures. He is a member of the Cherokee Nation. Contacts: Hobbs, Straus, Dean and Wilder, 1819 H Street, N.W., Suite 800. Washington, D.C., 20006, USA. Telephone: 202-783-5100. Fax: 202-296-8834.

Index